THOMAS PAINE

THOMAS PAINE

Moncure D. Conway
Introduction by
Professor Eric Foner
The City University of New York

Volume II

AMERICAN MEN AND WOMEN
OF LETTERS SERIES
General Editor
Professor Daniel Aaron

CHELSEA HOUSE
NEW YORK 1983

**This edition is an edited reprint of the
1892 edition by G.P. Putnam's Sons.**

Copyright © 1983 by Chelsea House Publishers
All rights reserved
Printed and bound in the United States of America

ISBN: 0-87754-172-8

THE LIFE OF THOMAS PAINE.

CHAPTER I.

"KILL THE KING, BUT NOT THE MAN."

DUMAS' hero, Dr. Gilbert (in "Ange Pitou"), an idealization of Paine, interprets his hopes and horrors on the opening of the fateful year 1793. Dr. Gilbert's pamphlets had helped to found liberty in the New World, but sees that it may prove the germ of total ruin to the Old World.

"A new world," repeated Gilbert; "that is to say, a vast open space, a clear table to work upon,—no laws, but no abuses; no ideas, but no prejudices. In France, thirty thousand square leagues of territory for thirty millions of people; that is to say, should the space be equally divided, scarcely room for a cradle or a grave for each. Out yonder, in America, two hundred thousand square leagues for three millions of people; frontiers which are ideal, for they border on the desert, which is to say, immensity. In those two hundred thousand leagues, navigable rivers, having a course of a thousand leagues; virgin forests, of which God alone knows the limits,—that is to say, all the elements of life, of civilization, and of a brilliant future. Oh, how easy it is, Billot, when a man is called Lafayette, and is accustomed to wield a sword; when a man is called Washington, and is accustomed to reflect deeply,—how easy is it to combat against walls of wood, of earth, of stone, of human flesh! But when, instead of founding, it is necessary to destroy; when we see in the old order things that we are obliged to attack,—walls of bygone, crumbling ideas; and that behind the ruins even of these walls crowds of people and of interests still take refuge; when, after having found the idea, we find that in order to make the people adopt it, it will be necessary perhaps to decimate that people, from the old who remember to the child who has still to learn; from the recollection which is the monument to the instinct that is its germ—then, oh then, Billot, it is a task that will make all shudder who can see beneath the horizon. . . . I shall, however, persevere, for although I see obstacles, I can perceive the end; and that end is splendid, Billot. It is not the liberty of France alone that I dream of; it is the liberty of the whole world. It is not the physical equality; it is equality before the law,—equality of rights. It is not only the fraternity of our own citizens, but of all nations. . . . Forward, then, and over the heaps of our dead bodies may one day march the generations of which this boy here is in the advanced guard!"

Though Dr. Gilbert has been in the Bastille, though he barely escapes the bullet of a revolutionist, he tries to unite the throne and the people. So, as we have seen, did Paine struggle until the King took flight, and, over his own signature, branded all his pledges as extorted lies. Henceforth for the King personally he has no respect; yet the whole purpose of his life is now to save that of the prisoner. Besides his humane horror of capital punishment, especially in a case which involves the heads of thousands, Paine foresees Nemesis fashioning her wheels in every part of Europe, and her rudder across the ocean,—where America beholds in Louis XVI. her deliverer.

Paine's outlawry, announced by Kersaint in Convention, January 1st, was more eloquent for wrath

than he for clemency. Under such menaces the
majority for sparing Louis shrank with the New
Year; French pride arose, and with Danton was
eager to defy despots by tossing to them the head
of a king. Poor Paine found his comrades retreat-
ing. What would a knowledge of the French
tongue have been worth to this leading republican
of the world, just then the one man sleeplessly
seeking to save a King's life! He could not plead
with his enraged republicans, who at length over-
powered even Brissot, so far as to draw him into the
fatal plan of voting for the King's death, coupled
with submission to the verdict of the people. Paine
saw that there was at the moment no people, but
only an infuriated clan. He was now defending a
forlorn hope, but he struggled with a heroism that
would have commanded the homage of Europe
had not its courts been also clans. He hit on a
scheme which he hoped might, in that last extremity,
save the real revolution from a suicidal inhumanity.
It was the one statesmanlike proposal of the time:
that the King should be held as a hostage for the
peaceful behavior of other kings, and, when their
war on France had ceased, banished to the United
States.

On January 15th, before the vote on the King's
punishment was put, Paine gave his manuscript
address to the president: debate closed before it
could be read, and it was printed. He argued that
the Assembly, in bringing back Louis when he had
abdicated and fled, was the more guilty; and against
his transgressions it should be remembered that by
his aid the shackles of America were broken.

"Let then those United States be the guard and the asylum of Louis Capet. There, in the future, remote from the miseries and crimes of royalty, he may learn, from the constant presence of public prosperity, that the true system of government consists not in monarchs, but in fair, equal, and honorable representation. In recalling this circumstance, and submitting this proposal, I consider myself a citizen of both countries. I submit it as an American who feels the debt of gratitude he owes to every Frenchman. I submit it as a man, who, albeit an adversary of kings, forgets not that they are subject to human frailties. I support my proposal as a citizen of the French Republic, because it appears to me the best and most politic measure that can be adopted. As far as my experience in public life extends, I have ever observed that the great mass of people are always just, both in their intentions and their object; but the true method of attaining such purpose does not always appear at once. The English nation had groaned under the Stuart despotism. Hence Charles I. was executed; but Charles II. was restored to all the powers his father had lost. Forty years later the same family tried to re-establish their oppression; the nation banished the whole race from its territories. The remedy was effectual; the Stuart family sank into obscurity, merged itself in the masses, and is now extinct."

He reminds the Convention that the king had two brothers out of the country who might naturally desire his death: the execution of the king might make them presently plausible pretenders to the throne, around whom their foreign enemies would rally: while the man recognized by foreign powers as the rightful monarch of France was living there could be no such pretender.

"It has already been proposed to abolish the penalty of death, and it is with infinite satisfaction that I recollect the humane and excellent oration pronounced by Robespierre on the subject, in the constituent Assembly. Monarchical governments have trained the human race to sanguinary punishments, but the people should not follow the examples of their oppressors in such vengeance. As France has been the first of European nations to abolish royalty, let her also be the first to abolish the punishment of death, and to find out a milder and more effectual substitute."

This was admirable art. Under shelter of Robespierre's appeal against the death penalty, the "Mountain"[1] could not at the moment break the force of Paine's plea by reminding the Convention of his Quaker sentiments. It will be borne in mind that up to this time Robespierre was not impressed, nor Marat possessed, by the homicidal demon. Marat had felt for Paine a sort of contemptuous kindness, and one day privately said to him : " It is you, then, who believe in a republic ; you have too much sense to believe in such a dream." Robespierre, according to Lamartine, " affected for the cosmopolitan radicalism of Paine the respect of a neophite for ideas not understood." Both leaders now suspected that Paine had gone over to the " Brissotins," as the Girondists were beginning to be called. However, the Brissotins, though a majority, had quailed before the ferocity with which the Jacobins had determined on the king's death. M. Taine declares that the victory of the minority in this case was the familiar one of reckless violence over the more civilized— the wild beast over the tame. Louis Blanc denies that the Convention voted, as one of them said, under poignards ; but the signs of fear are unmis-

[1] So called from the high benches on which these members sat. The seats of the Girondists on the floor were called the " Plain," and after their overthrow the " Marsh."

takable. Vergniaud had declared it an insult for any one to suppose he would vote for the king's death, but he voted for it. Villette was threatened with death if he did not vote for that of the king. Sieyès, who had attacked Paine for republicanism, voted death. "What," he afterward said—"what were the tribute of my glass of wine in that torrent of brandy?" But Paine did not withhold his cup of cold water. When his name was called he cried out: "I vote for the detention of Louis till the end of the war, and after that his perpetual banishment." He spoke his well prepared vote in French, and may have given courage to others. For even under poignards—the most formidable being liability to a charge of royalism—the vote had barely gone in favor of death.[1]

The fire-breathing Mountain felt now that its supremacy was settled. It had learned its deadly art of conquering a thinking majority by recklessness. But suddenly another question was sprung upon the Convention: Shall the execution be immediate, or shall there be delay? The Mountain groans and hisses as the question is raised, but the dictation had not extended to this point, and the question must be discussed. Here is one more small chance for Paine's poor royal client. Can the execution only be postponed it will probably never be executed. Unfortunately Marat, whose

[1] Upwards of three hundred voted with Paine, who says that the majority by which death was carried, unconditionally, was twenty-five. As a witness who had watched the case, his testimony may correct the estimate of Carlyle:

"Death by a small majority of Fifty-three. Nay, if we deduct from the one side, and add to the other, a certain Twenty-six who said Death but coupled some faintest ineffectual surmise of mercy with it, the majority will be but *One*." See also Paine's "Mémoire, etc., à Monroe."

thirst for the King's blood is almost cannibalistic, can read on Paine's face his elation. He realizes that this American, with Washington behind him, has laid before the Convention a clear and consistent scheme for utilizing the royal prisoner. The king's neck under a suspended knife, it will rest with the foreign enemies of France whether it shall fall or not; while the magnanimity of France and its respect for American gratitude will prevail. Paine, then, must be dealt with somehow in this new debate about delay.

He might, indeed, have been dealt with summarily had not the *Moniteur* done him an opportune service; on January 17th and 18th it printed Paine's unspoken argument for mercy, along with Erskine's speech at his trial in London, and the verdict. So on the 19th, when Paine entered the Convention, it was with the prestige not only of one outlawed by Great Britain for advocating the Rights of Man, but of a representative of the best Englishmen and their principles. It would be vain to assail the author's loyalty to the republic. That he would speak that day was certain, for on the morrow (20th) the final vote was to be taken. The Mountain could not use on Paine their weapon against Girondins; they could not accuse the author of the "Rights of Man" of being royalist. When he had mounted the tribune, and the clerk (Bancal, Franklin's friend) was beginning to read his speech, Marat cried, "I submit that Thomas Paine is incompetent to vote on this question; being a Quaker his religious principles are opposed to the death-penalty." There was great confusion for a time. The anger of the Jacobins was extreme, says Guizot, and "they refused to listen to the speech of Paine, the American, till respect for his courage gained him a hearing."[1] Demands for freedom of speech gradually subdued the interruptions, and the secretary proceeded:

"Very sincerely do I regret the Convention's vote of yesterday for death. I have the advantage of some experience; it is near twenty years that I have been engaged in the cause of liberty, having contributed something to it in the revolution of the United States of America. My language has always been that of liberty *and* humanity, and I know by experience that nothing so exalts a nation as the union of these two principles, under all circumstances. I know that the public mind of France, and particularly that of Paris, has been heated and irritated by the dangers to which they have been exposed; but could we carry our thoughts into the future, when the dangers are ended, and the irritations forgotten, what to-day seems an act of justice may then appear an act of vengeance. [*Murmurs.*] My anxiety for the cause of France has become for the moment concern for its honor. If, on my return to America, I should employ myself on a history of the French Revolution, I had rather record a thousand errors dictated by humanity, than one inspired by a justice too severe. I voted against an appeal to the people, because it appeared to me that the Convention was needlessly wearied on that point; but I so voted in the hope that this Assembly would pronounce against death, and for the same punishment that the nation would have voted, at least in my opinion, that is, for reclusion during the war and banishment thereafter. That is the punishment most efficacious, because it includes the whole family at once, and none other can so operate. I am still against the appeal to the primary assemblies, because there is a better method. This Convention has been elected to form a Constitution, which will be submitted to the primary assemblies. After its acceptance a necessary consequence will be an election, and another Assembly. We cannot suppose that the

[1] "History of France," vi., p. 136.

present Convention will last more than five or six months. The choice of new deputies will express the national opinion on the propriety or impropriety of your sentence, with as much efficacy as if those primary assemblies had been consulted on it. As the duration of our functions here cannot be long, it is a part of our duty to consider the interests of those who shall replace us. If by any act of ours the number of the nation's enemies shall be needlessly increased, and that of its friends diminished,—at a time when the finances may be more strained than to-day,—we should not be justifiable for having thus unnecessarily heaped obstacles in the path of our successors. Let us therefore not be precipitate in our decisions.

"France has but one ally—the United States of America. That is the only nation that can furnish France with naval provisions, for the kingdoms of northern Europe are, or soon will be, at war with her. It happens, unfortunately, that the person now under discussion is regarded in America as a deliverer of their country. I can assure you that his execution will there spread universal sorrow, and it is in your power not thus to wound the feelings of your ally. Could I speak the French language I would descend to your bar, and in their name become your petitioner to respite the execution of the sentence on Louis."

Here were loud murmurs from the "Mountain," answered with demands for liberty of opinion. Thuriot sprang to his feet crying, "This is not the language of Thomas Paine." Marat mounted the tribune and asked Paine some questions, apparently in English, then descending he said to the Assembly in French: "I denounce the interpreter, and I maintain that such is not the opinion of Thomas Paine. It is a wicked and faithless translation."[1] These words, audacious as mendacious,

[1] "Venant d'un démocrate tel que Thomas Paine, d'un homme qui avait vécu parmi les Américains, d'un penseur, cette déclaration parut si dangereuse à Marat que, pour en détruire l'effet, il n'hésita pas à s'écrier : 'Je dénonce le truchement. Je soutiens que ce n'est point là l'opinion de Thomas Paine. C'est une traduction infidèle.'"—Louis Blanc. See also "Histoire Parliamentaire," xxiii., p. 250.

caused a tremendous uproar. Garran came to the rescue of the frightened clerk, declaring that he had read the original, and the translation was correct. Paine stood silent and calm during the storm. The clerk proceeded :

"Your Executive Committee will nominate an ambassador to Philadelphia; my sincere wish is that he may announce to America that the National Convention of France, out of pure friendship to America, has consented to respite Louis. That people, your only ally, have asked you by my vote to delay the execution.

"Ah, citizens, give not the tyrant of England the triumph of seeing the man perish on a scaffold who helped my dear brothers of America to break his chains!"

At the conclusion of this speech Marat "launched himself into the middle of the hall" and cried out that Paine had "voted against the punishment of death because he was a preacher." Paine replied, "I voted against it both morally and politically."

Had the vote been taken that day perhaps Louis might have escaped. Brissot, shielded from charges of royalism by Paine's republican fame, now strongly supported his cause. "A cruel precipitation," he cried, "may alienate our friends in England, Ireland, America. Take care! The opinion of European peoples is worth to you armies!" But all this only brought out the Mountain's particular kind of courage; they were ready to defy the world—Washington included—in order to prove that a King's neck was no more than any other man's. Marat's clan—the "Nihilists" of the time, whose strength was that they stopped at nothing

—had twenty-four hours to work in; they surrounded the Convention next day with a mob howling for "justice!" Fifty-five members were absent; of the 690 present a majority of seventy decided that Louis XVI. should die within twenty-four hours.

A hundred years have passed since that tragedy of poor Louis; graves have given up their dead; secrets of the hearts that then played their part are known. The world can now judge between England's Outlaw and England's King of that day. For it is established, as we have seen, both by English and French archives, that while Thomas Paine was toiling night and day to save the life of Louis that life lay in the hand of the British Ministry. Some writers question the historic truth of the offer made by Danton, but none can question the refusal of intercession, urged by Fox and others at a time when (as Count d'Estaing told Morris) the Convention was ready to give Pitt the whole French West Indies to keep him quiet. It was no doubt with this knowledge that Paine declared from the tribune that George III. would triumph in the execution of the King who helped America to break England's chains. Brissot also knew it when with weighed words he reported for his Committee (January 12th): "The grievance of the British Cabinet against France is not that Louis is in judgment, but that Thomas Paine wrote 'The Rights of Man.'" "The militia were armed," says Louis Blanc, "in the south-east of England troops received order to march to London, the meeting of Parliament was advanced forty days, the Tower was reinforced by a new garrison, in fine there was unrolled a formidable preparation of war against —Thomas Paine's book on the Rights of Man!"[1]

Incredible as this may appear the debates in the House of Commons, on which it is fairly founded, would be more incredible were they not duly reported in the "Parliamentary History."[2] In the debates on the Alien Bill, permitting the King to order any foreigner out of the country at will, on making representations to the French Convention in behalf of the life of Louis, on augmenting the military forces with direct reference to France, the recent trial of Paine was rehearsed, and it was plainly shown that the object of the government was to suppress freedom of the press by Terror. Erskine was denounced for defending Paine and for afterwards attending a meeting of the "Society of Friends of the Liberty of the Press," to whose resolutions on Paine's case his name was attached. Erskine found gallant defenders in the House, among them Fox, who demanded of Pitt: "Can you not prosecute Paine without an army?" Burke at this time enacted a dramatic scene. Having stated that three thousand daggers had been ordered at Birmingham by an Englishman, he drew from his pocket a dagger, cast it on the floor of the House of Commons, and cried: "That is what we are to get from an alliance with France!" Paine—Paine—Paine—was the burden laid on Pitt, who had said to Lady Hester Stanhope: "Tom Paine is quite right." That Thomas Paine and his

[1] "Histoire de la Révolution," vol. viii., p. 96.
[2] Vol. xxv.

"Rights of Man" were the actual cause of the English insults to which their declaration of war replied was so well understood in the French Convention that its first answer to the menaces was to appoint Paine and Condorcet to write an address to the English people.[1]

It is noticeable that on the question whether the judgment on the King's fate should be submitted to the people, Paine voted "No." His belief in the right of all to representation implied distrust of the immediate voice of the masses. The King had said that if his case were referred to the people "he should be massacred." Gouverneur Morris had heard this, and no doubt communicated it to Paine, who was in consultation with him on his plan of sending Louis to America.[2] Indeed, it is probable that popular suffrage would have ratified the decree. Nevertheless, it was a fair "appeal to the people" which Paine made, after the fatal verdict, in expressing to the Convention his belief that the people would not have done so. For after the decree the helplessness of the prisoner appealed to popular compassion, and on the fatal day the tide had turned. Four days after the execution the American Minister writes to Jefferson: "The greatest care was taken to prevent a concourse of people. This proves a conviction that the majority was not favorable to that severe measure. In fact the great mass of the people mourned the fate of their unhappy prince."

[1] "Le Département des Affaires Étrangères pendant la Révolution, 1787–1804." Par Frédéric Masson, Bibliothécaire du Ministère des Affaires Étrangères. Paris, 1877, p. 273.

[2] Morris' "Diary," ii., pp. 19, 27, 32.

To Paine the death of an "unhappy prince" was no more a subject for mourning than that of the humblest criminal—for, with whatever extenuating circumstances, a criminal he was to the republic he had sworn to administer. But the impolicy of the execution, the resentment uselessly incurred, the loss of prestige in America, were felt by Paine as a heavy blow to his cause—always the international republic. He was, however, behind the scenes enough to know that the blame rested mainly on America's old enemy and his league of foreign courts against liberated France. The man who, when Franklin said "Where liberty is, there is my country," answered "Where liberty is not, there is mine," would not despair of the infant republic because of its blunders. Attributing these outbursts to maddening conspiracies around and within the new-born nation, he did not believe there could be peace in Europe so long as it was ruled by George III. He therefore set himself to the struggle, as he had done in 1776. Moreover, Paine has faith in Providence.[1]

At this time, it should be remembered, opposition to capital punishment was confined to very

[1] "The same spirit of fortitude that insured success to America will insure it to France, for it is impossible to conquer a nation determined to be free. . . . Man is ever a stranger to the ways by which Providence regulates the order of things. The interference of foreign despots may serve to introduce into their own enslaved countries the principles they come to oppose. Liberty and equality are blessings too great to be the inheritance of France alone. It is honour to her to be their first champion; and she may now say to her enemies, with a mighty voice, 'O, ye Austrians, ye Prussians! ye who now turn your bayonets against us, it is for you, it is for all Europe, it is for all mankind, and not for France alone, that she raises the standard of Liberty and Equality!'"—Paine's address to the Convention (September 25, 1792) after taking his seat.

few outside of the despised sect of Quakers. In the debate three, besides Paine, gave emphatic expression to that sentiment, Manuel, Condorcet, —Robespierre! The former, in giving his vote against death, said: "To Nature belongs the right of death. Despotism has taken it from her; Liberty will return it." As for Robespierre, his argument was a very powerful reply to Paine, who had reminded him of the bill he had introduced into the old National Assembly for the abolition of capital punishment. He did, indeed, abhor it, he said; it was not his fault if his views had been disregarded. But why should men who then opposed him suddenly revive the claims of humanity when the penalty happened to fall upon a King? Was the penalty good enough for the people, but not for a King? If there were any exception in favor of such a punishment, it should be for a royal criminal.

This opinion of Robespierre is held by some humane men. The present writer heard from Professor Francis W. Newman—second to none in philanthropy and compassionateness—a suggestion that the death penalty should be reserved for those placed at the head of affairs who betray their trust, or set their own above the public interests to the injury of a Commonwealth.

The real reasons for the execution of the King closely resemble those of Washington for the execution of Major André, notwithstanding the sorrow of the country, with which the Commander sympathized. The equal nationality of the United States, repudiated by Great Britain, was in question. To hang spies was, however illogically, a conventional usage among nations. Major André must die, therefore, and must be refused the soldier's death for which he petitioned. For a like reason Europe must be shown that the French Convention is peer of their scornful Parliaments; and its fundamental principle, the equality of men, could not admit a King's escape from the penalty which would be unhesitatingly inflicted on a "Citizen." The King had assumed the title of Citizen, had worn the republican cockade; the apparent concession of royal inviolability, in the moment of his betrayal of the compromise made with him, could be justified only on the grounds stated by Paine,—impolicy of slaying their hostage, creating pretenders, alienating America; and the honor of exhibiting to the world, by a salient example, the Republic's magnanimity in contrast with the cruelty of Kings.

CHAPTER II.

AN OUTLAWED ENGLISH AMBASSADOR.

Soon after Paine had taken his seat in the Convention, Lord Fortescue wrote to Miles, an English agent in Paris, a letter fairly expressive of the feelings, fears, and hopes of his class.

"Tom Paine is just where he ought to be—a member of the Convention of Cannibals. One would have thought it impossible that any society upon the face of the globe should have been fit for the reception of such a being until the late deeds of the National Convention have shown them to be most fully qualified. His vocation will not be complete, nor theirs either, till his head finds its way to the top of a pike, which will probably not be long first."[1]

[1] This letter, dated September 26, 1792, appears in the Miles Correspondence (London, 1890). There are indications that Miles was favorably disposed towards Paine, and on that account, perhaps, was subjected to influence by his superiors. As an example of the way in which just minds were poisoned towards Paine, a note of Miles may be mentioned. He says he was "told by Col. Bosville, a declared friend of Paine, that his manners and conversation were coarse, and he loved the brandy bottle." But just as this Miles Correspondence was appearing in London, Dr. Grece found the manuscript diary of Rickman, who had discovered (as two entries show) that this "declared friend of Paine," Col. Bosville, and professed friend of himself, was going about uttering injurious falsehoods concerning him (Rickman), seeking to alienate his friends at the moment when he most needed them. Rickman was a bookseller engaged in circulating Paine's works. There is little doubt that this wealthy Col. Bosville was at the time unfriendly to the radicals. He was staying in Paris on Paine's political credit, while depreciating him.

But if Paine was so fit for such a Convention, why should they behead him? The letter betrays a real perception that Paine possesses humane principles, and an English courage, which would bring him into danger. This undertone of Fortescue's invective represented the profound confidence of Paine's adherents in England. When tidings came of the King's trial and execution, whatever glimpses they gained of their outlawed leader showed him steadfast as a star caught in one wave and another of that turbid tide. Many, alas, needed apologies, but Paine required none. That one Englishman, standing on the tribune for justice and humanity, amid three hundred angry Frenchmen in uproar, was as sublime a sight as Europe witnessed in those days. To the English radical the outlawry of Paine was as the tax on light, which was presently walling up London windows, or extorting from them the means of war against ideas.[1] The trial of Paine had elucidated nothing, except that, like Jupiter, John Bull had the thunderbolts, and Paine the arguments. Indeed, it is difficult to discover any other Englishman who at the moment pre-eminently stood for principles now proudly called English.

But Paine too presently held thunderbolts. Although his efforts to save Louis had offended the

[1] In a copy of the first edition of "The Rights of Man," which I bought in London, I found, as a sort of book-mark, a bill for 1*l*. 6*s*. 8*d*., two quarters' window-tax, due from Mr. Williamson, Upper Fitzroy Place. Windows closed with bricks are still seen in some of the gloomiest parts of London. I have in manuscript a bitter anathema of the time:

"God made the Light, and saw that it was good:
Pitt laid a tax on it,—G— d— his blood!"

"Mountain," and momentarily brought him into the danger Lord Fortescue predicted, that party was not yet in the ascendant. The Girondists were still in power, and though some of their leaders had bent before the storm, that they might not be broken, they had been impressed both by the courage and the tactics of Paine. "The Girondists consulted Paine," says Lamartine, "and placed him on the Committee of Surveillance." At this moment many Englishmen were in France, and at a word from Paine some of their heads might have mounted on the pike which Lord Fortescue had imaginatively prepared for the head that wrote "The Rights of Man." There remained, for instance, Mr. Munro, already mentioned. This gentleman, in a note preserved in the English Archives, had written to Lord Grenville (September 8, 1792) concerning Paine: "What must a nation come to that has so little discernment in the election of their representatives, as to elect such a fellow?" But having lingered in Paris after England's formal declaration of war (February 11th), Munro was cast into prison. He owed his release to that "fellow" Paine, and must be duly credited with having acknowledged it, and changed his tone for the rest of his life,—which he probably owed to the English committeeman. Had Paine met with the fate which Lords Gower and Fortescue hoped, it would have gone hard with another eminent countryman of theirs,—Captain Grimstone, R.A. This personage, during a dinner party at the Palais Égalité, got into a controversy with Paine, and, forgetting that the English Jove could not in Paris safely answer argument with thunder, called Paine a traitor to his country and struck him a violent blow. Death was the penalty of striking a deputy, and Paine's friends were not unwilling to see the penalty inflicted on this stout young Captain who had struck a man of fifty-six. Paine had much trouble in obtaining from Barrère, of the Committee of Public Safety, a passport out of the country for Captain Grimstone, whose travelling expenses were supplied by the man he had struck.

In a later instance, related by Walter Savage Landor, Paine's generosity amounted to quixotism. The story is finely told by Landor, who says in a note: "This anecdote was communicated to me at Florence by Mr. Evans, a painter of merit, who studied under Lawrence, and who knew personally (Zachariah) Wilkes and Watt. In religion and politics he differed widely from Paine."

"Sir," said he, "let me tell you what he did for me. My name is Zachariah Wilkes. I was arrested in Paris and condemned to die. I had no friend here ; and it was a time when no friend would have served me : Robespierre ruled. 'I am innocent!' I cried in desperation. 'I am innocent, so help me God! I am condemned for the offence of another.' I wrote a statement of my case with a pencil; thinking at first of addressing it to my judge, then of directing it to the president of the Convention. The jailer, who had been kind to me, gave me a gazette, and told me not to mind seeing my name, so many were there before it.

"'O!' said I 'though you would not lend me your ink, do transmit this paper to the president.'

"'No, my friend!' answered he gaily. 'My head is as good as yours, and looks as well between the shoulders, to my liking. Why not send it (if you send it anywhere) to the deputy Paine here?' pointing to a column in the paper.

"'O God! he must hate and detest the name of Englishman: pelted, insulted, persecuted, plundered . . .'

"'I could give it to him,' said the jailer.

"'Do then!' said I wildly. 'One man more shall know my innocence.' He came within the half hour. I told him my name, that my employers were Watt and Boulton of Birmingham, that I had papers of the greatest consequence, that if I failed to transmit them, not only my life was in question, but my reputation. He replied: 'I know your employers by report only; there are no two men less favourable to the principles I profess, but no two upon earth are honester. You have only one great man among you: it is Watt; for Priestley is gone to America. The church-and-king men would have japanned him. He left to these philosophers of the rival school his house to try experiments on; and you may know, better than I do, how much they found in it of carbon and calx, of silex and argilla.'

"He examined me closer than my judge had done; he required my proofs. After a long time I satisfied him. He then said, 'The leaders of the Convention would rather have my life than yours. If by any means I can obtain your release on my own security, will you promise me to return within twenty days?' I answered, 'Sir, the security I can at present give you, is trifling . . . I should say a mere nothing.'

"'Then you do not give me your word?' said he.

"'I give it and will redeem it.'

"He went away, and told me I should see him again when he could inform me whether he had succeeded. He returned in the earlier part of the evening, looked fixedly upon me, and said, 'Zachariah Wilkes! if you do not return in twenty-four days (four are added) you will be the most unhappy of men; for had you not been an honest one, you could not be the agent of Watt and Boulton. I do not think I have hazarded much in offering to take your place on your failure: such is the condition.' I was speechless; he was unmoved. Silence was first broken by the jailer. 'He seems to get fond of the spot now he must leave it.' I had thrown my arms upon the table towards my liberator, who sat opposite, and I rested my head and breast upon it too, for my temples ached and tears had not yet relieved them. He said, 'Zachariah! follow me to the carriage.' The soldiers paid the respect due to his scarf, presenting arms, and drawing up in file as we went along. The jailer called for a glass of wine, gave it me, poured out another, and drank to our next meeting."[1]

Another instance may be related in Paine's own words, written (March 20, 1806) to a gentleman in New York.

"SIR,—I will inform you of what I know respecting General Miranda, with whom I first became acquainted at New York, about the year 1783. He is a man of talents and enterprise, and the whole of his life has been a life of adventures.

"I went to Europe from New York in April, 1787. Mr. Jefferson was then Minister from America to France, and Mr. Littlepage, a Virginian (whom Mr. Jay knows), was agent for the king of Poland, at Paris. Mr. Littlepage was a young man of extraordinary talents, and I first met with him at Mr. Jefferson's house at dinner. By his intimacy with the king of Poland, to whom also he was chamberlain, he became well acquainted with the plans and projects of the Northern Powers of Europe. He told me of Miranda's getting himself introduced to the Empress Catharine of Russia, and obtaining a sum of money from her, four thousand pounds sterling; but it did not appear to me what the object was for which the money was given; it appeared a kind of retaining fee.

"After I had published the first part of the 'Rights of Man' in England, in the year 1791, I met Miranda at the house of Turnbull and Forbes, merchants, Devonshire Square, London. He had been a little before this in the employ of Mr. Pitt, with respect to the affair of Nootka Sound, but I did not at that time know it; and I will, in the course of this letter, inform you how this connection between Pitt and Miranda ended; for I know it of my own knowledge.

[1] Zachariah Wilkes did not fail to return, or Paine to greet him with safety, and the words, "There is yet English blood in England." But here Landor passes off into an imaginative picture of villages rejoicing at the fall of Robespierre. Paine himself had then been in prison seven months; so we can only conjecture the means by which Zachariah was liberated.—Landor's Works, London, 1853, i., p. 296.

"I published the second part of the 'Rights of Man' in London, in February, 1792, and I continued in London till I was elected a member of the French Convention, in September of that year; and went from London to Paris to take my seat in the Convention, which was to meet the 20th of that month. I arrived in Paris on the 19th. After the Convention met, Miranda came to Paris, and was appointed general of the French army, under General Dumouriez. But as the affairs of that army went wrong in the beginning of the year 1793, Miranda was suspected, and was brought under arrest to Paris to take his trial. He summoned me to appear to his character, and also a Mr. Thomas Christie, connected with the house of Turnbull and Forbes. I gave my testimony as I believed, which was, that his leading object was and had been the emancipation of his country, Mexico, from the bondage of Spain; for I did not at that time know of his engagements with Pitt. Mr. Christie's evidence went to show that Miranda did not come to France as a necessitous adventurer; but believed he came from public-spirited motives, and that he had a large sum of money in the hands of Turnbull and Forbes. The house of Turnbull and Forbes was then in a contract to supply Paris with flour. Miranda was acquitted.

"A few days after his acquittal he came to see me, and in a few days afterwards I returned his visit. He seemed desirous of satisfying me that he was independent, and that he had money in the hands of Turnbull and Forbes. He did not tell me of his affair with old Catharine of Russia, nor did I tell him that I knew of it. But he entered into conversation with respect to Nootka Sound, and put into my hands several letters of Mr. Pitt's to him on that subject; amongst which was one which I believe he gave me by mistake, for when I had opened it, and was beginning to read it, he put forth his hand and said, ' O, that is not the letter I intended'; but as the letter was short I soon got through with it, and then returned it to him without making any remarks upon it. The dispute with Spain was then compromised; and Pitt compromised with Miranda for his services by giving him twelve hundred pounds sterling, for this was the contents of the letter.

"Now if it be true that Miranda brought with him a credit upon certain persons in New York for sixty thousand pounds sterling, it is not difficult to suppose from what quarter the money came ; for the opening of any proposals between Pitt and Miranda was already made by the affair of Nootka Sound. Miranda was in Paris when Mr. Monroe arrived there as Minister ; and as Miranda wanted to get acquainted with him, I cautioned Mr. Monroe against him, and told him of the affair of Nootka Sound, and the twelve hundred pounds.

"You are at liberty to make what use you please of this letter, and with my name to it."

Here we find a paid agent of Pitt calling on outlawed Paine for aid, by his help liberated from prison ; and, when his true character is accidentally discovered, and he is at the outlaw's mercy, spared,—no doubt because this true English ambassador, who could not enter England, saw that at the moment passionate vengeance had taken the place of justice in Paris. Lord Gower had departed, and Paine must try and shield even his English enemies and their agents, where, as in Miranda's case, the agency did not appear to affect France. This was while his friends in England were hunted down with ferocity.

In the earlier stages of the French Revolution there was much sympathy with it among literary men and in the universities. Coleridge, Southey, Wordsworth, were leaders in the revolutionary cult at Oxford and Cambridge. By 1792, and especially after the institution of Paine's prosecution, the repression became determined. The memoir of Thomas Poole, already referred to, gives the experiences of a Somerset gentleman, a friend of Coleridge. After the publication of Paine's "Rights of Man" (1791) he became a "political Ishmaelite." "He made his appearance amongst the wigs and powdered locks of his kinsfolk and acquaintance, male and female, without any of the customary powder in his hair, which innocent novelty was a scandal to all beholders, seeing that it was the outward and visible sign of a love of innovation, a well-known badge of sympathy with democratic ideas."

Among Poole's friends, at Stowey, was an attorney named Symes, who lent him Paine's "Rights of Man." After Paine's outlawry Symes met a cabinet-maker with a copy of the book, snatched it out of his hand, tore it up, and, having learned that it was lent him by Poole, propagated about the country that he (Poole) was distributing seditious literature about the country. Being an influential man, Poole prevented the burning of Paine in effigy at Stowey. As time goes on this country-gentleman and scholar finds the government opening his letters, and warning his friends that he is in danger.

"It was," he writes to a friend, "the boast an Englishman was wont to make that he could think, speak, and write whatever he thought proper, provided he violated no law, nor injured any individual. But now an absolute controul exists, not indeed over the imperceptible operations of the mind, for those no power of man can controul; but, what is the same thing, over the effects of those operations, and if among these effects, that of speaking is to be checked, the soul is as much enslaved as the body in a cell of the Bastille. The man who once feels, nay fancies, this, is a slave. It shows as if the suspicious secret government of an Italian Republic had replaced the open, candid government of the English laws."

As Thomas Poole well represents the serious and cultured thought of young England in that time, it is interesting to read his judgment on the king's execution and the imminent war.

"Many thousands of human beings will be sacrificed in the ensuing contest, and for what? To support three or four individuals, called arbitrary kings, in the situation which they have usurped. I consider every Briton who loses his life in the war us much murdered as the King of France, and every one who approves the war, as signing the death-warrant of each soldier or sailor that falls. . . . The excesses in France are great; but who are the authors of them? The Emperor of Germany, the King of Prussia, and Mr. Burke. Had it not been for their impertinent interference, I firmly believe the King of France would be at this moment a happy monarch, and that people would be enjoying every advantage of political liberty. . . . The slave-trade, you will see, will not be abolished, because to be humane and honest now is to be a traitor to the constitution, a lover of sedition and licentiousness! But this universal depression of the human mind cannot last long."

It was in this spirit that the defence of a free press was undertaken in England. That thirty years' war was fought and won on the works of Paine. There were some "Lost Leaders": the king's execution, the reign of terror, caused reaction in many a fine spirit; but the rank and file followed their Thomas Paine with a faith that crowned heads might envy. The London men knew Paine thoroughly. The treasures of the world would not draw him, nor any terrors drive him, to the side of cruelty and inhumanity. Their eye was upon him. Had Paine, after the king's execution, despaired of the republic there might have ensued some demoralization among his followers in London. But they saw him by the side of the delivered prisoner of the Bastille, Brissot, an author well known in England, by the side of Condorcet and others of Franklin's honored circle, engaged in death-struggle with the fire-breathing dragon called "The Mountain." That was the same unswerving man they had been following, and to all accusations against the revolution their answer was—Paine is still there!

A reign of terror in England followed the outlawry of Paine. Twenty-four men, at one time or another, were imprisoned, fined, or transported for uttering words concerning abuses such as now every Englishman would use concerning the same. Some who sold Paine's works were imprisoned before Paine's trial, while the seditious character of the books was not yet legally settled. Many were punished after the trial, by both fine and imprisonment. Newspapers were punished for printing extracts, and for having printed them before the trial.[1] For this kind of work old statutes passed for other purposes were impressed, new statutes framed, until Fox declared the Bill of Rights repealed, the con-

---

[1] The first trial after Paine's, that of Thomas Spence (February 26, 1793), for selling "The Rights of Man," failed through a flaw in the indictment, but the mistake did not occur again. At the same time William Holland was awarded a year's imprisonment and £100 fine for selling "Letter to the Addressers." H. D. Symonds, for publishing "Rights of Man," £20 fine and two years; for "Letter to the Addressers," one year, £100 fine, with sureties in £1,000 for three years, and imprisonment till the fine be paid and sureties given. April 17, 1793, Richard Phillips, printer, Leicester, eighteen months. May 8th, J. Ridgway, London, selling "Rights of Man," £100 and one year; "Letter to the Addressers," one year, £100 fine; in each case sureties in £1,000, with imprisonment until fines paid and sureties given. Richard Peart, "Rights" and "Letter," three months. William Belcher, "Rights" and "Letter," three months. Daniel Holt, £50, four years. Messrs. Robinson, £200. Eaton and Thompson, the latter in Birmingham, were acquitted. Clio Rickman escaped punish-

stitution cut up by the roots, and the obedience of the people to such "despotism" no longer "a question of moral obligation and duty, but of prudence."[1]

From his safe retreat in Paris bookseller Rickman wrote his impromptu:

> "Hail Briton's land! Hail freedom's shore!
>   Far happier than of old;
> For in thy blessed realms no more
>   The Rights of Man are sold!"

The famous town-crier of Bolton, who reported to his masters that he had been round that place "and found in it neither the rights of man nor common sense," made a statement characteristic of the time. The aristocracy and gentry had indeed lost their humanity and their sense under a disgraceful panic. Their serfs, unable to read, were fairly represented by those who, having burned Paine in effigy, asked their employer if there was "any other gemman he would like burnt, for a

---

ment by running over to Paris. Dr. Currie (1793) writes: "The prosecutions that are commenced all over England against printers, publishers, etc., would astonish you; and most of these are for offences committed many months ago. The printer of the *Manchester Herald* has had seven different indictments preferred against him for paragraphs in his paper; and six *different* indictments for selling or disposing of six different copies of Paine,—all previous to the *trial* of Paine. The man was opulent, supposed worth 20,000 *l.*; but these different actions will ruin him, as they were intended to do."—"Currie's Life," i., p. 185. See Buckle's "History of Civilization," etc., American ed., p. 352. In the cases where "gentlemen" were found distributing the works the penalties were ferocious. Fische Palmer was sentenced to seven years' transportation. Thomas Muir, for advising persons to read "the works of that wretched outcast Paine" (the Lord Advocate's words) was sentenced to fourteen years' transportation. This sentence was hissed. The tipstaff being ordered to take those who hissed into custody, replied: "My lord, they're all hissing."

[1] "Parl. Hist.," xxxii., p. 383.

glass o' beer." The White Bear (now replaced by the Criterion Restaurant) no longer knew its little circle of radicals. A symbol of how they were trampled out is discoverable in the " T. P." shoe-nails. These nails, with heads so lettered, were in great request among the gentry, who had only to hold up their boot-soles to show how they were trampling on Tom Paine and his principles. This at any rate was accurate. Manufacturers of vases also devised ceramic anathemas.[1]

In all of this may be read the frantic fears of the King and aristocracy which were driving the Ministry to make good Paine's aphorism, " There is no English Constitution." An English Constitution was, however, in process of formation,—in prisons, in secret conclaves, in lands of exile, and chiefly in Paine's small room in Paris. Even in that time of Parisian turbulence and peril the hunted liberals of

[1] There are two Paine pitchers in the Museum at Brighton, England. Both were made at Leeds, one probably before Paine's trial, since it presents a respectable full-length portrait, holding in his hand a book, and beneath, the words : " Mr. Thomas Paine, Author of The Rights of Man." The other shows a serpent with Paine's head, two sides being adorned with the following lines :

> " God save the King, and all his subjects too,
> Likewise his forces and commanders true,
> May he their rights forever hence Maintain
> Against all strife occasioned by Tom Paine."

> " Prithee Tom Paine why wilt thou meddling be
> In others' business which concerns not thee ;
> For while thereon thou dost extend thy cares
> Thou dost at home neglect thine own affairs."

> " God save the King ! "

> " Observe the wicked and malicious man
> Projecting all the mischief that he can."

England found more security in France than in their native land.[1] For the eyes of the English reformer of that period, seeing events from prison or exile, there was a perspective such as time has now supplied to the historian. It is still difficult to distribute the burden of shame fairly. Pitt was unquestionably at first anxious to avoid war. That the King was determined on the war is certain; he refused to notice Wilberforce when he appeared at court after his separation from Pitt on that point.

[1] When William Pitt died in 1806,—crushed under disclosures in the impeachment of Lord Melville,—the verdict of many sufferers was expressed in an "Epitaph Impromptu" (MS.) found among the papers of Thomas Rickman. It has some historic interest.

> "Reader! with eye indignant view this bier;
> The foe of all the human race lies here.
> With talents small, and those directed, too,
> Virtue and truth and wisdom to subdue,
> He lived to every noble motive blind,
> And died, the execration of mankind.
>
> "Millions were butchered by his damnèd plan
> To violate each sacred right of man;
> Exulting he o'er earth each misery hurled,
> And joyed to drench in tears and blood, the world.
>
> "Myriads of beings wretched he has made
> By desolating war, his favourite trade,
> Who, robbed of friends and dearest ties, are left
> Of every hope and happiness bereft.
>
> "In private life made up of fuss and pride,
> Not e'en his vices leaned to virtue's side;
> Unsound, corrupt, and rotten at the core,
> His cold and scoundrel heart was black all o'er;
> Nor did one passion ever move his mind
> That bent towards the tender, warm, and kind.
>
> "Tyrant, and friend to war! we hail the day
> When Death, to bless mankind, made thee his prey,
> And rid the earth of all could earth disgrace,—
> The foulest, bloodiest scourge of man's oppressèd race."

But the three attempts on his life, and his mental infirmity, may be pleaded for George III. Paine, in his letter to Dundas, wrote " Madjesty"; when Rickman objected, he said : " Let it stand." And it stands now as the best apology for the King, while it rolls on Pitt's memory the guilt of a twenty-two years' war for the subjugation of thought and freedom. In that last struggle of the barbarism surviving in civilization, it was shown that the madness of a populace was easily distanced by the cruelty of courts. Robespierre and Marat were humanitarian beside George and his Ministers; the Reign of Terror, and all the massacres of the French Revolution put together, were child's-play compared with the anguish and horrors spread through Europe by a war whose pretext was an execution England might have prevented.

CHAPTER III.

REVOLUTION *VS.* CONSTITUTION.

The French revolutionists have long borne responsibility for the first declaration of war in 1793. But from December 13, 1792, when the Painophobia Parliament began its debates, to February 1st, when France proclaimed itself at war with England, the British government had done little else than declare war—and prepare war—against France. Pitt, having to be re-elected, managed to keep away from Parliament for several days at its opening, and the onslaught was assumed by Burke. He began by heaping insults on France. On December 15th he boasted that he had not been cajoled by promise of promotion or pension, though he presently, on the same evening, took his seat for the first time on the Treasury bench. In the "Parliamentary History" (vols. xxx. and xxxi.) may be found Burke's epithets on France,—the "republic of assassins," "Cannibal Castle," "nation of murderers," "gang of plunderers," "murderous atheists," "miscreants," "scum of the earth." His vocabulary grew in grossness, of course, after the King's execution and the declaration of war, but from the first it was ribaldry and abuse. And this did not come from a private member, but from the Treasury bench. He was supported by a furious majority which stopped at no injustice. Thus the Convention was burdened with guilt of the September massacres, though it was not then in existence. Paine's works being denounced, Erskine reminded the House of the illegality of so influencing a trial not yet begun. He was not listened to. Fox and fifty other earnest men had a serious purpose of trying to save the King's life, and proposed to negotiate with the Convention. Burke fairly foamed at the motions to that end, made by Fox and Lord Lansdowne. What, negotiate with such villains! To whom is our agent to be accredited? Burke draws a comic picture of the English ambassador entering the Convention, and, when he announces himself as from "George Third, by the grace of God," denounced by Paine. "Are we to humble ourselves before Judge Paine?" At this point Whetstone made a disturbance and was named. There were some who found Burke's trifling intolerable. Mr. W. Smith reminded the House that Cromwell's ambassadors had been received by Louis XIV. Fox drew a parallel between the contemptuous terms used toward the French, and others about "Hancock and his crew," with whom Burke advised treaty, and with whom His Majesty did treat. All this was answered by further insults to France, these corresponding with a series of practical injuries. Lord Gower had been recalled August 17th, after the formation of a republic, and all intercourse with the French Minister in London, Chauvelin, was terminated. In violation of the treaty of 1786, the agents of France were refused permission to purchase grain and arms in England, and their vessels loaded with provisions seized. The circulation of French bonds, issued in 1790, was prohibited in England. A coalition had been formed with the enemies of France, the Emperor of Austria and the King of Prussia. Finally, on the execution of Louis XVI., Chauvelin was ordered (January 24th) to leave England in eight days. Talleyrand remained, but Chauvelin was kicked out of the country, so to say, simply because the Convention had recognized him. This appeared a plain *casus belli*, and was answered by the declaration of the Convention in that sense (February 1st), which England answered ten days later.[1]

In all this Paine recognized the hand of Burke. While his adherents in England, as we have seen, were finding in Pitt a successor to Satan, there is a notable absence from Paine's writings and letters of any such animosity towards that Minister. He

[1] " It was stipulated in the treaty of commerce between France and England, concluded at Paris [1786] that the sending away an ambassador by either party, should be taken as an act of hostility by the other party. The declaration of war (February, 1793) by the Convention . . . was made in exact conformity to this article in the treaty; for it was not a declaration of war against England, but a declaration that the French republic is *in* war with England; the first act of hostility having been committed by England. The declaration was made on Chauvelin's return to France, and in consequence of it."—Paine's " Address to the People of France " (1797). The words of the declaration of war, following the list of injuries, are: " La Convention Nationale déclaré, au nom de la nation Française, qu'attendu les actes multipliés et d'agressions ci-dessus mentionnés, la république Française est en guerre avec le roi d'Angleterre." The solemn protest of Lords Lauderdale, Lansdowne, and Derby, February 1st, against the address in answer to the royal message, before France had spoken, regards that address as a demonstration of universal war. The facts and the situation are carefully set forth by Louis Blanc, " Histoire de la Révolution," tome viii., p. 93 *seq.*

regarded Pitt as a victim. "The father of Pitt," he once wrote, "when a member of the House of Commons, exclaiming one day, during a former war, against the enormous and ruinous expense of German connections, as the offspring of the Hanover succession, and borrowing a metaphor from the story of Prometheus, cried out: 'Thus, like Prometheus, is Britain chained to the barren rock of Hanover, whilst the imperial eagle preys upon her vitals.'" It is probable that on the intimations from Pitt, at the close of 1792, of his desire for private consultations with friendly Frenchmen, Paine entered into the honorable though unauthorized conspiracy for peace which was terminated by the expulsion of Chauvelin. In the light of later events, and the desertion of Dumouriez, these overtures of Pitt made through Talleyrand (then in London) were regarded by the French leaders, and are still regarded by French writers, as treacherous. But no sufficient reason is given for doubting Pitt's good faith in that matter. Writing to the President (Washington), December 28, 1792, the American Minister, Gouverneur Morris, states the British proposal to be:

"France shall deliver the royal family to such branch of the Bourbons as the King may choose, and shall recall her troops from the countries they now occupy. In this event Britain will send hither a Minister and acknowledge the Republic, and mediate a peace with the Emperor and King of Prussia. I have several reasons to believe that this information is not far from the truth."

It is true that Pitt had no agent in France whom he might not have disavowed, and that after the fury with which the Painophobia Parliament, under lead of Burke, inspired by the King, had opened, could hardly have maintained any peaceful terms. Nevertheless, the friends of peace in France secretly acted on this information, which Gouverneur Morris no doubt received from Paine. A grand dinner was given by Paine, at the Hôtel de Ville, to Dumouriez, where this brilliant General met Brissot, Condorcet, Santerre, and several eminent English radicals, among them Sampson Perry. At this time it was proposed to send Dumouriez secretly to London, to negotiate with Pitt, but this was abandoned. Maret went, and he found Pitt gracious and pacific. Chauvelin, however, advised the French government of this illicit negotiation, and Maret was ordered to return. Such was the situation when Louis was executed. That execution, as we have seen, might have been prevented had Pitt provided the money; but it need not be supposed that, with Burke now on the Treasury bench, the refusal is to be ascribed to anything more than his inability to cope with his own majority, whom the King was patronizing. So completely convinced of Pitt's pacific disposition were Maret and his allies in France that the clandestine ambassador again departed for London. But on arriving at Dover, he learned that Chauvelin had been expelled, and at once returned to France.[1]

Paine now held more firmly than ever the first article of his faith as to practical politics: the chief

[1] See Louis Blanc's "Histoire," etc., tome viii., p. 100, for the principal authorities concerning this incident.—*Annual Register*, 1793, ch. vi.; "Mémoires tirés des papiers d'un homme d'État.," ii., p. 157; "Mémoires de Dumouriez," t. iii., p. 384.

task of republicanism is to break the Anglo-German sceptre. France is now committed to war; it must be elevated to that European aim. Lord North and America reappear in Burke and France.

Meanwhile what is said of Britain in his "Rights of Man" was now more terribly true of France— it had no Constitution. The Committee on the Constitution had declared themselves ready to report early in the winter, but the Mountaineers managed that the matter should be postponed until after the King's trial. As an American who prized his citizenship, Paine felt chagrined and compromised at being compelled to act as a legislator and a judge because of his connection with a Convention elected for the purpose of framing a legislative and judicial machinery. He and Condorcet continued to add touches to this Constitution, the Committee approving, and on the first opportunity it was reported again. This was February 15, 1793. But, says the *Moniteur*, "the struggles between the Girondins and the Mountain caused the examination and discussion to be postponed." It was, however, distributed.

Gouverneur Morris, in a letter to Jefferson (March 7th), says this Constitution "was read to the Convention, but I learnt the next morning that a Council had been held on it overnight, by which it was condemned." Here is evidence in our American archives of a meeting or "Council" condemning the Constitution on the night of its submission. It must have been secret, for it does not appear in French histories, so far as I can discover. Durand de Maillane says that "the exclusion of Robespierre and Couthon from this eminent task [framing a Constitution] was a new matter for discontent and jealousy against the party of Pétion "—a leading Girondin,—and that Robespierre and his men desired " to render their work useless." [1] No indication of this secret condemnation of the Paine-Condorcet Constitution, by a conclave appeared on March 1st, when the document was again submitted. The Convention now set April 15th for its discussion, and the Mountaineers fixed that day for the opening of their attack on the Girondins. The Mayor of Paris appeared with a petition, adopted by the Communal Council of the thirty-five sections of Paris, for the arrest of twenty-two members of the Convention, as slanderers of Paris,—" presenting the Parisians to Europe as men of blood,"—friends of Roland, accomplices of the traitor Dumouriez, enemies of the clubs. The deputies named were: Brissot, Guadet, Vergniaud, Gensonné, Grangeneuve, Buzot, Barbaroux, Salles, Biroteau, Pontécoulant, Pétion, Lanjuinais, Valazé, Hardy, Louvet, Lehardy, Gorsas, Abbé Fauchet, Lanthenas, Lasource, Valady, Chambon. Of this list five were members of the Committee on the Constitution, and two supplementary members.[2] Besides this, two of the arraigned—Louvet and Lasource—had been especially active in pressing forward the Constitution. The Mountaineers turned the discord they thus

---

[1] "Histoire de la Convention Nationale," p. 50. Durand-Maillane was "the silent member" of the Convention, but a careful observer and well-informed witness. I follow him and Louis Blanc in relating the fate of the Paine-Condorcet Constitution.

[2] See vol. i., p. 357.

caused into a reason for deferring discussion of the Constitution. They declared also that important members were absent, levying troops, and especially that Marat's trial had been ordered. The discussion on the petition against the Girondins, and whether the Constitution should be considered, proceeded together for two days, when the Mountaineers were routed on both issues. The Convention returned the petition to the Mayor, pronouncing it " calumnious," and it made the Constitution the order of the day. Robespierre, according to Durand-Maillane, showed much spite at this defeat. He adroitly secured a decision that the preliminary " Declaration of Rights " should be discussed first, as there could be endless talk on those generalities.[1]

[1] This Declaration, submitted by Condorcet, April 17th, being largely the work of Paine, is here translated: The end of all union of men in society being maintenance of their natural rights, civil and political, these rights should be the basis of the social pact : their recognition and their declaration ought to precede the Constitution which secures and guarantees them. 1. The natural rights, civil and political, of men are liberty, equality, security, property, social protection, and resistance to oppression. 2. Liberty consists in the power to do whatever is not contrary to the rights of others ; thus, the natural rights of each man has no limits other than those which secure to other members of society enjoyment of the same rights. 3. The preservation of liberty depends on the sovereignty of the Law, which is the expression of the general will. Nothing unforbidden by law can be impeached, and none may be constrained to do what it does not command. 4. Every man is free to make known his thought and his opinions. 5. Freedom of the press (and every other means of publishing one's thoughts) cannot be prohibited, suspended, or limited. 6. Every citizen shall be free in the exercise of his worship [*culte*]. 7. Equality consists in the power of each to enjoy the same rights. 8. The Law should be equal for all, whether in recompense, punishment, or restraint. 9. All citizens are admissible to all public positions, employments, and functions. Free peoples can recognise no grounds of preference except talents and virtues. 10. Security consists in the protection accorded by society to each citizen for the preservation of his person, property, and rights. 11. None should be sued, accused, arrested, or detained, save in cases determined by the law, and in accordance with forms prescribed by it. Every other act against a

It now appears plain that Robespierre, Marat, and the Mountaineers generally were resolved that there should be no new government. The difference between them and their opponents was fundamental: to them the Revolution was an end, to the others a means. The Convention was a purely revolutionary body. It had arbitrarily absorbed all legislative and judicial functions, exercising them without responsibility to any code or constitution. For instance, in State Trials French law required three fourths of the voices for condemnation; had the rule been followed Louis XVI. would not have perished. Lanjuinais had pressed the point, and it was answered that the sentence on Louis was political, for the interest of the State; *salus populi suprema lex*. This implied that the Convention,

citizen is arbitrary and null. 12. Those who solicit, promote, sign, execute or cause to be executed such arbitrary acts are culpable, and should be punished. 13. Citizens against whom the execution of such acts is attempted have the right of resistance by force. Every citizen summoned or arrested by the authority of law, and in the forms prescribed by it, should instantly obey; he renders himself guilty by resistance. 14. Every man being presumed innocent until declared guilty, should his arrest be judged indispensable, all rigor not necessary to secure his person should be severely repressed by law. 15. None should be punished save in virtue of a law established and promulgated previous to the offence, and legally applied. 16. A law that should punish offences committed before its existence would be an arbitrary Act. Retroactive effect given to any law is a crime. 17. Law should award only penalties strictly and evidently necessary to the general security; they should be proportioned to the offence and useful to society. 18. The right of property consists in a man's being master in the disposal, at his will, of his goods, capital, income, and industry. 19. No kind of work, commerce, or culture can be interdicted for any one; he may make, sell, and transport every species of production. 20. Every man may engage his services, and his time; but he cannot sell himself; his person is not an alienable property. 21. No one may be deprived of the least portion of his property without his consent, unless because of public necessity, legally determined, exacted openly, and under the condition of a just indemnity in advance. 22. No tax shall be established except for the general utility, and to relieve public needs. All citizens have the right to co-operate, turning aside from its appointed functions, had, in anticipation of the judicial forms it meant to establish, constituted itself into a Vigilance Committee to save the State in an emergency. But it never turned back again to its proper work. Now when the Constitution was framed, every possible obstruction was placed in the way of its adoption, which would have relegated most of the Mountaineers to private life.

Robespierre and Marat were in luck. The Paine-Condorcet Constitution omitted all mention of a Deity. Here was the immemorial and infallible recipe for discord, of which Robespierre made the most. He took the "Supreme Being" under his protection ; he also took morality under his protection, insisting that the Paine-Condorcet Constitution

personally or by their representatives, in the establishment of public contributions. 23. Instruction is the need of all, and society owes it equally to all its members. 24. Public succors are a sacred debt of society, and it is for the law to determine their extent and application. 25. The social guarantee of the rights of man rests on the national sovereignty. 26. This sovereignty is one, indivisible, imprescriptible, and inalienable. 27. It resides essentially in the whole people, and each citizen has an equal right to co-operate in its exercise. 28. No partial assemblage of citizens, and no individual may attribute to themselves sovereignty, to exercise authority and fill any public function, without a formal delegation by the law. 29. Social security cannot exist where the limits of public administration are not clearly determined by law, and where the responsibility of all public functionaries is not assured. 30. All citizens are bound to co-operate in this guarantee, and to enforce the law when summoned in its name. 31. Men united in society should have legal means of resisting oppression. In every free government the mode of resisting different acts of oppression should be regulated by the Constitution. 32. It is oppression when a law violates the natural rights, civil and political, which it should ensure. It is oppression when the law is violated by public officials in its application to individual cases. It is oppression when arbitrary acts violate the rights of citizens against the terms of the law. 33. A people has always the right to revise, reform, and change its Constitution. One generation has no right to bind future generations, and all heredity in offices is absurd and tyrannical.

gave liberty even to illicit traffic. While these discussions were going on Marat gained his triumphant acquittal from the charges made against him by the Girondins. This damaging blow further demoralized the majority which was eager for the Constitution. By violence, by appeals against atheism, by all crafty tactics, the Mountaineers secured recommitment of the Constitution. To the Committee were added Hérault de Séchelles, Ramel, Mathieu, Couthon, Saint-Just,—all from the Committee of Public Safety. The Constitution as committed was the most republican document of the kind ever drafted, as remade it was a revolutionary instrument; but its preamble read: " In the presence and under the guidance (*auspices*) of the Supreme Being, the French People declare," etc.

God was in the Constitution; but when it was reported (June 10th) the Mountaineers had their opponents *en route* for the scaffold. The arraignment of the twenty-two, declared by the Convention " calumnious " six weeks before, was approved on June 2d. It was therefore easy to pass such a constitution as the victors desired. Some had suggested, during the theological debate, that " many crimes had been sanctioned by this King of kings,"—no doubt with emphasis on the discredited royal name. Robespierre identified his " Supreme Being " with NATURE, of whose ferocities the poor Girondins soon had tragical evidence.[1]

---

[1] " Les rois, les aristocrates, les tyrans qu'ils soient, sont des esclaves révoltés contre le souverain de la terre, qui est le *genre humain*, et contre le législateur de l'univers, qui est la *nature*."—Robespierre's final article of "' Rights," adopted by the Jacobins, April 21, 1793. Should not slaves revolt?

The Constitution was adopted by the Convention on June 25th; it was ratified by the Communes August 10th. When it was proposed to organize a government under it, and dissolve the Convention, Robespierre remarked: *That sounds like a suggestion of Pitt!* Thereupon the Constitution was suspended until universal peace, and the Revolution superseded the Republic as end and aim of France.[1]

Some have ascribed to Robespierre a phrase he borrowed, on one occasion, from Voltaire, *Si Dieu n'existait pas, il faudrait l'inventer*. Robespierre's originality was that he did invent a god, made in his own image, and to that idol offered human sacrifices,—beginning with his own humanity. That he was genuinely superstitious is suggested by the plausibility with which his enemies connected him

[1] "I observed in the french revolutions that they always proceeded by stages, and made each stage a stepping stone to another. The Convention, to amuse the people, voted a constitution, and then voted to suspend the practical establishment of it till after the war, and in the meantime to carry on a revolutionary government. When Robespierre fell they proposed bringing forward the *suspended* Constitution, and apparently for this purpose appointed a committee to frame what they called *organic laws*, and these organic laws turned out to be a new Constitution (the Directory Constitution which was in general a good one). When Bonaparte overthrew this Constitution he got himself appointed first *Consul* for ten years, then for life, and now Emperor with an hereditary succession."—Paine to Jefferson. MS. (Dec. 27, 1804). The Paine-Condorcet Constitution is printed in *Œuvres Complètes de Condorcet*, vol. xviii. That which superseded it may be read (the Declaration of Rights omitted) in the "Constitutional History of France. By Henry C. Lockwood." (New York, 1890). It is, *inter alia*, a sufficient reason for describing the latter as revolutionary, that it provides that a Convention, elected by a majority of the departments, and a tenth part of the primaries, to revise or alter the Constitution, shall be "formed in like manner as the legislatures, and unite in itself the highest power." In other words, instead of being limited to constitutional revision, may exercise all legislative and other functions, just as the existing Convention was doing.

with the "prophetess," Catharine Théot, who pronounced him the reincarnate "Word of God." Certain it is that he revived the old forces of fanaticism, and largely by their aid crushed the Girondins, who were rationalists. Condorcet had said that in preparing a Constitution for France they had not consulted Numa's nymph or the pigeon of Mahomet; they had found human reason sufficient.

Corruption of best is worst. In the proportion that a humane deity would be a potent sanction for righteous laws, an inhuman deity is the sanction of inhuman laws. He who summoned a nature-god to the French Convention let loose the scourge on France. Nature inflicts on mankind, every day, a hundred-fold the agonies of the Reign of Terror. Robespierre had projected into nature a sentimental conception of his own, but he had no power to master the force he had evoked. That had to take the shape of the nature-gods of all time, and straightway dragged the Convention down to the savage plane where discussion becomes an exchange of thunder-stones. Such relapses are not very difficult to effect in revolutionary times. By killing off sceptical variations, and cultivating conformity, a cerebral evolution proceeded for ages by which kind-hearted people were led to worship jealous and cruel gods, who, should they appear in human form, would be dealt with as criminals. Unfortunately, however, the nature-god does not so appear; it is represented in euphemisms, while at the same time it coerces the social and human standard. Since the nature-god punishes hereditarily, kills every man at last, and so tortures millions that the suggestion of hell seems only too probable to those sufferers, a political system formed under the legitimacy of such a superstition must subordinate crimes to sins, regard atheism as worse than theft, acknowledge the arbitrary principle, and confuse retaliation with justice. From the time that the shekinah of the nature-god settled on the Mountain, offences were measured, not by their injury to man, but as insults to the Mountain-god, or to his anointed. In the mysterious counsels of the Committee of Public Safety the rewards are as little harmonious with the human standard as in the ages when sabbath-breaking and murder met the same doom. Under the paralyzing splendor of a divine authority, any such considerations as the suffering or death of men become petty. The average Mountaineer was unable to imagine that those who tried to save Louis had other than royalist motives. In this Armageddon the Girondins were far above their opponents in humanity and intelligence, but the conditions did not admit of an entire adherence to their honorable weapons of argument and eloquence. They too often used deadly threats, without meaning them; the Mountaineers, who did mean them, took such phrases seriously, and believed the struggle to be one of life and death. Such phenomena of bloodshed, connected with absurdly inadequate causes, are known in history only where gods mingle in the fray. Reign of Terror? What is the ancient reign of the god of battles, jealous, angry every day, with everlasting tortures of fire prepared for the unorthodox, however upright, even more than for the immoral? In France too it was a suspicion of unorthodoxy in the revolutionary creed that plunged most of the sufferers into the lake of fire and brimstone.

From the time of Paine's speeches on the King's fate he was conscious that Marat's evil eye was on him. The American's inflexible republicanism had inspired the vigilance of the powerful journals of Brissot and Bonneville, which barred the way to any dictatorship. Paine was even propagating a doctrine against presidency, thus marring the example of the United States, on which ambitious Frenchmen, from Marat to the Napoleons, have depended for their stepping-stone to despotism. Marat could not have any doubt of Paine's devotion to the Republic, but knew well his weariness of the Revolution. In the simplicity of his republican faith Paine had made a great point of the near adoption of the Constitution, and dissolution of the Convention in five or six months, little dreaming that the Mountaineers were concentrating themselves on the aim of becoming masters of the existing Convention and then rendering it permanent. Marat regarded Paine's influence as dangerous to revolutionary government, and, as he afterwards admitted, desired to crush him. The proposed victim had several vulnerable points: he had been intimate with Gouverneur Morris, whose hostility to France was known; he had been intimate with Dumouriez, declared a traitor; and he had no connection with any of the Clubs, in which so many found asylum. He might have joined one of them had he known the French language, and perhaps it would have been prudent to unite himself with the "Cordeliers," in whose *esprit de corps* some of his friends found refuge.

However, the time of intimidation did not come for two months after the King's death, and Paine was busy with Condorcet on the task assigned them, of preparing an Address to the People of England concerning the war of their government against France. This work, if ever completed, does not appear to have been published. It was entrusted (February 1st) to Barrère, Paine, Condorcet, and M. Faber. As Frédéric Masson, the learned librarian and historian of the Office of Foreign Affairs, has found some trace of its being assigned to Paine and Condorcet, it may be that further research will bring to light the Address. It could hardly have been completed before the warfare broke out between the Mountain and the Girondins, when anything emanating from Condorcet and Paine would have been delayed, if not suppressed. There are one or two brief essays in Condorcet's works—notably "The French Republic to Free Men"—which suggest collaboration with Paine, and may be fragments of their Address.[1]

[1] "Œuvres Complètes de Condorcet," Paris, 1804, t. xvi., p. 16: "La République Française aux hommes libres." In 1794, when Paine was in prison, a pamphlet was issued by the revolutionary government, entitled: "An Answer to the Declaration of the King of England, respecting his Motives for Carrying on the Present War, and his Conduct towards France." This anonymous pamphlet, which is in English, replies to the royal proclamation of October 29th, and bears evidence of being written while the English still occupied Toulon or early in November, 1793. There are passages in it that suggest the hand of Paine, along with others which he could not have written. It is possible that some composition of his, in pursuance of the task assigned him and Condorcet, was utilized by the Committee of Public Safety in its answer to George III.

At this time the long friendship between Paine and Condorcet, and the Marchioness too, had become very intimate. The two men had acted together on the King's trial at every step, and their speeches on bringing Louis to trial suggest previous consultations between them.

Early in April Paine was made aware of Marat's hostility to him. General Thomas Ward reported to him a conversation in which Marat had said: "Frenchmen are mad to allow foreigners to live among them. They should cut off their ears, let them bleed a few days, and then cut off their heads." "But you yourself are a foreigner," Ward had replied, in allusion to Marat's Swiss birth.[1] The answer is not reported. At length a tragical incident occurred, just before the trial of Marat (April 13th), which brought Paine face to face with this enemy. A wealthy young Englishman, named Johnson, with whom Paine had been intimate in London, had followed him to Paris, where he lived in the same house with his friend. His love of Paine amounted to worship. Having heard of Marat's intention to have Paine's life taken, such was the young enthusiast's despair, and so terrible the wreck of his republican dreams, that he resolved on suicide. He made a will bequeathing his property to Paine, and stabbed himself. Fortunately he was saved by some one who entered just as he was about to give himself the third blow. It may have been Paine himself who then saved his friend's life; at any rate, he did so eventually.

---

[1] "Englishmen in the French Revolution." By John G. Alger. London, 1889, p. 176. (A book of many blunders.)

The decree for Marat's trial was made amid galleries crowded with his adherents, male and female ("Dames de la Fraternité"), who hurled cries of wrath on every one who said a word against him. All were armed, the women ostentatious of their poignards. The trial before the Revolutionary Tribunal was already going in Marat's favor, when it was determined by the Girondins to bring forward this affair of Johnson. Paine was not, apparently, a party to this move, though he had enjoined no secrecy in telling his friend Brissot of the incident, which occurred before Marat was accused. On April 16th there appeared in Brissot's journal *Le Patriote Français*, the following paragraph:

"A sad incident has occurred to apprise the anarchists of the mournful fruits of their frightful teaching. An Englishman, whose name I reserve, had abjured his country because of his detestation of kings; he came to France hoping to find there liberty; he saw only its mask on the hideous visage of anarchy. Heart-broken by this spectacle, he determined on self-destruction. Before dying, he wrote the following words, which we have read, as written by his own trembling hand, on a paper which is in the possession of a distinguished foreigner:—'I had come to France to enjoy Liberty, but Marat has assassinated it. Anarchy is even more cruel than despotism. I am unable to endure this grievous sight, of the triumph of imbecility and inhumanity over talent and virtue.'"

The acting editor of *Le Patriote Français*, Girey-Dupré, was summoned before the Tribunal, where Marat was on trial, and testified that the note published had been handed to him by Brissot, who assured him that it was from the original, in the hands of Thomas Paine. Paine deposed that he had been unacquainted with Marat before the Convention assembled; that he had not supposed Johnson's note to have any connection with the accusations against Marat.

> *President.*—Did you give a copy of the note to Brissot?
> *Paine.*—I showed him the original.
> *President.*—Did you send it to him as it is printed?
> *Paine.*—Brissot could only have written this note after what I read to him, and told him. I would observe to the tribunal that Johnson gave himself two blows with the knife after he had understood that Marat would denounce him.
> *Marat.*—Not because I would denounce the youth who stabbed himself, but because I wish to denounce Thomas Paine.[1]
> *Paine (continuing).*—Johnson had for some time suffered mental anguish. As for Marat, I never spoke to him but once. In the lobby of the Convention he said to me that the English people are free and happy; I replied, they groan under a double despotism.[2]

No doubt it had been resolved to keep secret the fact that young Johnson was still alive. The moment was critical; a discovery that Brissot had written or printed "avant de mourir" of one still alive might have precipitated matters.

It came out in the trial that Marat, addressing a club ("Friends of Liberty and Equality"), had asked them to register a vow to recall from the Convention "all of those faithless members who had betrayed their duties in trying to save a tyrant's life," such deputies being "traitors, royalists, or fools."

Meanwhile the Constitution was undergoing discussion in the Convention, and to that Paine now

---

[1] It would appear that Paine had not been informed until Marat declared it, and was confirmed by the testimony of Choppin, that the attempted suicide was on his account.

[2] *Moniteur*, April 24, 1793.

gave his entire attention. On April 20th the Convention, about midnight, when the Moderates had retired and the Mountaineers found themselves masters of the field, voted to entertain the petition of the Parisian sections against the Girondins. Paine saw the star of the Republic sinking. On "April 20th, 2d year of the Republic," he wrote as follows to Jefferson :

" My dear Friend,—The gentleman (Dr. Romer) to whom I entrust this letter is an intimate acquaintance of Lavater ; but I have not had the opportunity of seeing him, as he had sett off for Havre prior to my writing this letter, which I forward to him under cover from one of his friends, who is also an acquaintance of mine.

" We are now in an extraordinary crisis, and it is not altogether without some considerable faults here. Dumouriez, partly from having no fixed principles of his own, and partly from the continual persecution of the Jacobins, who act without either prudence or morality, has gone off to the Enemy, and taken a considerable part of the Army with him. The expedition to Holland has totally failed and all Brabant is again in the hands of the Austrians.

" You may suppose the consternation which such a sudden reverse of fortune has occasioned, but it has been without commotion. Dumouriez threatened to be in Paris in three weeks. It is now three weeks ago ; he is still on the frontier near to Mons with the Enemy, who do not make any progress. Dumouriez has proposed to re-establish the former Constitution, in which plan the Austrians act with him. But if France and the National Convention act prudently this project will not succeed. In the first place there is a popular disposition against it, and there is force sufficient to prevent it. In the next place, a great deal is to be taken into the calculation with respect to the Enemy. There are now so many powers accidentally jumbled together as to render it exceedingly difficult to them to agree upon any common object.

" The first object, that of restoring the old Monarchy, is

evidently given up by the proposal to re-establish the late Constitution. The object of England and Prussia was to preserve Holland, and the object of Austria was to recover Brabant; while those separate objects lasted, each party having one, the Confederation could hold together, each helping the other; but after this I see not how a common object is to be formed. To all this is to be added the probable disputes about opportunity, the expense, and the projects of reimbursements. The Enemy has once adventured into France, and they had the permission or the good fortune to get back again. On every military calculation it is a hazardous adventure, and armies are not much disposed to try a second time the ground upon which they have been defeated.

"Had this revolution been conducted consistently with its principles, there was once a good prospect of extending liberty through the greatest part of Europe; but I now relinquish that hope. Should the Enemy by venturing into France put themselves again in a condition of being captured, the hope will revive; but this is a risk that I do not wish to see tried, lest it should fail.

"As the prospect of a general freedom is now much shortened, I begin to contemplate returning home. I shall await the event of the proposed Constitution, and then take my final leave of Europe. I have not written to the President, as I have nothing to communicate more than in this letter. Please to present to him my affection and compliments, and remember me among the circle of my friends. Your sincere and affectionate friend,

"THOMAS PAINE.

"P. S. I just now received a letter from General Lewis Morris, who tells me that the house and Barn on my farm at N. Rochelle are burnt down. I assure you I shall not bring money enough to build another."

Four days after this letter was written Marat, triumphant, was crowned with oak leaves. Foufrede in his speech (April 16th) had said: "Marat has formally demanded dictatorship." This was the mob's reply: *Bos locutus est.*

With Danton, Paine had been on friendly terms, though he described as "rose water" the author's pleadings against the guillotine. On May 6th, Paine wrote to Danton a letter brought to light by Taine, who says: "Compared with the speeches and writings of the time, it produces the strangest effect by its practical good sense."[1] Dr. Robinet also finds here evidence of "a lucid and wise intellect."[2]

"PARIS, May 6th, 2nd year of the Republic (1793).

"CITOYEN DANTON:
"As you read English, I write this letter to you without passing it through the hands of a translator. I am exceedingly disturbed at the distractions, jealousies, discontents and uneasiness that reign among us, and which, if they continue, will bring ruin and disgrace on the Republic. When I left America in the year 1787, it was my intention to return the year following, but the French Revolution, and the prospect it afforded of extending the principles of liberty and fraternity through the greater part of Europe, have induced me to prolong my stay upwards of six years. I now despair of seeing the great object of European liberty accomplished, and my despair arises not from the combined foreign powers, not from the intrigues of aristocracy and priestcraft, but from the tumultuous misconduct with which the internal affairs of the present revolution is conducted.

"All that now can be hoped for is limited to France only, and I agree with your motion of not interfering in the government of any foreign country, nor permitting any foreign country to interfere in the government of France. This decree was necessary as a preliminary toward terminating the war. But while these internal contentions continue, while the hope remains to the enemy of seeing the Republic fall to pieces, while not only the representatives of the departments but representation itself is publicly insulted, as it has lately

[1] "La Révolution," ii., pp. 382, 413, 414.
[2] "Danton Emigré," p. 177.

been and now is by the people of Paris, or at least by the tribunes, the enemy will be encouraged to hang about the frontiers and await the issue of circumstances.

"I observe that the confederated powers have not yet recognised Monsieur, or D'Artois, as regent, nor made any proclamation in favour of any of the Bourbons; but this negative conduct admits of two different conclusions. The one is that of abandoning the Bourbons and the war together; the other is that of changing the object of the war and substituting a partition scheme in the place of their first object, as they have done by Poland. If this should be their object, the internal contentions that now rage will favour that object far more than it favoured their former object. The danger every day increases of a rupture between Paris and the departments. The departments did not send their deputies to Paris to be insulted, and every insult shown to them is an insult to the departments that elected and sent them. I see but one effectual plan to prevent this rupture taking place, and that is to fix the residence of the Convention, and of the future assemblies, at a distance from Paris.

"I saw, during the American Revolution, the exceeding inconvenience that arose by having the government of Congress within the limits of any Municipal Jurisdiction. Congress first resided in Philadelphia, and after a residence of four years it found it necessary to leave it. It then adjourned to the State of Jersey. It afterwards removed to New York; it again removed from New York to Philadelphia, and after experiencing in every one of these places the great inconvenience of a government, it formed the project of building a Town, not within the limits of any municipal jurisdiction, for the future residence of Congress. In any one of the places where Congress resided, the municipal authority privately or openly opposed itself to the authority of Congress, and the people of each of those places expected more attention from Congress than their equal share with the other States amounted to. The same thing now takes place in France, but in a far greater excess.

"I see also another embarrassing circumstance arising in Paris of which we have had full experience in America. I mean that of fixing the price of provisions. But if this measure is to be attempted it ought to be done by the Municipality. The Convention has nothing to do with regulations of this kind; neither can they be carried into practice. The people of Paris may say they will not give more than a certain price for provisions, but as they cannot compel the country people to bring provisions to market the consequence will be directly contrary to their expectations, and they will find dearness and famine instead of plenty and cheapness. They may force the price down upon the stock in hand, but after that the market will be empty.

"I will give you an example. In Philadelphia we undertook, among other regulations of this kind, to regulate the price of Salt; the consequence was that no Salt was brought to market, and the price rose to thirty-six shillings sterling per Bushel. The price before the war was only one shilling and sixpence per Bushel; and we regulated the price of flour (farine) till there was none in the market, and the people were glad to procure it at any price.

"There is also a circumstance to be taken into the account which is not much attended to. The assignats are not of the same value they were a year ago, and as the quantity increases the value of them will diminish. This gives the appearance of things being dear when they are not so in fact, for in the same proportion that any kind of money falls in value articles rise in price. If it were not for this the quantity of assignats would be too great to be circulated. Paper money in America fell so much in value from this excessive quantity of it, that in the year 1781 I gave three hundred paper dollars for one pair of worsted stockings. What I write you upon this subject is experience, and not merely opinion.

"I have no personal interest in any of these matters, nor in any party disputes. I attend only to general principles.

"As soon as a constitution shall be established I shall return to America; and be the future prosperity of France ever so great, I shall enjoy no other part of it than the happiness of knowing it. In the mean time I am distressed to see matters so badly conducted, and so little attention paid to moral principles. It is these things that injure the character of the Revolution and discourage the progress of liberty all over the world.

"When I began this letter I did not intend making it so lengthy, but since I have gone thus far I will fill up the remainder of the sheet with such matters as occur to me.

"There ought to be some regulation with respect to the spirit of denunciation that now prevails. If every individual is to indulge his private malignacy or his private ambition, to denounce at random and without any kind of proof, all confidence will be undermined and all authority be destroyed. Calumny is a species of Treachery that ought to be punished as well as any other kind of Treachery. It is a private vice productive of public evils ; because it is possible to irritate men into disaffection by continual calumny who never intended to be disaffected. It is therefore, equally as necessary to guard against the evils of unfounded or malignant suspicion as against the evils of blind confidence. It is equally as necessary to protect the characters of public officers from calumny as it is to punish them for treachery or misconduct. For my own part I shall hold it a matter of doubt, until better evidence arises than is known at present, whether Dumouriez has been a traitor from policy or from resentment. There was certainly a time when he acted well, but it is not every man whose mind is strong enough to bear up against ingratitude, and I think he experienced a great deal of this before he revolted. Calumny becomes harmless and defeats itself when it attempts to act upon too large a scale. Thus the denunciation of the Sections [of Paris] against the twenty-two deputies falls to the ground. The departments that elected them are better judges of their moral and political characters than those who have denounced them. This denunciation will injure Paris in the opinion of the departments because it has the appearance of dictating to them what sort of deputies they shall elect. Most of the acquaintances that I have in the convention are among those who are in that list, and I know there are not better men nor better patriots than what they are.

"I have written a letter to Marat of the same date as this but not on the same subject. He may show it to you if he chuse.

"Votre Ami,

"THOMAS PAINE.

"Citoyen Danton."

It is to be hoped that Paine's letter to Marat may be discovered in France; it is shown by the Cobbett papers, printed in the Appendix, that he kept a copy, which there is reason to fear perished with General Bonneville's library in St. Louis. Whatever may be the letter's contents, there is no indication that thereafter Marat troubled Paine. Possibly Danton and Marat compared their letters, and the latter got it into his head that hostility to this American, anxious only to cross the ocean, could be of no advantage to him. Or perhaps he remembered that if a hue and cry were raised against "foreigners" it could not stop short of his own leaf-crowned Neufchatel head. He had shown some sensitiveness about that at his trial. Samson-Pegnet had testified that, at conversations in Paine's house, Marat had been reported as saying that it was necessary to massacre all the foreigners, especially the English. This Marat pronounced an "atrocious calumny, a device of the statesmen [his epithet for Girondins] to render me odious." Whatever his motives, there is reason to believe that Marat no longer included Paine in his proscribed list. Had it been otherwise a fair opportunity of striking down Paine presented itself on the occasion, already alluded to, when Paine gave his testimony in favor of General Miranda. Miranda was tried before the Revolutionary Tribunal on May 12th, and three days following. He had served under Dumouriez, was defeated, and was suspected of connivance with his treacherous commander. Paine was known to have been friendly with Dumouriez, and his testimony in favor of Miranda might naturally have been used against both men. Miranda was, however, acquitted, and that did not make Marat better disposed towards that adventurer's friends, all Girondins, or, like Paine, who belonged to no party, hostile to Jacobinism. Yet when, on June 2d, the doomed Girondins were arrested, there were surprising exceptions : Paine and his literary collaborateur, Condorcet. Moreover, though the translator of Paine's works, Lanthenas, was among the proscribed, his name was erased on Marat's motion.

On June 7th Robespierre demanded a more stringent law against foreigners, and one was soon after passed ordering their imprisonment. It was understood that this could not apply to the two foreigners in the Convention—Paine and Anacharsis Clootz,—though it was regarded as a kind of warning to them. I have seen it stated, but without authority, that Paine had been admonished by Danton to stay away from the Convention on June 2d, and from that day there could not be the slightest utility in his attendance. The Mountaineers had it all their own way. For simply criticising the Constitution they brought forward in place of that of the first committee, Condorcet had to fly from prosecution. Others also fled, among them Brissot and Duchatel. What with the arrestations and flights Paine found himself, in June, almost alone. In the Convention he was sometimes the solitary figure left on the Plain, where but now sat the brilliant statesmen of France. They, his beloved friends, have started in procession towards the guillotine, for even flight must end there ; daily others are pressed into their ranks; his own summons, he feels, is only a question of a few weeks or days. How Paine loved those men—Brissot, Condorcet, Lasource, Duchatel, Vergniaud, Gensonné! Never was man more devoted to his intellectual comrades. Even across a century one may realize what it meant to him, that march of some of his best friends to the scaffold, while others were hunted through France, and the agony of their families, most of whom he well knew.

Alas, even this is not the worst! For what were the personal fate of himself or any compared with the fearful fact that the harvest is past and the republic not saved! Thus had ended all his labors, and his visions of the Commonwealth of Man. The time had come when many besides poor Johnson sought peace in annihilation. Paine, heartbroken, sought oblivion in brandy. Recourse to such anæsthetic, of which any affectionate man might fairly avail himself under such incredible agony as the ruin of his hopes and the approaching murder of his dearest friends, was hitherto unknown in Paine's life. He drank freely, as was the custom of his time; but with the exception of the evidence of an enemy at his trial in England, that he once saw him under the influence of wine after a dinner party (1792), which he admitted was "unusual," no intimation of excess is discoverable in any contemporary record of Paine until this his fifty-seventh year. He afterwards told his friend Rickman that, "borne down by public and private affliction, he had been driven to excesses in Paris"; and, as it was about this time that Gouverneur Morris and Colonel

Bosville, who had reasons for disparaging Paine, reported stories of his drunkenness (growing ever since), we may assign the excesses mainly to June. It will be seen by comparison of the dates of events and documents presently mentioned that Paine could not have remained long in this pardonable refuge of mental misery. Charlotte Corday's poignard cut a rift in the black cloud. After that tremendous July 13th there is positive evidence not only of sobriety, but of life and work on Paine's part that make the year memorable.

Marat dead, hope springs up for the arrested Girondins. They are not yet in prison, but under "arrestation in their homes"; death seemed inevitable while Marat lived, but Charlotte Corday has summoned a new leader. Why may Paine's imperilled comrades not come forth again? Certainly they will if the new chieftain is Danton, who under his radical rage hides a heart. Or if Marat's mantle falls on Robespierre, would not that scholarly lawyer, who would have abolished capital punishment, reverse Marat's cruel decrees? Robespierre had agreed to the new Constitution (reported by Paine's friend, Hérault de Séchelles) and when even that dubious instrument returns with the popular sanction, all may be well. The Convention, which is doing everything except what it was elected to do, will then dissolve, and the happy Republic remember it only as a nightmare. So Paine takes heart again, abandons the bowl of forgetfulness, and becomes a republican Socrates instructing disciples in an old French garden.

CHAPTER IV.

A GARDEN IN THE FAUBOURG ST. DENIS.

SIR GEORGE TREVELYAN has written a pregnant passage, reminding the world of the moral burden which radicals in England had to bear a hundred years ago.

"When to speak or write one's mind on politics is to obtain the reputation, and render one's self liable to the punishment of a criminal, social discredit, with all its attendant moral dangers, soon attaches itself to the more humble opponents of a ministry. To be outside the law as a publisher or a pamphleteer is only less trying to conscience and conduct than to be outside the law as' a smuggler or a poacher ; and those who, ninety years ago, placed themselves within the grasp of the penal statutes as they were administered in England and barbarously perverted in Scotland were certain to be very bold men, and pretty sure to be unconventional up to the uttermost verge of respectability. As an Italian Liberal was sometimes half a bravo, and a Spanish patriot often more than half a brigand, so a British Radical under George the Third had generally, it must be confessed, a dash of the Bohemian. Such, in a more or less mitigated form, were Paine and Cobbett, Hunt, Hone, and Holcroft ; while the same causes in part account for the elfish vagaries of Shelley and the grim improprieties of Godwin. But when we recollect how these, and the like of these, gave up every hope of worldly prosperity, and set their life and liberty in continual hazard for the sake of that personal and political freedom which we now exercise as unconsciously as we breathe the air, it would be too exacting to require that each and all of them should have lived as decorously as Perceval, and died as solvent as Bishop Tomline."[1]

To this right verdict it may be added that, even at the earlier period when it was most applicable, the radicals could only produce one rival in profligacy (John Wilkes) to their aristocratic oppressors. It may also be noted as a species of homage that the slightest failings of eminent reformers become historic. The vices of Burke and Fox are forgotten. Who remembers that the younger Pitt was brought to an early grave by the bottle? But every fault of those who resisted his oppression is placed under a solar microscope. Although, as Sir George affirms, the oppressors largely caused the faults, this homage to the higher moral standard of the reformers may be accepted.[2]

It was, indeed, a hard time for reformers in England. Among them were many refined gentlemen who felt that it was no country for a thinker and scholar to live in. Among the pathetic pictures of the time was that of the twelve scholars, headed by Coleridge and Southey, and twelve ladies, who found the atmosphere of England too impure for

[1] " Early History of Charles James Fox," American ed., p. 440.

[2] The following document was found among the papers of Mr. John Hall, originally of Leicester, England, and has been forwarded to me by his descendant, J. Dutton Steele, Jr., of Philadelphia.

" A Copy of a Letter from the chairman of a meeting of the Gentry and Clergy at Atherstone, written in consequence of an envious schoolmaster and two or three others who informed the meeting that the Excise Officers of Polesworth were employed in distributing the Rights of Man ; but which was very false.

" Sir : I should think it unnecessary to inform you, that the purport of his Majesty's proclamation in the Month of May last, and the numerous meetings which are daily taking place both in Town and Country, are for the avowed purpose of suppressing treasonable and seditious writings amongst which

any but slaves to breathe, and proposed to seek in America some retreat where their pastoral "pantisocrasy" might be realized. Lack of funds prevented the fulfilment of this dream, but that it should have been an object of concert and endeavor, in that refined circle at Bristol, is a memorable sign of that dreadful time. In the absence of means to form such communities, preserving the culture and charm of a society evolved out of barbarism, apart from the walls of a remaining political barbarism threatening it with their ruins, some scholars were compelled, like Coleridge, to rejoin the feudalists, and help them to buttress the crumbling castle. They secured themselves from the social deterioration of living on wild "honey-dew" in a wilderness, at cost of wearing intellectual masks. Some fled to America, like Cobbett. But others fixed their abode in Paris, where radicalism was fashionable and invested with the charm of the *salon* and the theatre.

Before the declaration of war Paine had been on friendly terms with some eminent Englishmen in Paris: he dined every week with Lord Lauder-

Mr. Payne's Rights of Man ranks most conspicuous. Were I not informed you have taken some pains in spreading that publication, I write to say If you don't from this time adopt a different kind of conduct you will be taken notice of in such way as may prove very disagreeable.

"The Eyes of the Country are upon you and you will do well in future to shew yourself faithful to the Master who employs you.

"I remain,
"Your Hble servant,
"(Signed) Jos. Boultbee.
"Baxterby, 15th Decr., 92.

"N. B. The letter was written the next morning after the Meeting where most of the Loyal souls got drunk to an uncommon degree. They drank his Majesty's health so often the reckoning amounted to 7s. 6d. each. One of the informers threw down a shilling and ran away."

dale, Dr. John Moore, an author, and others in some restaurant. After most of these had followed Lord Gower to England he had to be more guarded. A British agent, Major Semple, approached him under the name of Major Lisle. He professed to be an Irish patriot, wore the green cockade, and desired introduction to the Minister of War. Paine fortunately knew too many Irishmen to fall into this snare.[1] But General Miranda, as we have seen, fared better. Paine was, indeed, so overrun with visitors and adventurers that he appropriated two mornings of each week at the Philadelphia House for levees. These, however, became insufficient to stem the constant stream of visitors, including spies and lion-hunters, so that he had little time for consultation with the men and women whose co-operation he needed in public affairs. He therefore leased an out-of-the-way house, reserving knowledge of it for particular friends, while still retaining his address at the Philadelphia Hotel, where the levees were continued.

The irony of fate had brought an old mansion of Madame de Pompadour to become the residence of Thomas Paine and his half dozen English disciples. It was then, and still is, No. 63 Faubourg St. Denis. Here, where a King's mistress held her merry fêtes, and issued the decrees of her reign—sometimes of terror,—the little band of English humanitarians read and conversed, and sported in the garden. In a little essay on "Forgetfulness," addressed to his friend, Lady Smith, Paine described these lodgings.

[1] Rickman, p. 129.

"They were the most agreeable, for situation, of any I ever had in Paris, except that they were too remote from the Convention, of which I was then a member. But this was recompensed by their being also remote from the alarms and confusion into which the interior of Paris was then often thrown. The news of those things used to arrive to us, as if we were in a state of tranquillity in the country. The house, which was enclosed by a wall and gateway from the street, was a good deal like an old mansion farm-house, and the court-yard was like a farm yard, stocked with fowls,—ducks, turkies, and geese ; which, for amusement, we used to feed out of the parlor window on the ground floor. There were some hutches for rabbits, and a sty with two pigs. Beyond was a garden of more than an acre of ground, well laid out, and stocked with excellent fruit trees. The orange, apricot, and greengage plum were the best I ever tasted ; and it is the only place where I saw the wild cucumber. The place had formerly been occupied by some curious person.

"My apartments consisted of three rooms ; the first for wood, water, etc.; the next was the bedroom ; and beyond it the sitting room, which looked into the garden through a glass door ; and on the outside there was a small landing place railed in, and a flight of narrow stairs almost hidden by the vines that grew over it, by which I could descend into the garden without going down stairs through the house. . . . I used to find some relief by walking alone in the garden, after dark, and cursing with hearty good will the authors of that terrible system that had turned the character of the Revolution I had been proud to defend. I went but little to the Convention, and then only to make my appearance, because I found it impossible to join in their tremendous decrees, and useless and dangerous to oppose them. My having voted and spoken extensively, more so than any other member, against the execution of the king, had already fixed a mark upon me ; neither dared any of my associates in the Convention to translate and speak in French for me anything I might have dared to have written. . . . Pen and ink were then of no use to me ; no good could be done by writing, and no printer dared to print ; and whatever I might have written, for my private amusement, as anecdotes of the times, would have been continually exposed to be examined, and tortured into any meaning that the rage of party might fix upon it. And as to softer subjects, my heart was in distress at the fate of my friends, and my harp hung upon the weeping willows.

"As it was summer, we spent most of our time in the garden, and passed it away in those childish amusements that serve to keep reflection from the mind,—such as marbles, Scotch hops, battledores, etc., at which we were all pretty expert. In this retired manner we remained about six or seven weeks, and our landlord went every evening into the city to bring us the news of the day and the evening journal."

The "we" included young Johnson, Mr. and Mrs. Christie, Mr. Choppin, probably Mr. Shapworth, an American, and M. Laborde, a scientific friend of Paine. These appear to have entered with Paine into co-operative housekeeping, though taking their chief meals at the restaurants. In the evenings they were joined by others,—the Brissots (before the arrest), Nicholas Bonneville, Joel Barlow, Captain Imlay, Mary Wollstonecraft, the Rolands. Mystical Madame Roland dreaded Paine's power, which she considered more adapted to pull down than to build, but has left a vivid impression of "the boldness of his conceptions, the originality of his style, the striking truths he throws out bravely among those whom they offend." The Mr. Shapworth alluded to is mentioned in a manuscript journal of Daniel Constable, sent me by his nephew, Clair J. Grece, LL.D. This English gentleman visited Baton Rouge and Shapworth's plantation in 1822. "Mr. S.," he says, "has a daughter married to the Governor [Robinson], has travelled in Europe, married a French

lady. He is a warm friend of Thomas Paine, as
is his son-in-law. He lived with Paine many
months at Paris. He [Paine] was then a sober,
correct gentleman in appearance and manner."
The English refugees, persecuted for selling the
"Rights of Man," were, of course, always welcomed
by Paine, and poor Rickman was his guest during
this summer of 1793.[1] The following reminiscence
of Paine, at a time when Gouverneur Morris was
(for reasons that presently appear) reporting him
to his American friends as generally drunk, was
written by Rickman:

"He usually rose about seven. After breakfast he usually
strayed an hour or two in the garden, where he one morning
pointed out the kind of spider whose web furnished him with the
first idea of constructing his iron bridge ; a fine model of which,
in mahogany, is preserved in Paris. The little happy circle
who lived with him will ever remember those days with delight:
with these select friends he would talk of his boyish days,
played at chess, whist, piquet, or cribbage, and enliven the
moments by many interesting anecdotes : with these he would

[1] Rickman appears to have escaped from England in 1792, according to
the following sonnet sent me by Dr. Grece. It is headed : "Sonnet to my
Little Girl, 1792. Written at Calais, on being pursued by cruel prosecution
and persecution."

> "Farewell, sweet babe ! and mayst thou never know,
>   Like me, the pressure of exceeding woe.
> Some griefs (for they are human nature's right)
>   On life's eventful stage will be thy lot ;
> Some generous cares to clear thy mental sight,
>   Some pains, in happiest hours, perhaps, begot ;
> But mayst thou ne'er be, like thy father, driven
>   From a loved partner, family, and home,
> Snatched from each heart-felt bliss, domestic heaven !
>   From native shores, and all that's valued, roam.
> Oh, may bad governments, the source of human woe,
> Ere thou becom'st mature, receive their deadly blow ;
> Then mankind's greatest curse thou ne'er wilt know."

play at marbles, scotch hops, battledores, etc.: on the broad and fine gravel walk at the upper end of the garden, and then retire to his boudoir, where he was up to his knees in letters and papers of various descriptions. Here he remained till dinner time; and unless he visited Brissot's family, or some particular friend, in the evening, which was his frequent custom, he joined again the society of his favorites and fellow-boarders, with whom his conversation was often witty and cheerful, always acute and improving, but never frivolous. Incorrupt, straightforward, and sincere, he pursued his political course in France, as everywhere else, let the government or clamor or faction of the day be what it might, with firmness, with clearness, and without a shadow of turning."

In the spring of 1890 the present writer visited the spot. The lower front of the old mansion is divided into shops,—a Fruiterer being appropriately next the gateway, which now opens into a wide thoroughfare. Above the rooms once occupied by Paine was the sign "Ecrivain Publique,"—placed there by a Mademoiselle who wrote letters and advertisements for humble neighbors not expert in penmanship. At the end of what was once the garden is a Printer's office, in which was a large lithograph portrait of Victor Hugo. The printer, his wife, and little daughter were folding publications of the "Extreme Left." Near the door remains a veritable survival of the garden and its living tenants which amused Paine and his friends. There were two ancient fruit trees, of which one was dying, but the other budding in the spring sunshine. There were ancient coops with ducks, and pigeon-houses with pigeons, also rabbits, and some flowers. This little nook, of perhaps forty square feet, and its animals, had been there—so an old inhabitant told me—time out of mind. They belonged to nobody in particular; the pigeons were fed by the people around; the fowls were probably kept there by some poultryman. There were eager groups attending every stage of the investigation. The exceptional antiquity of the mansion had been recognized by its occupants,—several families,—but without curiosity, and perhaps with regret. Comparatively few had heard of Paine.

Shortly before I had visited the garden near Florence which Boccaccio's immortal tales have kept in perennial beauty through five centuries. It may be that in the far future some brother of Boccace will bequeath to Paris as sweet a legend of the garden where beside the plague of blood the prophet of the universal Republic realized his dream in microcosm. Here gathered sympathetic spirits from America, England, France, Germany, Holland, Switzerland, freed from prejudices of race, rank, or nationality, striving to be mutually helpful, amusing themselves with Arcadian sports, studying nature, enriching each other by exchange of experiences. It is certain that in all the world there was no group of men and women more disinterestedly absorbed in the work of benefiting their fellow-beings. They could not, however, like Boccaccio's ladies and gentlemen "kill Death" by their witty tales; for presently beloved faces disappeared from their circle, and the cruel axe was gleaming over them.

And now the old hotel became the republican capitol of Europe. There sat an international Premier with his Cabinet, concentrated on the work of saving the Girondins. He was indeed treated by the Executive government as a Minister. It was supposed by Paine and believed by his adherents that Robespierre had for him some dislike. Paine in later years wrote of Robespierre as a "hypocrite," and the epithet may have a significance not recognized by his readers. It is to me probable that Paine considered himself deceived by Robespierre with professions of respect, if not of friendliness before being cast into prison; a conclusion naturally based on requests from the Ministers for opinions on public affairs. The archives of the Revolution contain various evidences of this, and several papers by Paine evidently in reply to questions. We may feel certain that every subject propounded was carefully discussed in Paine's little cosmopolitan Cabinet before his opinion was transmitted to the revolutionary Cabinet of Committees. In reading the subjoined documents it must be borne in mind that Robespierre had not yet been suspected of the cruelty presently associated with his name. The Queen and the Girondist leaders were yet alive. Of these leaders Paine was known to be the friend, and it was of the utmost importance that he should be suavely loyal to the government that had inherited these prisoners from Marat's time.

The first of these papers is erroneously endorsed "January 1793. Thom. Payne. Copie," in the French State Archives.[1] Its reference to the defeat of the Duke of York at Dunkirk assigns its date to the late summer. It is headed, "Observa-

[1] États Unis. Vol. 37. Document 39.

tions on the situation of the Powers joined against France."

"It is always useful to know the position and the designs of one's enemies. It is much easier to do so by combining and comparing the events, and by examining the consequences which result from them, than by forming one's judgment by letters found or intercepted. These letters could be fabricated with the intention of deceiving, but events or circumstances have a character which is proper to them. If in the course of our political operations we mistake the designs of our enemy, it leads us to do precisely that which he desired we should do, and it happens, by the fact, but against our intentions, that we work for him.

"It appears at first sight that the coalition against France is not of the nature of those which form themselves by a treaty. It has been the work of circumstances. It is a heterogeneous mass, the parts of which dash against each other, and often neutralise themselves. They have but one single point of reunion, the re-establishment of the monarchical government in France. Two means can conduct them to the execution of this plan. The first is, to re-establish the Bourbons, and with them the Monarchy; the second, to make a division similar to that which they have made in Poland, and to reign themselves in France. The political questions to be solved are, then, to know on which of these two plans it is most probable, the united Powers will act; and which are the points of these plans on which they will agree or disagree.

"Supposing their aim to be the re-establishment of the Bourbons, the difficulty which will present itself, will be, to know who will be their Allies?

"Will England consent to the re-establishment of the compact of family in the person of the Bourbons, against whom she has machinated and fought since her existence? Will Prussia consent to re-establish the alliance which subsisted between France and Austria, or will Austria wish to re-establish the ancient alliance between France and Prussia, which was directed against her? Will Spain, or any other maritime Power, allow France and her Marine to ally themselves to

England? In fine, will any of these Powers consent to furnish forces which could be directed against herself? However, all these cases present themselves in the hypothesis of the restoration of the Bourbons.

"If we suppose that their plan be the dismemberment of France, difficulties will present themselves under another form, but not of the same nature. It will no longer be question, in this case, of the Bourbons, as their position will be worse; for if their preservation is a part of their first plan, their destruction ought to enter in the second; because it is necessary for the success of the dismembering that not a single pretendant to the Crown of France should exist.

"As one must think of all the probabilities in political calculations, it is not unlikely that some of the united Powers, having in view the first of these plans, and others the second, —that this may be one of the causes of their disagreement. It is to be remembered that Russia recognised a Regency from the beginning of Spring; not one of the other Powers followed her example. The distance of Russia from France, and the different countries by which she is separated from her, leave no doubt as to her dispositions with regard to the plan of division; and as much as one can form an opinion on the circumstances, it is not her scheme.

"The coalition directed against France, is composed of two kinds of Powers. The Maritime Powers, not having the same interest as the others, will be divided, as to the execution of the project of division.

"I do not hesitate to believe that the politic of the English Government is to foment the scheme of dismembering, and the entire destruction of the Bourbon family.

"The difficulty which must arise, in this last hypothesis, between the united Maritime Powers proceeds from their views being entirely opposed.

"The trading vessels of the Northern Nations, from Holland to Russia, must pass through the narrow Channel, which lies between Dunkirk and the coasts of England; and consequently not one of them, will allow this latter Power to have forts on both sides of this Strait. The audacity with which she has seized the neutral vessels ought to demonstrate to all Nations how much her schemes increase their danger, and menace the security of their present and future commerce.

"Supposing then that the other Nations oppose the plans of England, she will be forced to cease the war with us; or, if she continues it, the Northern Nations will become interested in the safety of France.

"There are three distinct parties in England at this moment: the Government party, the Revolutionary party, and an intermedial party,—which is only opposed to the war on account of the expense it entails, and the harm it does commerce and manufacture. I am speaking of the People, and not of the Parliament. The latter is divided into two parties: the Ministerial, and the Anti-Ministerial. The Revolutionary party, the intermedial party and the Anti-Ministerial party will all rejoice, publicly or privately, at the defeat of the Duke of York's army, at Dunkirk. The intermedial party, because they hope that this defeat will finish the war. The Antiministerial party, because they hope it will overthrow the Ministry. And all the three because they hate the Duke of York. Such is the state of the different parties in England.

"Signed: THOMAS PAINE."

In the same volume of the State Archives (Paris) is the following note by Paine, with its translation:

"You mentioned to me that saltpetre was becoming scarce. I communicate to you a project of the late Captain Paul Jones, which, if successfully put in practice, will furnish you with that article.

"All the English East India ships put into St. Helena, off the coast of Africa, on their return from India to England. A great part of their ballast is saltpetre. Captain Jones, who had been at St. Helena, says that the place can be very easily taken. His proposal was to send off a small squadron for that purpose, to keep the English flag flying at port. The English vessels will continue coming in as usual. By this means it will be a long time before the Government of England can have any knowledge of what has happened. The success of this depends so much upon secrecy that I wish you would translate this yourself, and give it to Barrère."

In the next volume (38) of the French Archives, marked "États Unis, 1793," is a remarkable document (No. 39), entitled "A Citizen of America to the Citizens of Europe." The name of Paine is only pencilled on it, and it was probably written by him; but it purports to have been written in America, and is dated "Philadelphia, July 28, 1793; 18th Year of Independence." It is a clerk's copy, so that it cannot now be known whether the ruse of its origin in Philadelphia was due to Paine or to the government. It is an extended paper, and repeats to some extent, though not literally, what is said in the "Observations" quoted above. Possibly the government, on receiving that paper (Document 39 also), desired Paine to write it out as an address to the "Citizens of Europe." It does not appear to have been published. The first four paragraphs of this paper, combined with the "Observations," will suffice to show its character.

"Understanding that a proposal is intended to be made at the ensuing meeting of the Congress of the United States of America, to send Commissioners to Europe to confer with the Ministers of all the Neutral Powers, for the purpose of negociating preliminaries of Peace, I address this letter to you on that subject, and on the several matters connected therewith.

"In order to discuss this subject through all its circumstances, it will be necessary to take a review of the state of Europe, prior to the French revolution. It will from thence appear, that the powers leagued against France are fighting to attain an object, which, were it possible to be attained, would be injurious to themselves.

"This is not an uncommon error in the history of wars and governments, of which the conduct of the English government in the war against America is a striking instance. She commenced that war for the avowed purpose of subjugating America; and after wasting upwards of one hundred millions sterling, and then abandoning the object, she discovered in the course of three or four years, that the prosperity of England was increased, instead of being diminished, by the independence of America. In short, every circumstance is pregnant with some natural effect, upon which intentions and opinions have no influence; and the political error lies in misjudging what the effect will be. England misjudged it in the American war, and the reasons I shall now offer will shew, that she misjudges it in the present war.—In discussing this subject, I leave out of the question every thing respecting forms and systems of government; for as all the governments of Europe differ from each other, there is no reason that the government of France should not differ from the rest.

"The clamours continually raised in all the countries of Europe were, that the family of the Bourbons was become too powerful; that the intrigues of the court of France endangered the peace of Europe. Austria saw with a jealous eye the connection of France with Prussia; and Prussia, in her turn became jealous of the connection of France with Austria; England had wasted millions unsuccessfully in attempting to prevent the family compact with Spain; Russia disliked the alliance between France and Turkey; and Turkey became apprehensive of the inclination of France towards an alliance with Russia. Sometimes the quadruple alliance alarmed some of the powers, and at other times a contrary system alarmed others, and in all those cases the charge was always made against the intrigues of the Bourbons."

In each of these papers a plea for the imperilled Girondins is audible. Each is a reminder that he, Thomas Paine, friend of the Brissotins, is continuing their anxious and loyal vigilance for the Republic. And during all this summer Paine had good reason to believe that his friends were safe. Robespierre was eloquently deprecating useless effusion of blood. As for Paine himself, he was not only consulted on public questions, but trusted in practical affairs. He was still able to help Americans and Englishmen who invoked his aid. Writing to Lady Smith concerning two applications of that kind, he says :

"I went into my chamber to write and sign a certificate for them, which I intended to take to the guard house to obtain their release. Just as I had finished it, a man came into my room, dressed in the Parisian uniform of a captain, and spoke to me in good English, and with a good address. He told me that two young men, Englishmen, were arrested and detained in the guard house, and that the section (meaning those who represented and acted for the section) had sent him to ask me if I knew them, in which case they would be liberated. This matter being soon settled between us, he talked to me about the Revolution, and something about the 'Rights of Man,' which he had read in English; and at parting offered me, in a polite and civil manner, his services. And who do you think the man was who offered me his services? It was no other than the public executioner, Samson, who guillotined the King and all who were guillotined in Paris, and who lived in the same street with me."

There appeared no reason to suppose this a domiciliary visit, or that it had any relation to anything except the two Englishmen. Samson was not a detective. It soon turned out, however, that there was a serpent creeping into Paine's little garden in the Faubourg St. Denis. He and his guests knew it not, however, until all their hopes fell with the leaves and blossoms amid which they had passed a summer to which Paine, from his prison, looked back with fond recollection.

CHAPTER V.

A CONSPIRACY.

"HE suffered under Pontius Pilate." Pilate's gallant struggle to save Jesus from lynchers survives in no kindly memorial save among the peasants of Oberammergau. It is said that the impression once made in England by the Miracle Play has left its relic in the miserable puppet-play Punch and Judy (*Pontius cum Judæis*); but meanwhile the Church repeats, throughout Christendom, "He suffered under Pontius Pilate." It is almost normal in history that the brand of infamy falls on the wrong man. This is the penalty of personal eminence, and especially of eloquence. In the opening years of the French Revolution the two men in Europe who seemed omnipotent were Pitt and Robespierre. By reason of their eloquence, their ingenious defences, their fame, the columns of credit and discredit were begun in their names, and have so continued. English liberalism, remembering the imprisoned and flying writers, still repeats, "They suffered under William Pitt." French republics transmit their legend of Condorcet, Camille Desmoulins, Brissot, Malesherbes, "They suffered under Robespierre." The friends, disciples, biographers, of Thomas Paine have it in their creed that he suffered under both Pitt and Robespierre. It is certain that neither Pitt nor Robespierre was so strong as he appeared. Their hands cannot be cleansed, but they are historic scapegoats of innumerable sins they never committed.

Unfortunately for Robespierre's memory, in England and America especially, those who for a century might have been the most ready to vindicate a slandered revolutionist have been confronted by the long imprisonment of the author of the "Rights of Man," and by the discovery of his virtual death-sentence in Robespierre's handwriting. Louis Blanc, Robespierre's great vindicator, could not, we may assume, explain this ugly fact, which he passes by in silence. He has proved, conclusively as I think, that Robespierre was among the revolutionists least guilty of the Terror; that he was murdered by a conspiracy of those whose cruelties he was trying to restrain; that, when no longer alive to answer, they burdened him with their crimes, as the only means of saving their heads. Robespierre's doom was sealed when he had real power, and used it to prevent any organization of the constitutional government which might have checked revolutionary excesses. He then, because of a superstitious faith in the auspices of the Supreme Being, threw the reins upon the neck of the revolution he afterwards vainly tried to curb. Others, who did not wish to restrain it, seized the reins and when the precipice was reached took care that Robespierre should be hurled over it.

Many allegations against Robespierre have been disproved. He tried to save Danton and Camille Desmoulins, and did save seventy-three deputies whose death the potentates of the Committee of Public Safety had planned. But against him still lies that terrible sentence found in his Note Book, and reported by a Committee to the Convention: " Demand that Thomas Payne be decreed of accusation for the interests of America as much as of France."[1]

The Committee on Robespierre's papers, and especially Courtois its Chairman, suppressed some things favorable to him (published long after), and it can never be known whether they found anything further about Paine. They made a strong point of the sentence found, and added: " Why Thomas Payne more than another? Because he helped to establish the liberty of both worlds."

An essay by Paine on Robespierre has been lost, and his opinion of the man can be gathered only from occasional remarks. After the Courtois report he had to accept the theory of Robespierre's malevolence and hypocrisy. He then, for the first time, suspected the same hand in a previous act of hostility towards him. In August, 1793, an address had been sent to the Convention from Arras, a town in his constituency, saying that they had lost confidence in Paine. This failed of success because a counter-address came from St. Omer. Robespierre being a native of Arras, it now seemed clear that he had instigated the address. It was,

[1] " Demander que Thomas Payne soit décréte d'accusation pour les intérêts de l'Amerique autant que de la France."

however, almost certainly the work of Joseph Lebon, who, as Paine once wrote, "made the streets of Arras run with blood." Lebon was his *suppléant*, and could not sit in the Convention until Paine left it.

But although Paine would appear to have ascribed his misfortunes to Robespierre at the time, he was evidently mystified by the whole thing. No word against him had ever fallen from Robespierre's lips, and if that leader had been hostile to him why should he have excepted him from the accusations of his associates, have consulted him through the summer, and even after imprisonment, kept him unharmed for months? There is a notable sentence in Paine's letter (from prison) to Monroe, elsewhere considered, showing that while there he had connected his trouble rather with the Committee of Public Safety than with Robespierre.

"However discordant the late American Minister Gouverneour Morris, and the late French Committee of Public Safety, were, it suited the purposes of both that I should be continued in arrestation. The former wished to prevent my return to America, that I should not expose his misconduct; and the latter lest I should publish to the world the history of its wickedness. Whilst that Minister and that Committee continued, I had no expectation of liberty. I speak here of the Committee of which Robespierre was a member."

Paine wrote this letter on September 10, 1794. Robespierre, three months before that, had ceased to attend the Committee, disavowing responsibility for its actions: Paine was not released. Robespierre, when the letter to Monroe was written, had been dead more than six months: Paine was not released. The prisoner had therefore good reason to look behind Robespierre for his enemies; and although the fatal sentence found in the Note Book, and a private assurance of Barrère, caused him to ascribe his wrongs to Robespierre, farther reflection convinced him that hands more hidden had also been at work. He knew that Robespierre was a man of measured words, and pondered the sentence that he should "be decreed of accusation for the interests of America as much as of France." In a letter written in 1802, Paine said: "There must have been a coalition in sentiment, if not in fact, between the terrorists of America and the terrorists of France, and Robespierre must have known it, or he could not have had the idea of putting America into the bill of accusation against me." Robespierre, he remarks, assigned no reason for his imprisonment.

The secret for which Paine groped has remained hidden for a hundred years. It is painful to reveal it now, but historic justice, not only to the memory of Paine, but to that of some eminent contemporaries of his, demands that the facts be brought to light.

The appointment of Gouverneur Morris to be Minister to France, in 1792, passed the Senate by 16 to 11 votes. The President did not fail to advise him of this reluctance, and admonish him to be more cautious in his conduct. In the same year Paine took his seat in the Convention. Thus the royalist and republican tendencies, whose struggles made chronic war in Washington's Cabinet, had their counterpart in Paris, where our Minister

Morris wrote royalist, and Paine republican, manifestoes. It will have been seen, by quotations from his diary already given, that Gouverneur Morris harbored a secret hostility towards Paine; and it is here assumed that those entries and incidents are borne in mind. The Diary shows an appearance of friendly terms between the two; Morris dines Paine and receives information from him. The royalism of Morris and humanity of Paine brought them into a common desire to save the life of Louis.

But about the same time the American Minister's own position became a subject of anxiety to him. He informs Washington (December 28, 1792) that Genêt's appointment as Minister to the United States had not been announced to him (Morris). "Perhaps the Ministry think it is a trait of republicanism to omit those forms which were anciently used to express good will." His disposition towards Paine was not improved by finding that it was to him Genêt had reported. "I have not yet seen M. Genêt," writes Morris again, "but Mr. Paine is to introduce him to me." Soon after this Morris became aware that the French Ministry had asked his recall, and had Paine also known this the event might have been different. The Minister's suspicion that Paine had instigated the recall gave deadliness to his resentment when the inevitable break came between them.

The occasion of this arose early in the spring. When war had broken out between England and France, Morris, whose sympathies were with England, was eager to rid America of its treaty obligations to France. He so wrote repeatedly to Jefferson, Secretary of State. An opportunity presently occurred for acting on this idea. In reprisal for the seizure by British cruisers of American ships conveying provisions to France, French cruisers were ordered to do the like, and there were presently ninety-two captured American vessels at Bordeaux. They were not allowed to reload and go to sea lest their cargoes should be captured by England. Morris pointed out to the French Government this violation of the treaty with America, but wrote to Jefferson that he would leave it to them in Philadelphia to insist on the treaty's observance, or to accept the "unfettered" condition in which its violation by France left them. Consultation with Philadelphia was a slow business, however, and the troubles of the American vessels were urgent. The captains, not suspecting that the American Minister was satisfied with the treaty's violation, were angry at his indifference about their relief, and applied to Paine. Unable to move Morris, Paine asked him "if he did not feel ashamed to take the money of the country and do nothing for it." It was, of course, a part of Morris' scheme for ending the treaty to point out its violation and the hardships resulting, and this he did; but it would defeat his scheme to obtain the practical relief from those hardships which the untheoretical captains demanded. On August 20th, the captains were angrily repulsed by the American Minister, who, however, after they had gone, must have reflected that he had gone too far, and was in an untenable position; for on the same day he wrote to the French Minister a statement of the complaint.

"I do not [he adds] pretend to interfere in the internal concerns of the French Republic, and I am persuaded that the Convention has had weighty reasons for laying upon Americans the restriction of which the American captains complain. The result will nevertheless be that this prohibition will severely aggrieve the parties interested, and put an end to the commerce between France and the United States."

The note is half-hearted, but had the captains known it was written they might have been more patient. Morris owed his subsequent humiliation partly to his bad manners. The captains went off to Paine, and proposed to draw up a public protest against the American Minister. Paine advised against this, and recommended a petition to the Convention. This was offered on August 22d. In this the captains said: "We, who know your political situation, do not come to you to demand the rigorous execution of the treaties of alliance which unite us to you. We confine ourselves to asking for the present, to carry provisions to your colonies." To this the Convention promptly and favorably responded.

It was a double humiliation to Morris that the first important benefit gained by Americans since his appointment should be secured without his help, and that it should come through Paine. And it was a damaging blow to his scheme of transferring to England our alliance with France. A "violation" of the treaty excused by the only sufferers could not be cited as "releasing" the United States. A cruel circumstance for Morris was that the French Minister wrote (October 14th) : "You must be satisfied, sir, with the manner in which the request presented by the American captains from Bordeaux, has been received"—and so forth. Four days before, Morris had written to Jefferson, speaking of the thing as mere "mischief," and belittling the success, which "only served an ambition so contemptible that I shall draw over it the veil of oblivion."

The "contemptible ambition" thus veiled from Paine's friend, Jefferson, was revealed by Morris to others. Some time before (June 25th), he had written to Robert Morris :

"I suspected that Paine was intriguing against me, although he put on a face of attachment. Since that period I am confirmed in the idea, for he came to my house with Col. Oswald, and being a little more drunk than usual, behaved extremely ill, and through his insolence I discovered clearly his vain ambition."

This was probably written after Paine's rebuke already quoted. It is not likely that Colonel Oswald would have taken a tipsy man eight leagues out to Morris' retreat, Sainport, on business, or that the tipsy man would remember the words of his rebuke two years after, when Paine records them in his letter to Washington. At any rate, if Morris saw no deeper into Paine's physical than into his mental condition, the "insolent" words were those of soberness. For Paine's private letters prove him ignorant of any intrigue against Morris, and under an impression that the Minister had himself asked for recall; also that, instead of being ambitious to succeed Morris, he was eager to get out of France and back to America. The first expression of French dissatisfaction with Morris had been made through De Ternant, (February 20th, 1793,) whom he had himself been the means of sending as Minister to the United States. The positive recall was made through Genêt.[1] It would appear that Morris must have had sore need of a scapegoat to fix on poor Paine, when his intrigues with the King's agents, his trust of the King's money, his plot for a second attempt of the King to escape, his concealment of royalist leaders in his house, had been his main ministerial performances for some time after his appointment. Had the French known half as much as is now revealed in Morris' Diary, not even his office could have shielded him from arrest. That the executive there knew much of it, appears in the revolutionary archives. There is reason to believe that Paine, instead of intriguing against Morris, had, in ignorance of his intrigues, brought suspicion on himself by continuing his intercourse with the Minister. The following letter

[1] On September 1, 1792, Morris answered a request of the executive of the republic that he could not comply until he had received "orders from his Court," (*les ordres de ma cour*). The representatives of the new-born republic were scandalized by such an expression from an American Minister, and also by his intimacy with Lord and Lady Gower. They may have suspected what Morris' "Diary" now suggests, that he (Morris) owed his appointment to this English Ambassador and his wife. On August 17, 1792, Lord Gower was recalled, in hostility to the republic, but during the further weeks of his stay in Paris the American Minister frequented their house. From the recall Morris was saved for a year by the intervention of Edmund Randolph. (See my "Omitted Chapters of History," etc, p. 149.) Randolph met with a Morrisian reward. Morris ("Diary," ii., p. 98) records an accusation of Randolph, to which he listened in the office of Lord Grenville, Secretary of State, which plainly meant his (Randolph's) ruin, which followed. He knew it to be untrue, but no defence is mentioned.

of Paine to Barrère, chief Committeeman of Public Safety, dated September 5th, shows him protecting Morris while he is trying to do something for the American captains.

"I send you the papers you asked me for.

"The idea you have to send Commissioners to Congress, and of which you spoke to me yesterday, is excellent, and very necessary at this moment. Mr. Jefferson, formerly Minister of the United States in France, and actually Minister for Foreign Affairs at Congress, is an ardent defender of the interests of France. Gouverneur Morris, who is here now, is badly disposed towards you. I believe he has expressed the wish to be recalled. The reports which he will make on his arrival will not be to the advantage of France. This event necessitates the sending direct of Commissioners from the Convention. Morris is not popular in America. He has set the Americans who are here against him, as also the Captains of that Nation who have come from Bordeaux, by his negligence with regard to the affair they had to treat about with the Convention. *Between us* [*sic*] he told them: 'That they had thrown themselves into the lion's mouth, and it was for them to get out of it as best they could.' I shall return to America on one of the vessels which will start from Bordeaux in the month of October. This was the project I had formed, should the rupture not take place between America and England; but now it is necessary for me to be there as soon as possible. The Congress will require a great deal of information, independently of this. It will soon be seven years that I have been absent from America, and my affairs in that country have suffered considerably through my absence. My house and farm buildings have been entirely destroyed through an accidental fire.

"Morris has many relations in America, who are excellent patriots. I enclose you a letter which I received from his brother, General Louis Morris, who was a member of the Congress at the time of the Declaration of Independence. You will see by it that he writes like a good patriot. I only mention this so that you may know the true state of things. It will be fit to have respect for Gouverneur Morris, on account of his relations, who, as I said above, are excellent patriots.

"There are about 45 American vessels at Bordeaux, at the present moment. If the English Government wished to take revenge on the Americans, these vessels would be very much exposed during their passage. The American Captains left Paris yesterday. I advised them, on leaving, to demand a convoy of the Convention, in case they heard it said that the English had begun reprisals against the Americans, if only to conduct as far as the Bay of Biscay, at the expense of the American Government. But if the Convention determines to send Commissioners to Congress, they will be sent in a ship of the line. But it would be better for the Commissioners to go in one of the best American sailing vessels, and for the ship of the line to serve as a convoy; it could also serve to convoy the ships that will return to France charged with flour. I am sorry that we cannot converse together, but if you could give me a rendezvous, where I could see Mr. Otto, I shall be happy and ready to be there. If events force the American captains to demand a convoy, it will be to me that they will write on the subject, and not to Morris, against whom they have grave reasons of complaint. Your friend, etc.

THOMAS PAINE."[1]

This is the only letter written by Paine to any one in France about Gouverneur Morris, so far as I can discover, and not knowing French he could only communicate in writing. The American Archives are equally without anything to justify the Minister's suspicion that Paine was intriguing against him, even after his outrageous conduct about the captains. Morris had laid aside the functions of a Minister to exercise those of a treaty-making government. During this excursion into

[1] State Archives, Paris. États Unis, Vol. 38, No. 93. Endorsed: "No. 6. Translation of a letter from Thomas Payne to Citizen Barrère." It may be noted that Paine and Barrère, though they could read each other's language, could converse only in their own tongue.

presidential and senatorial power, for the injury of the country to which he was commissioned, his own countrymen in France were without an official Minister, and in their distress imposed ministerial duties on Paine. But so far from wishing to supersede Morris, Paine, in the above letter to Barrère, gives an argument for his retention, namely, that if he goes home he will make reports disadvantageous to France. He also asks respect for Morris on account of his relations, "excellent patriots."

Barrère, to whom Paine's letter is written, was chief of the Committee of Public Safety, and had held that powerful position since its establishment, April 6, 1793. To this all-powerful Committee of Nine Robespierre was added July 27th. On the day that Paine wrote the letter, September 5th, Barrère opened the Terror by presenting a report in which it is said, "Let us make terror the order of the day!" This Barrère was a sensualist, a crafty orator, a sort of eel which in danger turned into a snake. His "supple genius," as Louis Blanc expresses it, was probably appreciated by Morris, who was kept well informed as to the secrets of the Committee of Public Safety. This omnipotent Committee had supervision of foreign affairs and appointments. At this time the Minister of Foreign Affairs was Deforgues, whose secretary was the M. Otto alluded to in Paine's letter to Barrère. Otto spoke English fluently; he had been in the American Legation. Deforgues became Minister June 5th, on the arrest of his predecessor (Lebrun), and was anxious lest he should follow Lebrun to prison also,—as he ultimately did. Deforgues and his secretary, Otto, confided to Morris their strong desire to be appointed to America, Genêt having been recalled.[1]

Despite the fact that Morris' hostility to France was well known, he had become an object of awe. So long as his removal was daily expected in reply to a request twice sent for his recall, Morris was weak, and even insulted. But when ship after ship came in without such recall, and at length even with the news that the President had refused the Senate's demand for Morris' entire correspondence, everything was changed.[2] "So long," writes Morris to Washington, "as they believed in the success of their demand, they treated my representations with indifference and contempt; but at last, hearing nothing from their minister on that subject, or, indeed, on any other, they took it into their heads that I was immovable, and made overtures for conciliation." It must be borne in mind that at this time America was the only ally of France; that already there were fears that Washington was feeling his way towards a treaty with England. Soon after the overthrow of the monarchy Morris had hinted that the treaty between the United States and France, having been made with the King, might be represented by the English Ministry in America as void under the revolution; and that "it would be well to evince a degree of good will to America." When Robespierre first became a leader he had particular charge of diplo-

---

[1] Morris' letter to Washington, Oct. 18, 1793. The passage is omitted from the letter as quoted in his "Diary and Letters," ii., p. 53.
[2] See my "Life of Edmund Randolph," p. 214.

matic affairs. It is stated by Frédéric Masson that Robespierre was very anxious to recover for the republic the initiative of the alliance with the United States, which was credited to the King; and "although their Minister Gouverneur Morris was justly suspected, and the American republic was at that time aiming only to utilize the condition of its ally, the French republic cleared it at a cheap rate of its debts contracted with the King."[1] Such were the circumstances which, when Washington seemed determined to force Morris on France, made this Minister a power. Lebrun, the ministerial predecessor of Deforgues, may indeed have been immolated to placate Morris, who having been, under his administration, subjected to a domiciliary visit, had gone to reside in the country. That was when Morris' removal was supposed near; but now his turn came for a little reign of terror on his own account. In addition to Deforgues' fear of Lebrun's fate, should he anger Washington's immovable representative, he knew that his hope of succeeding Genêt in America must depend on Morris. The terrors and schemes of Deforgues and Otto brought them to the feet of Morris.

About the time when the chief of the Committee of Public Safety, Barrère, was consulting Paine about sending Commissioners to America, Deforgues was consulting Morris on the same point. The interview was held shortly after the humiliation which Morris had suffered, in the matter of the captains, and the defeat of his scheme for utilizing

[1] "Le Département des Affaires Étrangères pendant la Révolution," p. 295.

their grievance to release the United States from their alliance. The American captains had appointed Paine their Minister, and he had been successful. Paine and his clients had not stood in awe of Morris; but he now had the strength of a giant, and proceeded to use it like a giant.

The interview with Deforgues was not reported by Morris to the Secretary of State (Paine's friend, Jefferson), but in a confidential letter to Washington,—so far as was prudent.

> "I have insinuated [he writes] the advantages which might result from an early declaration on the part of the new minister that, as France has announced the determination not to meddle with the interior affairs of other nations, he can know only the *government* of America. In union with this idea, I told the minister that I had observed an overruling influence in their affairs which seemed to come from the other side of the channel, and at the same time had traced the intention to excite a seditious spirit in America; that it was impossible to be on a friendly footing with such persons, but that at present a different spirit seemed to prevail, etc. This declaration produced the effect I intended." [1]

In thus requiring that the new minister to America shall recognize only the "government" (and not negotiate with Kentucky, as Genêt had done), notice is also served on Deforgues that the Convention must in future deal only with the American Minister, and not with Paine or sea-captains in matters affecting his countrymen. The reference to an influence from the other side of the channel could only refer to Paine, as there were then no Englishmen in Paris outside his gar-

[1] Letter to Washington, Oct. 18, 1793.

den in the Faubourg St. Denis. By this ingenious phrase Morris already disclaims jurisdiction over Paine, and suggests that he is an Englishman worrying Washington through Genêt. This was a clever hint in another way. Genêt, now recalled, evidently for the guillotine, had been introduced to Morris by Paine, who no doubt had given him letters to eminent Americans. Paine had sympathized warmly with the project of the Kentuckians to expel the Spanish from the Mississippi, and this was patriotic American doctrine even after Kentucky was admitted into the Union (June 1, 1792). He had corresponded with Dr. O'Fallon, a leading Kentuckian on the subject. But things had changed, and when Genêt went out with his blank commissions he found himself confronted with a proclamation of neutrality which turned his use of them to sedition. Paine's acquaintance with Genêt, and his introductions, could now be plausibly used by Morris to involve him. The French Minister is shown an easy way of relieving his country from responsibility for Genêt, by placing it on the deputy from "the other side of the channel."

"This declaration produced the effect I intended," wrote Morris. The effect was indeed swift. On October 3d, Amar, after the doors of the Convention were locked, read the memorable accusation against the Girondins, four weeks before their execution. In that paper he denounced Brissot for his effort to save the King, for his intimacy with the English, for injuring the colonies by his labors for negro emancipation! In this denunciation Paine had the honor to be included.

"At that same time the Englishman Thomas Paine, called by the faction [Girondin] to the honor of representing the French nation, dishonored himself by supporting the opinion of Brissot, and by promising us in his fable the dissatisfaction of the United States of America, our natural allies, which he did not blush to depict for us as full of veneration and gratitude for the tyrant of France."

On October 19th the Minister of Foreign Affairs, Deforgues, writes to Morris:

"I shall give the Council an account of the punishable conduct of their agent in the United States [Genêt], and I can assure you beforehand that they will regard the strange abuse of their confidence by this agent, as I do, with the liveliest indignation. The President of the United States has done justice to our sentiments in attributing the deviations of the citizen Genêt to causes entirely foreign to his instructions, and we hope that the measures to be taken will more and more convince the head and members of your Government that so far from having authorized the proceedings and manœuvres of Citizen Genêt our only aim has been to maintain between the two nations the most perfect harmony."

One of "the measures to be taken" was the imprisonment of Paine, for which Amar's denunciation had prepared the way. But this was not so easy. For Robespierre had successfully attacked Amar's report for extending its accusations beyond the Girondins. How then could an accusation be made against Paine, against whom no charge could be brought, except that he had introduced a French minister to his friends in America! A deputy must be formally accused by the Convention before he could be tried by the Revolutionary Tribunal. An indirect route must be taken to reach the deputy secretly accused by the American Minister, and the latter had pointed it out by alluding to Paine as an influence "from across the channel." There was a law passed in June for the imprisonment of foreigners belonging to countries at war with France. This was administered by the Committees. Paine had not been liable to this law, being a deputy, and never suspected of citizenship in the country which had outlawed him, until Morris suggested it. Could he be got out of the Convention the law might be applied to him without necessitating any public accusation and trial, or anything more than an announcement to the Deputies.

Such was the course pursued. Christmas day was celebrated by the terrorist Bourdon de l'Oise with a denunciation of Paine: "They have boasted the patriotism of Thomas Paine. *Eh bien!* Since the Brissotins disappeared from the bosom of this Convention he has not set foot in it. And I know that he has intrigued with a former agent of the bureau of Foreign Affairs." This accusation could only have come from the American Minister and the Minister of Foreign Affairs—from Gouverneur Morris and Deforgues. Genêt was the only agent of Deforgues' office with whom Paine could possibly have been connected; and what that connection was the reader knows. That accusation is associated with the terrorist's charge that Paine had declined to unite with the murderous decrees of the Convention.

After the speech of Bourdon de l'Oise, Bentabole moved the "exclusion of foreigners from every public function during the war." Bentabole was a leading member of the Committee of General

Surety. "The Assembly," adds *The Moniteur*, " decreed that no foreigner should be admitted to represent the French people." The Committee of General Surety assumed the right to regard Paine as an Englishman; and as such out of the Convention, and consequently under the law of June against aliens of hostile nations. He was arrested next day, and on December 28th committed to the Luxembourg prison.

CHAPTER VI.

A TESTIMONY UNDER THE GUILLOTINE.

WHILE Paine was in prison the English gentry were gladdened by a rumor that he had been guillotined, and a libellous leaflet of "The Last Dying Words of Thomas Paine" appeared in London. Paine was no less confident than his enemies that his execution was certain—after the denunciation in Amar's report, October 3d—and did indeed utter what may be regarded as his dying words—"The Age of Reason." This was the task which he had from year to year adjourned to his maturest powers, and to it he dedicates what brief remnant of life may await him. That completed, it will be time to die with his comrades, awakened by his pen to a dawn now red with their blood.

The last letter I find written from the old Pompadour mansion is to Jefferson, under date of October 20th:

"DEAR SIR,—I wrote you by Captain Dominick who was to sail from Havre about the 20th of this month. This will probably be brought you by Mr. Barlow or Col. Oswald. Since my letter by Dominick I am every day more convinced and impressed with the propriety of Congress sending Commissioners to Europe to confer with the Ministers of the Jesuitical Powers on the means of terminating the war. The enclosed printed paper will shew there are a variety of subjects to be taken into consideration which did not appear at first, all of which have some tendency to put an end to the war. I see not how this war is to terminate if some intermediate power does not step forward. There is now no prospect that France can carry revolutions thro' Europe on the one hand, or that the combined powers can conquer France on the other hand. It is a sort of defensive War on both sides. This being the case how is the War to close? Neither side will ask for peace though each may wish it. I believe that England and Holland are tired of the war. Their Commerce and Manufactures have suffered most exceedingly—and besides this it is to them a war without an object. Russia keeps herself at a distance. I cannot help repeating my wish that Congress would send Commissioners, and I wish also that yourself would venture once more across the Ocean as one of them. If the Commissioners rendezvous at Holland they would then know what steps to take. They could call Mr. Pinckney to their Councils, and it would be of use, on many accounts, that one of them should come over from Holland to France. Perhaps a long truce, were it proposed by the neutral Powers, would have all the effects of a Peace, without the difficulties attending the adjustment of all the forms of Peace.—Yours affectionately   THOMAS PAINE."[1]

Thus has finally faded the dream of Paine's life—an international republic.

It is notable that in this letter Paine makes no mention of his own danger. He may have done so in the previous letter, unfound, to which he alludes. Why he made no attempt to escape after Amar's report seems a mystery, especially as he was assisting others to leave the country. Two of his friends, Johnson and Choppin—the last to part from him in the old garden,—escaped to Switzerland. John-

[1] I am indebted for this letter to Dr. John S. H. Fogg, of Boston. The letter is endorsed by Jefferson, "Rec'd Mar. 3." [1794.]

son will be remembered as the young man who attempted suicide on hearing of Marat's menaces against Paine. Writing to Lady Smith of these two friends, he says :

"He [Johnson] recovered, and being anxious to get out of France, a passport was obtained for him and Mr. Choppin ; they received it late in the evening, and set off the next morning for Basle, before four, from which place I had a letter from them, highly pleased with their escape from France, into which they had entered with an enthusiasm of patriotic devotion. Ah, France ! thou hast ruined the character of a revolution virtuously begun, and destroyed those who produced it. I might also say like Job's servant, 'and I only am escaped.'

"Two days after they were gone I heard a rapping at the gate, and looking out of the window of the bedroom I saw the landlord going with the candle to the gate, which he opened ; and a guard with muskets and fixed bayonets entered. I went to bed again and made up my mind for prison, for I was the only lodger. It was a guard to take up Johnson and Choppin, but, I thank God, they were out of their reach.

"The guard came about a month after, in the night, and took away the landlord, Georgeit. And the scene in the house finished with the arrestation of myself. This was soon after you called on me, and sorry I was that it was not in my power to render to Sir [Robert Smith] the service that you asked."

All then had fled. Even the old landlord had been arrested. In the wintry garden this lone man—in whose brain and heart the republic and the religion of humanity have their abode—moves companionless. In the great mansion, where once Madame de Pompadour glittered amid her courtiers, where in the past summer gathered the Round Table of great-hearted gentlemen and ladies,

Thomas Paine sits through the watches of the night at his devout task.[1]

"My friends were falling as fast as the guillotine could cut their heads off, and as I expected, every day, the same fate, I resolved to begin my work. I appeared to myself to be on my death bed, for death was on every side of me, and I had no time to lose. This accounts for my writing at the time I did, and so nicely did the time and intention meet, that I had not finished the first part of the work more than six hours before I was arrested and taken to prison. The people of France were running headlong into atheism, and I had the work translated in their own language, to stop them in that career, and fix them to the first article of every man's creed, who has any creed at all—*I believe in God.*"[2]

The second Christmas of the new republican era dawns. Where is the vision that has led this way-worn pilgrim? Where the star he has followed so long, to find it hovering over the new birth of humanity? It may have been on that day that, amid the shades of his slain friends, he wrote, as with

---

[1] It was a resumed task. Early in the year Paine had brought to his colleague Lanthenas a manuscript on religion, probably entitled "The Age of Reason." Lanthenas translated it, and had it printed in French, though no trace of its circulation appears. At that time Lanthenas may have apprehended the proscription which fell on him, with the other Girondins, in May, and took the precaution to show Paine's essay to Couthon, who, with Robespierre, had religious matters particularly in charge. Couthon frowned on the work and on Paine, and reproached Lanthenas for translating it. There was no frown more formidable than that of Couthon, and the essay (printed only in French) seems to have been suppressed. At the close of the year Paine wrote the whole work *de novo*. The first edition in English, now before me, was printed in Paris, by Barrois, 1794. In his preface to Part II., Paine implies a previous draft in saying: "I had not finished it more than six hours, *in the state it has since appeared*, before a guard came," etc. (The italics are mine.) The fact of the early translation appears in a letter of Lanthenas to Merlin de Thionville.

[2] Letter to Samuel Adams. The execution of the Girondins took place on October 31st.

blood about to be shed, the tribute to one that was pierced in trying to benefit mankind.

"Nothing that is here said can apply, even with the most distant disrespect, to the real character of Jesus Christ. He was a virtuous and amiable man. The morality that he preached and practised was of the most benevolent kind; and though similar systems of morality had been preached by Confucius, and by some of the Greek philosophers, many years before, by the Quakers since, and by good men in all ages, it has not been exceeded by any. . . . He preached most excellent morality, and the equality of man; but he preached also against the corruption and avarice of the Jewish priests, and this brought upon him the hatred and vengeance of the whole order of priesthood. The accusation which those priests brought against him was that of sedition and conspiracy against the Roman government, to which the Jews were then subject and tributary; and it is not improbable that the Roman government might have some secret apprehension of the effect of his doctrine, as well as the Jewish priests; neither is it improbable that Jesus Christ had in contemplation the delivery of the Jewish nation from the bondage of the Romans. Between the two, however, this virtuous reformer and religionist lost his life. . . . He was the son of God in like manner that every other person is—for the Creator is the Father of All. . . . Jesus Christ founded no new system. He called men to the practice of moral virtues, and the belief of one God. The great trait in his character is philanthropy."

Many Christmas sermons were preached in 1793, but probably all of them together do not contain so much recognition of the humanity of Jesus as these paragraphs of Paine. The Christmas bells ring in the false, but shall also ring in the true. While he is writing, on that Christmas night, word comes that he has been denounced by Bourdon de l'Oise, and expelled from the Convention. He now enters the Dark Valley. "Conceiving, after this, that I had but a few days of liberty I sat down, and brought the work to a close as speedily as possible."

In the "Age of Reason" there is a page of personal recollections. I have a feeling that this little episode marks the hour when Paine was told of his doom. From this overshadowed Christmas, likely to be his last, the lonely heart—as loving a heart as ever beat—here wanders across tempestuous years to his early Norfolkshire home. There is a grateful remembrance of the Quaker meeting, the parental care, the Grammar School; of his pious aunt who read him a printed sermon, and the garden steps where he pondered what he had just heard,—a Father demanding his Son's death for the sake of making mankind happier and better. He "perfectly recollects the spot" in the garden where, even then, but seven or eight years of age, he felt sure a man would be executed for doing such a thing, and that God was too good to act in that way. So clearly come out the scenes of childhood under the shadow of death.

He probably had an intimation on December 27th that he would be arrested that night. The place of his abode, though well known to the authorities, was not in the Convention's Almanach. Officially, therefore, his residence was still in the Passage des Petits Pères. There the officers would seek him, and there he should be found. "For that night only he sought a lodging there," reported the officers afterwards. He may have feared, too, that his manuscript would be destroyed if he were taken in his residence.

His hours are here traceable. On the evening of December 27th, in the old mansion, Paine reaches the last page of the "Age of Reason." They who have supposed him an atheist, may search as far as Job, who said "Though He slay me I will trust in Him," before finding an author who, caught in the cruel machinery of destructive nature, could write that last page.

"The creation we behold is the real and ever existing word of God, in which we cannot be deceived. It proclaimeth his power, it demonstrates his wisdom, it manifests his goodness and beneficence. The moral duty of man consists in imitating the moral goodness and beneficence of God manifested in the creation towards all his creatures. That seeing, as we daily do, the goodness of God to all men, it is an example calling upon all men to practise the same towards each other, and consequently that everything of persecution and revenge between man and man, and everything of cruelty to animals, is a violation of moral duty."

In what "Israel" is greater faith found? Having written these words, the pen drops from our world-wanderer's hand. It is nine o'clock of the night. He will now go and bend his neck under the decree of the Convention—provided by "the goodness of God to all men." Through the Faubourg, past Porte St. Martin, to the Rue Richelieu, to the Passage des Petits Pères, he walks in the wintry night. In the house where he wrote his appeal that the Convention would slay not the man in destroying the monarch, he asks a lodging "for that night only."

As he lays his head on the pillow, it is no doubt with a grateful feeling that the good God has prolonged his freedom long enough to finish a defence of true religion from its degradation by superstition or destruction by atheism,—these, as he declares, being the two purposes of his work. It was providently if not providentially timed. "I had not finished it more than six hours, in the state it has since appeared, before a guard came, about three in the morning, with an order, signed by the two Committees of Public Safety and Surety General, for putting me in arrestation as a foreigner, and conveying me to the prison of the Luxembourg."

The following documents are translated for this work from the originals in the National Archives of France.

"NATIONAL CONVENTION.

"Committee of General Surety and Surveillance of the National Convention.

"On the 7th Nivose [December 27th] of the 2d year of the French Republic, one and indivisible.

"TO THE DEPUTIES:

"The Committee resolves, that the persons named Thomas Paine and Anacharsis Clootz, formerly Deputies to the National Convention, be arrested and imprisoned, as a measure of General Surety; that an examination be made of their papers, and those found suspicious put under seal and brought to the Committee of General Surety.

"Citizens Jean Baptiste Martin and Lamy, bearers of the present decree are empowered to execute it,—for which they ask the help of the Civil authorities and, if need be, of the army.

"The representatives of the nation, members of the Committee of General Surety—Signed: M. Bayle, Voulland, Jagot, Amar, Vadier, Élie Lacoste, Guffroy, Louis (du bas Rhin) La Vicomterie, Panis."

"This day, the 8th Nivose of the 2d year of the French Republic, one and indivisible, to execute and fulfil the order given us, we have gone to the residence of Citizen Thomas Paine, Passage des Petits Pères, number seven, Philadelphia House. Having requested the Commander of the [Police] post, William Tell Section, to have us escorted, according to the order we showed him, he obeyed by assigning us four privates and a corporal, to search the above-said lodging; where we requested the porter to open the door, and asked him whether he knew all who lodged there; and as he did not affirm it, we desired him to take us to the principal agent, which he did; having come to the said agent, we asked him if he knew by name all the persons to whom he rented lodgings; after having repeated to him the name mentioned in our order, he replied to us, that he had come to ask him a lodging for that night only; which being ascertained, we asked him to conduct us to the bedroom of Citizen Thomas Paine, where we arrived; then seeing we could not be understood by him, an American, we begged the manager of the house, who knows his language, to kindly interpret for him, giving him notice of the order of which we were bearers; whereupon the said Citizen Thomas Paine submitted to be taken to Rue Jacob, Great Britain Hotel, which he declared through his interpreter to be the place where he had his papers; having recognized that his lodging contained none of them, we accompanied the said Thomas Paine and his interpreter to Great Britain Hotel, Rue Jacob, Unity Section; the present minutes closed, after being read before the undersigned.

"(Signed):

    THOMAS PAINE.   J. B. MARTIN.
    DORLÉ, Commissary.
    GILLET, Commissary.
    F. DELLANAY.
    ACHILLE AUDIBERT, Witness.[1]
    LAMY."

"And as it was about seven or eight o'clock in the morning of this day 8th Nivose, being worn out with fatigue, and forced to take some food, we postponed the end of our proceeding till eleven o'clock of the same day, when, desiring to finish it, we

[1] It will be remembered that Audibert had carried to London Paine's invitation to the Convention.

went with Citizen Thomas Paine to Britain House, where we found Citizen Barlow, whom Citizen Thomas Paine informed that we, the Commissaries, were come to look into the papers, which he said were at his house, as announced in our preceding paragraph through Citizen Dellanay, his interpreter ; We, Commissary of the Section of the Unity, undersigned, with the Citizens order-bearers, requested Citizen Barlow to declare whether there were in his house, any papers or correspondence belonging to Citizen Thomas Paine ; on which, complying with our request, he declared there did not exist any ; but wishing to leave no doubt on our way of conducting the matter, we did not think it right to rely on what he said ; resolving, on the contrary, to ascertain by all legal ways that there did not exist any, we requested Citizen Barlow to open for us all his cupboards ; which he did, and after having visited them, we, the abovesaid Commissary, always in the presence of Citizen Thomas Paine, recognized that there existed no papers belonging to him; we also perceived that it was a subterfuge on the part of Citizen Thomas Paine who wished only to transfer himself to the house of Citizen Barlow, his native friend *(son ami natal)* whom we invited to ask of Citizen Thomas Paine his usual place of abode ; and the latter seemed to wish that his friend might accompany him and be present at the examination of his papers. Which we, the said Commissary granted him, as Citizen Barlow could be of help to us, together with Citizen Etienne Thomas Dessous, interpreter for the English language, and Deputy Secretary to the Committee of General Surety of the National Convention, whom we called, in passing by the said Committee, to accompany us to the true lodging of the said Paine, Faubourg du Nord, Nro. 63. At which place we entered his rooms, and gathered in the Sitting-room all the papers found in the other rooms of the said apartment. The said Sitting-room receives light from three windows, looking, one on the Garden and the two others on the Courtyard ; and after the most scrupulous examination of all the papers, that we had there gathered, none of them has been found suspicious, neither in French nor in English, according to what was affirmed to us by Citizen Dessous our interpreter who signed with us, and Citizen Thomas Paine ; and we, the undersigned Commissary, resolved that no seal should be placed, after the examination mentioned, and closed the said minutes, which we declare to contain the truth. Drawn up at the residence, and closed at 4 p.m. in the day and year abovenamed; and we have all signed after having read the minutes.

"(Signed):

THOMAS PAINE.   JOEL BARLOW.
DORLÉ, Commissary.   GILLET, Commissary.
DESSOUS.   J. B. MARTIN.   LAMY.

"And after having signed we have requested, according to the order of the Committee of General Surety of the National Convention, Citizen Thomas Paine to follow us, to be led to jail; to which he complied without any difficulty, and he has signed with us:

THOMAS PAINE.   J. B. MARTIN.
DORLÉ, Commissary.   LAMY.
GILLETT, Commissary."

"I have received from the Citizens Martin and Lamy, Deputy-Secretaries to the Committee of General Surety of the National Convention, the Citizens Thomas Paine and Anacharsis Clootz, formerly Deputies; by order of the said Committee.

"At the Luxembourg, this day 8th Nivose, 2nd year of the French Republic, One and Indivisible.

"Signed: BENOIT, *Concierge*."

"FOREIGN OFFICE—Received the 12th Ventose [March 2d]. Sent to the Committees of General Surety and Public Safety the 8th Pluviose [January 27th] this 2d year of the French Republic, One and indivisible.

"Signed: BASSOL, *Secretary*."

"CITIZENS LEGISLATORS!—The French nation has, by a universal decree, invited to France one of our countrymen, most worthy of honor, namely, Thomas Paine, one of the political founders of the independence and of the Republic of America.

"Our experience of twenty years has taught America to know and esteem his public virtues and the invaluable services he rendered her.

"Persuaded that his character of foreigner and ex-Deputy is the only cause of his provisional imprisonment, we come in the name of our country (and we feel sure she will be grateful to us for it), we come to you, Legislators, to reclaim our friend, our countryman, that he may sail with us for America, where he will be received with open arms.

"If it were necessary to say more in support of the Petition which, as friends and allies of the French Republic, we submit to her representatives, to obtain the liberation of one of the most earnest and faithful apostles of liberty, we would beseech the National Convention, for the sake of all that is dear to the glory and to the heart of freemen, not to give a cause of joy and triumph to the allied tyrants of Europe, and above all to the despotism of Great Britain, which did not blush to outlaw this courageous and virtuous defender of Liberty.

"But their insolent joy will be of short duration ; for we have the intimate persuasion that you will not keep longer in the bonds of painful captivity the man whose courageous and energetic pen did so much to free the Americans, and whose intentions we have no doubt whatever were to render the same services to the French Republic. Yes, we feel convinced that his principles and views were pure, and in that regard he is entitled to the indulgence due to human fallibility, and to the respect due to rectitude of heart ; and we hold all the more firmly our opinion of his innocence, inasmuch as we are informed that after a scrupulous examination of his papers, made by order of the Committee of General Surety, instead of anything to his charge, enough has been found rather to corroborate the purity of his principles in politics and morals.

"As a countryman of ours, as a man above all so dear to the Americans, who like yourselves are earnest friends of Liberty, we ask you, in the name of that goddess cherished of the only two Republics of the World, to give back Thomas Paine to his brethren and permit us to take him to his country which is also ours.

"If you require it, Citizens Representatives, we shall make ourselves warrant and security for his conduct in France during the short stay he may make in this land.

"Signed :

W. JACKSON, of Philadelphia. J. RUSSELL, of Boston. PETER WHITESIDE, of Philadelphia. HENRY JOHNSON, of Boston. THOMAS CARTER, of Newbury Port. JAMES COOPER of Philadelphia. JOHN WILLERT BILLOPP, of New York. THOMAS WATERS GRIFFITH, of Baltimore. TH. RAMSDEN, of Boston. SAMUEL P. BROOME, of New York. A. MEADENWORTH, of Connecticut. JOEL BARLOW, of Connecticut. MICHAEL ALCORN, of Philadelphia. M. ONEALY, of Baltimore. JOHN MCPHERSON, of Alexandria [Va.]. WILLIAM HASKINS, of Boston. J. GREGORY, of Petersburg, Virginia. JAMES INGRAHAM, of Boston."[1]

The following answer to the petitioning Americans was given by Vadier, then president of the Convention.

"CITIZENS: The brave Americans are our brothers in liberty; like us they have broken the chains of despotism; like us they have sworn the destruction of kings and vowed an eternal hatred to tyrants and their instruments. From this identity of principles should result a union of the two nations forever unalterable. If the tree of liberty already flourishes in the two hemispheres, that of commerce should, by this happy alliance, cover the poles with its fruitful branches. It is for France, it is for the United States, to combat and lay low, in concert, these proud islanders, these insolent dominators of the sea and the commerce of nations. When the sceptre of despotism is falling from the criminal hand of the tyrants of the earth, it is necessary also to break the trident which emboldens the insolence of these corsairs of Albion, these modern Carthaginians. It is time to repress the audacity and mercantile avarice of these pirate tyrants of the sea, and of the commerce of nations.

"You demand of us, citizens, the liberty of Thomas Paine; you wish to restore to your hearths this defender of the rights of man. One can only applaud this generous movement. Thomas Paine is a native of England; this is undoubtedly enough to apply to him the measures of security prescribed by the revolutionary laws. It may be added, citizens, that if Thomas Paine has been the apostle of liberty, if he has powerfully co-operated with the American Revolution, his genius has not understood that which has regenerated France; he has regarded the system only in accordance with the illusions with

[1] The preceding documents connected with the arrest are in the Archives Nationales, F. 4641.

which the false friends of our revolution have invested it. You must with us deplore an error little reconcilable with the principles admired in the justly esteemed works of this republican author.

"The National Convention will take into consideration the object of your petition, and invites you to its sessions."

A memorandum adds: "Reference of this petition is decreed to the Committees of Public Safety and General Surety, united."

It is said that Paine sent an appeal for intervention to the Cordeliers Club, and that their only reply was to return to him a copy of his speech in favor of preserving the life of Louis XVI. This I have not been able to verify.

On leaving his house for prison, Paine entrusted to Joel Barlow the manuscript of the "Age of Reason," to be conveyed to the printer. This was with the knowledge of the guard, whose kindness is mentioned by Paine.

CHAPTER VII.

A MINISTER AND HIS PRISONER.

BEFORE resuming the history of the conspiracy against Paine it is necessary to return a little on our steps. For a year after the fall of monarchy in France (August 10, 1792), the real American Minister there was Paine, whether for Americans or for the French Executive. The Ministry would not confer with a hostile and presumably decapitated agent, like Morris. The reader has (Chaps. IV. and V., Vol. II.) evidence of their consultations with Paine. Those communications of Paine were utilized in Robespierre's report to the Convention, November 17, 1793, on the foreign relations of France. It was inspired by the humiliating tidings that Genêt in America had reinforced the European intrigues to detach Washington from France. The President had demanded Genêt's recall, had issued a proclamation of "impartiality" between France and her foes, and had not yet decided whether the treaty formed with Louis XVI. should survive his death. And Morris was not recalled!

In his report Robespierre makes a solemn appeal to the "brave Americans." Was it "that crowned automaton called Louis XVI." who helped to rescue them from the oppressor's yoke, or our arm and armies? Was it his money sent over or the taxes of French labor? He declares that the Republic has been treacherously compromised in America.

"By a strange fatality the Republic finds itself still represented among their allies by agents of the traitors she has punished: Brissot's brother-in-law is Consul-General there; another man, named Genêt, sent by Lebrun and Brissot to Philadelphia as plenipotentiary agent, has faithfully fulfilled the views and instructions of the faction that appointed him."

The result is that "parallel intrigues" are observable—one aiming to bring France under the league, the other to break up the American republic into parts.[1]

In this idea of "parallel intrigues" the irremovable Morris is discoverable. It is the reappearance of what he had said to Deforgues about the simultaneous sedition in America (Genêt's) and "influence in their affairs from the other side of the channel" (Paine's). There was not, however, in Robespierre's report any word that might be construed into a suspicion of Paine; on the contrary, he declares the Convention now pure. The Convention instructed the Committee of Public Safety to provide for strictest fulfilment of its treaties with America, and caution to its agents to respect the government and territory of its allies. The first necessary step was to respect the President's Minister, Gouverneur Morris, however odious he might be, since it would be on his representations that the continuance of France's one important alliance

[1] "Hist. Parl.," xxx., p. 224.

might depend. Morris played cleverly on that string; he hinted dangers that did not exist, and dangled promises never to be fulfilled. He was master of the situation. The unofficial Minister who had practically superseded him for a year was now easily locked up in the Luxembourg.

But why was not Paine executed? The historic paradox must be ventured that he owed his reprieve—his life—to Robespierre. Robespierre had Morris' intercepted letters and other evidences of his treachery, yet as Washington insisted on him, and the alliance was at stake, he must be obeyed. On the other hand were evidences of Washington's friendship for Paine, and of Jefferson's intimacy with him. Time must therefore be allowed for the prisoner to communicate with the President and Secretary of State. They must decide between Paine and Morris. It was only after ample time had passed, and no word about Paine came from Washington or Jefferson, while Morris still held his position, that Robespierre entered his memorandum that Paine should be tried before the revolutionary tribunal.

Meanwhile a great deal happened, some of which, as Paine's experiences in the Luxembourg, must be deferred to a further chapter. The American Minister had his triumph. The Americans in Paris, including the remaining sea-captains, who had been looking to Paine as their Minister, were now to discover where the power was lodged. Knowing Morris' hatred for Paine, they repaired to the Convention with their petition. Major Jackson, a well known officer of the American Revolution, who headed the deputation (which included every unofficial American in Paris), utilized a letter of introduction he had brought from Secretary Jefferson to Morris by giving it to the Committee of General Surety, as an evidence of his right to act in the emergency.

Action was delayed by excitement over the celebration of the first anniversary of the King's execution. On that occasion (January 21st) the Convention joined the Jacobin Club in marching to the "Place de la Révolution," with music and banners; there the portraits of kings were burned, an act of accusation against all the kings of the earth adopted, and a fearfully realistic drama enacted. By a prearrangement unknown to the Convention four condemned men were guillotined before them. The Convention recoiled, and instituted an inquisition as to the responsibility for this scene. It was credited to the Committee of General Surety, justly no doubt, but its chief, Vadier, managed to relieve it of the odium. This Vadier was then president of the Convention. He was appropriately selected to give the first anniversary oration on the King's execution. A few days later it fell to Vadier to address the eighteen Americans at the bar of the Convention on their petition for Paine's release. The petition and petitioners being referred to the Committees of Public Safety and General Surety in joint session, the Americans were there answered, by Billaud-Varennes it was said, "that their reclamation was only the act of individuals, without any authority from the American government."

This was a plain direction. The American government, whether in Paris or Philadelphia, had Paine's fate in its hands.

At this time it was of course not known that Jefferson had retired from the Cabinet. To him Paine might have written, but—sinister coincidence!—immediately after the committees had referred the matter to the American government an order was issued cutting off all communication between prisoners and the outside world. That Morris had something to do with this is suggested by the fact that he was allowed to correspond with Paine in prison, though this was not allowed to his successor, Monroe. However, there is, unfortunately, no need to repair to suspicions for the part of Gouverneur Morris in this affair. His first ministerial mention of the matter to Secretary Jefferson is dated on the tragical anniversary, January 21st. "Lest I should forget it," he says of this small incident, the imprisonment of one whom Congress and the President had honored—

"Lest I should forget it, I must mention that Thomas Paine is in prison, where he amuses himself with publishing a pamphlet against Jesus Christ. I do not recollect whether I mentioned to you that he would have been executed along with the rest of the Brissotins if the advance party had not viewed him with contempt. I incline to think that if he is quiet in prison he may have the good luck to be forgotten, whereas, should he be brought much into notice, the long suspended axe might fall on him. I believe he thinks that I ought to claim him as an American citizen; but considering his birth, his naturalization in this country, and the place he filled, I doubt much the right, and I am sure that the claim would be, for the present at least, inexpedient and ineffectual."

Although this paragraph is introduced in such a casual way, there is calculation in every word. First of all, however, be it observed, Morris knows precisely how the authorities will act several days before they have been appealed to. It also appears that if Paine was not executed with the Brissotins on October 31st, it was not due to any interference on his part. The "contempt" which saved Paine may be estimated by a reference to the executive consultations with him, and to Amar's bitter denunciation of him (October 3d) after Morris had secretly accused this contemptible man of influencing the Convention and helping to excite sedition in the United States. In the next place, Jefferson is admonished that if he would save his friend's head he must not bring the matter into notice. The government at Philadelphia must, in mercy to Paine, remain silent. As to the "pamphlet against Jesus Christ," my reader has already perused what Paine wrote on that theme in the "Age of Reason." But as that may not be so likely to affect freethinking Jefferson, Morris adds the falsehood that Paine had been naturalized in France. The reader need hardly be reminded that if an application by the American Minister for the release would be "ineffectual," it must be because the said Minister would have it so. Morris had already found, as he tells Washington, that the Ministry, supposing him immovable, were making overtures of conciliation; and none can read the obsequious letter of the Foreign Minister, Deforgues (October 19, 1793), without knowing that a word from Morris would release Paine. The

American petitioners had indeed been referred to their own government—that is, to Morris.

The American Minister's version of what had occurred is given in a letter to Secretary Jefferson, dated March 6th:

"I have mentioned Mr. Paine's confinement. Major Jackson—who, by the by, has not given me a letter from you which he says was merely introductory, but left it with the Comité de Sûreté Générale, as a kind of letter of credence—Major Jackson, relying on his great influence with the leaders here, stepped forward to get Mr. Paine out of jail, and with several other Americans, has presented a petition to that effect, which was referred to that Committee and the Comité de Salut Public. This last, I understand, slighted the application as totally irregular; and some time afterwards Mr. Paine wrote me a note desiring I would claim him as an American, which I accordingly did, though contrary to my judgment, for reasons mentioned in my last. The Minister's letter to me of the 1st Ventose, of which I enclose a copy, contains the answer to my reclamation. I sent a copy to Mr. Paine, who prepared a long answer, and sent it to me by an Englishman, whom I did not know. I told him, as Mr. Paine's friend, that my present opinion was similar to that of the Minister, but I might, perhaps, see occasion to change it, and in that case, if Mr. Paine wished it, I would go on with the claim, but that it would be well for him to consider the result; that, if the Government meant to release him, they had already a sufficient ground; but if not, I could only push them to bring on his trial for the crimes imputed to him; seeing that whether he be considered as a Frenchman, or as an American, he must be amenable to the tribunals of France for his conduct while he was a Frenchman, and he may see in the fate of the Brissotins, that to which he is exposed. I have heard no more of the affair since; but it is not impossible that he may force on a decision, which, as far as I can judge, would be fatal to him: for in the best of times he had a larger share of every other sense than common sense, and lately the intemperate use of ardent spirits has, I am told, considerably impaired the small stock he originally possessed."

In this letter the following incidental points suggest comment :

1. "Several other Americans." The petitioners for Paine's release were eighteen in number, and seem to have comprised all the Americans then left in Paris, some of them eminent.

2. "The crimes imputed to him." There were none. Paine was imprisoned under a law against "foreigners." Those charged with his arrest reported that his papers were entirely innocent. The archives of France, now open to exploration, prove that no offence was ever imputed to him, showing his arrest due only to Morris' insinuation of his being objectionable to the United States. By this insinuation ("crimes imputed to him") Paine was asserted to be amenable to French laws for matters with which the United States would of course have nothing to do, and of which nothing could be known in Philadelphia.

3. "While he was a Frenchman." Had Paine ever been a Frenchman, he was one when Morris pretended that he had claimed him as an American. But Paine had been excluded from the Convention and imprisoned expressly because he was not a Frenchman. No word of the Convention's published action was transmitted by Morris.

4. "The fate of the Brissotins," etc. This of course would frighten Paine's friends by its hint of a French hostility to him which did not exist, and might restrain them from applying to America for interference. Paine was already restrained by the new order preventing him from

communicating with any one except the American Minister.

5. "Intemperate," etc. This is mere calumny. Since the brief lapse in June, 1793, when overwhelmed by the arrest of his friends, Paine's daily life is known from those who dwelt with him. During the months preceding his arrest he wrote the "Age of Reason"; its power, if alcoholic, might have recommended his cellar to Morris, or to any man living.

So much for the insinuations and *suggestiones falsi* in Morris' letter. The suppressions of fact are more deadly. There is nothing of what had really happened; nothing of the eulogy of Paine by the President of the Convention, which would have been a commentary on what Morris had said of the contempt in which he was held; not a word of the fact that the petitioners were reminded by the Committee that their application was unofficial,—in other words, that the determination on Paine's fate rested with Morris himself. This Morris hides under the phrase: "slighted the application as totally irregular."

But the fatal far-reaching falsehood of Morris' letter to Jefferson was his assertion that he had claimed Paine as an American. This falsehood, told to Washington, Jefferson, Edmund Randolph, paralyzed all action in America in Paine's behalf; told to the Americans in Paris, it paralyzed further effort of their own.

The actual correspondence between Morris and Deforgues is now for the first time brought to light.

MORRIS TO DEFORGUES.

"PARIS, 14th February 1794.

"SIR,—Thomas Paine has just applied to me to claim him as a Citizen of the United States. These (I believe) are the facts which relate to him. He was born in England. Having become a citizen of the United States, he acquired great celebrity there through his revolutionary writings. In consequence he was adopted as French Citizen, and then elected Member of the Convention. His behaviour since that epoch is out of my jurisdiction. I am ignorant of the reason for his present detention in the Luxembourg prison, but I beg you, Sir, if there be reasons which prevent his liberation, and which are unknown to me, be so good as to inform me of them, so that I may communicate them to the Government of the United States.—I have the honour to be, Sir, Your very humble servant,

"GOUV. MORRIS."[1]

DEFORGUES TO MORRIS.

"PARIS, 1st Ventose, 2nd year of the Republic.
[February 19, 1794.]

"The Minister of Foreign Affairs to the Minister of the United States.

"In your letter of the 26th of last month you reclaim the liberty of Thomas Payne, as an American Citizen. Born in England, this co-deputy has become successively an American and a French Citizen. In accepting this last title, and in occupying a place in the Legislative Corps, he submitted himself to the laws of the Republic, and has renounced the protection which the right of the people and treaties concluded with the United States could have assured him.

"I am ignorant of the motives of his detention, but I must presume they are well founded. I shall nevertheless submit the demand you have addressed me to the Committee of Public Safety, and I shall lose no time in letting you know its decision.

"DEFORGUES."

[1] "États Unis," vol. xl., Doc. 54. Endorsed: "Received the 28th of same [Pluviose, *i. e.*, Feb. 16th]. To declare reception and to tell him that the Minister will take the necessary steps." The French Minister's reply is Doc. 61 of the same volume.

The opening assertion of the French Minister's note reveals the collusion. Careful examination of the American Minister's letter, to find where he "reclaims the liberty of Thomas Payne as an American citizen," forces me to the conclusion that the Frenchman only discovered such reclamation there by the assistance of Morris.

The American Minister distinctly declares Paine to be a French citizen, and disclaims official recognition of him.

It will be borne in mind that this French Minister is the same Deforgues who had confided to Morris his longing to succeed Genêt in America, and to whom Morris had whispered his design against Paine. Morris resided at Sainport, twenty-seven miles away, but his note is written in Paris. Four days elapse before the reply. Consultation is further proved by the French Minister's speaking of Paine as "occupying a place in the Legislative Corps." No uninspired Frenchman could have so described the Convention, any more than an American would have described the Convention of 1787 as "Congress." Deforgues' phrase is calculated for Philadelphia, where it might be supposed that the recently adopted Constitution had been followed by the organization of a legislature, whose members must of course take an oath of allegiance, which the Convention had not required.[1] Deforgues also makes bold to declare—as far away as Philadelphia—that Paine is a French citizen, though he

[1] Deforgues' phrase "laws of the Republic" is also a deception. The Constitution had been totally suspended by the Convention; no government or law had been or ever was established under or by it. There was as yet no Republic, and only revolutionary or martial laws.

was excluded from the Convention and imprisoned because he was a "foreigner." The extreme ingenuity of the letter was certainly not original with this Frenchman. The American Minister, in response to his note declaring Paine a French citizen, and disclaiming jurisdiction over him, returns to Sainport with his official opiate for Paine's friends in America and Paris—a certificate that he has "reclaimed the liberty of Thomas Paine as an American citizen." The alleged reclamation suppressed, the certificate sent to Secretary Jefferson and to Paine, the American Minister is credited with having done his duty. In Washington's Cabinet, where the technicalities of citizenship had become of paramount importance, especially as regarded France, Deforgues' claim that Paine was not an American must be accepted—Morris consenting—as final.

It may be wondered that Morris should venture on so dangerous a game. But he had secured himself in anything he might choose to do. So soon as he discovered, in the previous summer, that he was not to be removed, and had fresh thunderbolts to wield, he veiled himself from the inspection of Jefferson. This he did in a letter of September 22, 1793. In the quasi-casual way characteristic of him when he is particularly deep, Morris then wrote: "*By the bye, I shall cease to send you copies of my various applications in particular cases, for they will cost you more in postage than they are worth.*" I put in italics this sentence, as one which merits memorable record in the annals of diplomacy.

The French Foreign Office being secret as the grave, Jefferson facile, and Washington confiding, there was no danger that Morris' letter to Deforgues would ever appear. Although the letter of Deforgues,—his certificate that Morris had reclaimed Paine as an American,—was a little longer than the pretended reclamation, postal economy did not prevent the American Minister from sending *that*, but his own was never sent to his government, and to this day is unknown to its archives.

It cannot be denied that Morris' letter to Deforgues is masterly in its way. He asks the Minister to give him such reasons for Paine's detention as may not be known to him (Morris), there being no such reasons. He sets at rest any timidity the Frenchman might have, lest Morris should be ensnaring him also, by begging—not demanding—such knowledge as he may communicate to his government. Philadelphia is at a safe distance in time and space. Deforgues is complacent enough, Morris being at hand, to describe it as a "demand," and to promise speedy action on the matter—which was then straightway buried, for a century's slumber.

Paine was no doubt right in his subsequent belief that Morris was alarmed at his intention of returning to America. Should Paine ever reach Jefferson and his adherents, Gouverneur Morris must instantly lose a position which, sustained by Washington, made him a power throughout Europe. Moreover, there was a Nemesis lurking near him. The revolutionists, aware of his relations with their enemies, were only withheld from laying hands on him by awe of Washington and anxiety about the alliance. The moment of his repudiation by his government would have been a perilous one. It so proved, indeed, when Monroe supplanted him. For the present, however, he is powerful. As the French Executive could have no interest merely to keep Paine, for six months, without suggestion of trial, it is difficult to imagine any reason, save the wish of Morris, why he was not allowed to depart with the Americans, in accordance with their petition.

Thus Thomas Paine, recognized by every American statesman and by Congress as a founder of their Republic, found himself a prisoner, and a man without a country. Outlawed by the rulers of his native land—though the people bore his defender, Erskine, from the court on their shoulders—imprisoned by France as a foreigner, disowned by America as a foreigner, and prevented by its Minister from returning to the country whose President had declared his services to it pre-eminent!

Never dreaming that his situation was the work of Morris, Paine (February 24th) appealed to him for help.

"I received your letter enclosing a copy of a letter from the Minister of foreign affairs. You must not leave me in the situation in which this letter places me. You know I do not deserve it, and you see the unpleasant situation in which I am thrown. I have made an essay in answer to the Minister's letter, which I wish you to make ground of a reply to him. They have nothing against me—except that they do not choose I should be in a state of freedom to write my mind freely upon things I have seen. Though you and I are not on terms of the best harmony, I apply to you as the Minister of America, and you may add to that service whatever you think my integrity deserves. At any rate I expect you to make Congress acquainted with my situation, and to send to them copies of the letters that have passed on the subject. A reply to the Minister's letter is absolutely necessary, were it only to continue the reclamation. Otherwise your silence will be a sort of consent to his observations."

Supposing, from the French Minister's opening assertion, that a reclamation had really been made, Paine's simplicity led him into a trap. He sent his argument to be used by the Minister in an answer of his own, so that Minister was able to do as he pleased with it, the result being that it was buried among his private papers, to be partly brought to light by Jared Sparks, who is candid enough to remark on the Minister's indifference and the force of Paine's argument. Not a word to Congress was ever said on the subject.

Jefferson, without the knowledge or expectation of Morris, had resigned the State Secretaryship at the close of 1793. Morris' letter of March 6th reached the hands of Edmund Randolph, Jefferson's successor, late in June. On June 25th Randolph writes Washington, at Mount Vernon, that he has received a letter from Morris, of March 6th, saying "that he has demanded Paine as an American citizen, but that the Minister holds him to be amenable to the French laws." Randolph was a just man and an exact lawyer; it is certain that if he had received a copy of the fictitious "reclamation" the imprisonment would have been curtailed. Under the false information before him, nothing could be done but await the statement of the causes of Paine's detention, which Deforgues would "lose no time" in transmitting. It was impossible to deny, without further knowledge, the rights over Paine apparently claimed by the French government.

And what could be done by the Americans in Paris, whom Paine alone had befriended? Joel Barlow, who had best opportunities of knowing the facts, says: "He [Paine] was always charitable to the poor beyond his means, a sure friend and protector to all Americans in distress that he found in foreign countries; and he had frequent occasions to exert his influence in protecting them during the Revolution in France." They were grateful and deeply moved, these Americans, but thoroughly deceived about the situation. Told that they must await the action of a distant government, which itself was waiting for action in Paris, alarmed by the American Minister's hints of danger that might ensue on any misstep or agitation, assured that he was proceeding with the case, forbidden to communicate with Paine, they were reduced to helplessness. Meanwhile, between silent America and these Americans, all so cunningly disabled, stood the remorseless French Committee, ready to strike or to release in obedience to any sign from the alienated ally, to soothe whom no sacrifice would be too great. Genêt had been demanded for the altar of sacred Alliance, but (to Morris' regret) refused by the American government. The Revolution would have preferred Morris as a victim, but was quite ready to offer Paine.

Six or seven months elapsed without bringing from President or Cabinet a word of sympathy for Paine. But they brought increasing indications that America was in treaty with England, and Washington disaffected towards France. Under these circumstances Robespierre resolved on the accusation and trial of Paine. It does not necessarily follow that Paine would have been condemned; but there were some who did not mean that he should escape, among whom Robespierre may or may not have been included. The probabilities, to my mind, are against that theory. Robespierre having ceased to attend the Committee of Public Safety when the order issued for Paine's death.

CHAPTER VIII.

SICK AND IN PRISON.

It was a strange world into which misfortune had introduced Paine. There was in prison a select and rather philosophical society, mainly persons of refinement, more or less released from conventional habit by the strange conditions under which they found themselves. There were gentlemen and ladies, no attempt being made to separate them until some scandal was reported. The Luxembourg was a special prison for the French nobility and the English, who had a good opportunity for cultivating democratic ideas. The gaoler, Benoit, was good-natured, and cherished his unwilling guests as his children, according to a witness. Paine might even have been happy there but for the ever recurring tragedies—the cries of those led forth to death. He was now and then in strange juxtapositions. One day Deforgues came to join him, he who had conspired with Morris. Instead of receiving for his crime diplomatic security in America he found himself beside his victim. Perhaps if Deforgues and Paine had known each other's language a confession might have passed. There were horrors on horrors. Paine's old friend, Hérault de Séchelles, was imprisoned for having humanely concealed in his house a poor officer who was hunted by the police; he parted from Paine for the scaffold. So also he parted from the brilliant Camille Desmoulins, and the fine dreamer, Anacharsis Clootz. One day came Danton, who, taking Paine's hand, said: "That which you did for the happiness and liberty of your country, I tried in vain to do for mine. I have been less fortunate, but not less innocent. They will send me to the scaffold; very well, my friends, I shall go gaily." Even so did Danton meet his doom.[1]

All of the English prisoners became Paine's friends. Among these was General O'Hara,—that same general who had fired the American heart at Yorktown by offering the surrendered sword of Cornwallis to Rochambeau instead of Washington. O'Hara's captured suite included two physicians— Bond and Graham—who attended Paine during an illness, as he gratefully records. What money Paine had when arrested does not appear to have been taken from him, and he was able to assist General O'Hara with £200 to return to his country; though by this and similar charities he was left without means when his own unexpected deliverance came.[2]

The first part of "The Age of Reason" was sent out with final revision at the close of January.

[1] "Mémoires sur les prisons," t. ii., p. 153.
[2] Among the anecdotes told of O'Hara in prison, one is related of an argument he held with a Frenchman, on the relative degrees of liberty in England and France. "In England," he said, "we are perfectly free to write and print, *George is a good King;* but you—why you are not even permitted to write, *Robespierre is a tiger!*"

In the second edition appeared the following inscription:

"To my fellow citizens of the United States of America.—I put the following work under your protection. It contains my opinion upon Religion. You will do me the justice to remember, that I have always strenuously supported the Right of every man to his opinion, however different that opinion might be to mine. He who denies to another this right, makes a slave of himself to his present opinion, because he precludes himself the right of changing it. The most formidable weapon against errors of every kind is Reason. I have never used any other, and I trust I never shall.—Your affectionate friend and fellow citizen,

"Thomas Paine."

This dedication is dated, "Luxembourg (Paris), 8th Pluviose, Second year of the French Republic, one and indivisible. January 27, O. S. 1794." Paine now addressed himself to the second part of "The Age of Reason," concerning which the following anecdote is told in the manuscript memoranda of Thomas Rickman:

"Paine, while in the Luxembourg prison and expecting to die hourly, read to Mr. Bond (surgeon of Brighton, from whom this anecdote came) parts of his *Age of Reason;* and every night, when Mr. Bond left him, to be separately locked up, and expecting not to see Paine alive in the morning, he [Paine] always expressed his firm belief in the principles of that book, and begged Mr. Bond should tell the world such were his dying sentiments. Paine further said, if he lived he should further prosecute the work and print it. Bond added, Paine was the most conscientious man he ever knew."

In after years, when Paine was undergoing persecution for "infidelity," he reminded the zealots that they would have to "accuse Providence of infidelity," for having "protected him in all his dangers." Incidentally he gives reminiscences of his imprisonment.

"I was one of the nine members that composed the first Committee of Constitution. Six of them have been destroyed. Sieyès and myself have survived—he by bending with the times, and I by not bending. The other survivor [Barrère] joined Robespierre; he was seized and imprisoned in his turn, and sentenced to transportation. He has since apologized to me for having signed the warrant, by saying he felt himself in danger and was obliged to do it. Hérault Séchelles, an acquaintance of Mr. Jefferson, and a good patriot, was my *suppleant* as member of the Committee of Constitution. . . . He was imprisoned in the Luxembourg with me, was taken to the tribunal and guillotined, and I, his principal, left. There were two foreigners in the Convention, Anacharsis Clootz and myself. We were both put out of the Convention by the same vote, arrested by the same order, and carried to prison together the same night. He was taken to the guillotine, and I was again left. . . . Joseph Lebon, one of the vilest characters that ever existed, and who made the streets of Arras run with blood, was my *suppleant*, as member of the Convention for the Pas de Calais. When I was put out of the Convention he came and took my place. When I was liberated from prison and voted again into the Convention, he was sent to the same prison and took my place there, and he was sent to the guillotine instead of me. He supplied my place all the way through.

"One hundred and sixty-eight persons were taken out of the Luxembourg in one night, and a hundred and sixty of them guillotined next day, of which I knew I was to be one; and the manner I escaped that fate is curious, and has all the appearance of accident. The room in which I lodged was on the ground floor, and one of a long range of rooms under a gallery, and the door of it opened outward and flat against the wall; so that when it was open the inside of the door appeared outward, and the contrary when it was shut. I had three comrades, fellow prisoners with me, Joseph Vanhuile of Bruges, since president of the municipality of that town, Michael and

Robbins Bastini of Louvain. When persons by scores and by hundreds were to be taken out of the prison for the guillotine it was always done in the night, and those who performed that office had a private mark or signal by which they knew what rooms to go to, and what number to take. We, as I have said, were four, and the door of our room was marked, unobserved by us, with that number in chalk; but it happened, if happening is the proper word, that the mark was put on when the door was open and flat against the wall, and thereby came on the inside when we shut it at night; and the destroying angel passed by it."

Paine did not hear of this chalk mark until afterwards. In his letter to Washington he says:

"I had been imprisoned seven months, and the silence of the executive part of the government of America (Mr. Washington) upon the case, and upon every thing respecting me, was explanation enough to Robespierre that he might proceed to extremities. A violent fever which had nearly terminated my existence was, I believe, the circumstance that preserved it. I was not in a condition to be removed, or to know of what was passing, or of what had passed, for more than a month. It makes a blank in my remembrance of life. The first thing I was informed of was the fall of Robespierre."

The probabilities are that the prison physician Marhaski, whom Paine mentions with gratitude, was with him when the chalk mark was made, and that there was some connivance in the matter. In the same letter he says:

"From about the middle of March (1794) to the fall of Robespierre, July 29, (9th of Thermidor,) the state of things in the prisons was a continued scene of horror. No man could count upon life for twenty-four hours. To such a pitch of rage and suspicion were Robespierre and his committee arrived, that it seemed as if they feared to leave a man to live. Scarcely a night passed in which ten, twenty, thirty, forty, fifty or more were not taken out of the prison, carried before a pretended tribunal in the morning, and guillotined before night. One hundred and sixty-nine were taken out of the Luxembourg one night in the month of July, and one hundred and sixty of them guillotined. A list of two hundred more, according to the report in the prison, was preparing a few days before Robespierre fell. In this last list I have good reason to believe I was included."

To this Paine adds the memorandum for his accusation found in Robespierre's note-book. Of course it was natural, especially with the memorandum, to accept the Robespierre mythology of the time without criticism. The massacres of July were not due to Robespierre, who during that time was battling with the Committee of Public Safety, at whose hands he fell on the 29th. At the close of June there was an alarm at preparations for an insurrection in Luxembourg prison, which caused a union of the Committee of Public Safety and the police, resulting in indiscriminate slaughter of prisoners. But Paine was discriminated. Barrère, long after, apologized to him for having signed "the warrant," by saying he felt himself in danger and was obliged to do it. Paine accepted the apology, and when Barrère had returned to France, after banishment, Paine introduced him to the English author, Lewis Goldsmith.[1] As Barrère did not sign the warrant for Paine's imprisonment, it must have been a warrant for his death, or for accusation at a moment when it was equivalent to a death sentence. Whatever danger Barrère had to fear, so great as to cause him to sacrifice Paine, it was

[1] "Mémoires de B. Barrère,"t. i., p. 80. Lewis Goldsmith was the author of "Crimes of the Cabinets."

not from Robespierre; else it would not have continued to keep Paine in prison three months after Robespierre's death. As Robespierre's memorandum was for a "decree of accusation" against Paine, separately, which might not have gone against him, but possibly have dragged to light the conspiracy against him, there would seem to be no ground for connecting that "demand" with the warrant signed by a Committee he did not attend.

Paine had good cause for writing as he did in praise of "Forgetfulness." During the period in which he was unconscious with fever the horrors of the prison reached their apogee. On June 19th the kindly gaoler, Benoit, was removed and tried; he was acquitted but not restored. His place was given to a cruel fellow named Gayard, who instituted a reign of terror in the prison.

There are many evidences that the good Benoit, so warmly remembered by Paine, evaded the rigid police regulations as to communications of prisoners with their friends outside, no doubt with precaution against those of a political character. It is pleasant to record an instance of this which was the means of bringing beautiful rays of light into Paine's cell. Shortly before his arrest an English lady had called on him, at his house in the Faubourg St. Denis, to ask his intervention in behalf of an Englishman of rank who had been arrested. Paine had now, however, fallen from power, and could not render the requested service. This lady was the last visitor who preceded the officers who arrested him. But while he was in prison there was brought to him a communication, in a lady's handwriting, signed "A little corner of the World." So far as can be gathered, this letter was of a poetical character, perhaps tinged with romance. It was followed by others, all evidently meant to beguile the weary and fearful hours of a prisoner whom she had little expectation of ever meeting again. Paine, by the aid of Benoit, managed to answer his "contemplative correspondent," as he called her, signing, "The Castle in the Air." These letters have never seen the light, but the sweetness of this sympathy did, for many an hour, bring into Paine's *oubliette* the oblivion of grief described in the letter on "Forgetfulness," sent to the lady after his liberation.

"Memory, like a beauty that is always present to hear herself flattered, is flattered by every one. But the absent and silent goddess, Forgetfulness, has no votaries, and is never thought of: yet we owe her much. She is the goddess of ease, though not of pleasure. When the mind is like a room hung with black, and every corner of it crowded with the most horrid images imagination can create, this kind, speechless maid, Forgetfulness, is following us night and day with her opium wand, and gently touching first one and then another, benumbs them into rest, and then glides away with the silence of a departing shadow."

Paine was not forgotten by his old friends in France. So soon as the excitement attending Robespierre's execution had calmed a little, Lanthenas (August 7th) sent Merlin de Thionville a copy of the "Age of Reason," which he had translated, and made his appeal.

"I think it would be in the well-considered interest of the Republic, since the fall of the tyrants we have overthrown, to re-examine the motives of Thomas Paine's imprisonment.

That re-examination is suggested by too many and sensible grounds to be related in detail. Every friend of liberty familiar with the history of our Revolution, and feeling the necessity of repelling the slanders with which despots are loading it in the eyes of nations, misleading them against us, will understand these grounds. Should the Committee of Public Safety, having before it no founded charge or suspicion against Thomas Paine, retain any scruples, and think that from my occasional conversation with that foreigner, whom the people's suffrage called to the national representation, and some acquaintance with his language, I might perhaps throw light upon their doubt, I would readily communicate to them all that I know about him. I request Merlin de Thionville to submit these considerations to the Committee."

Merlin was now a leading member of the Committee. On the following day Paine sent (in French) the following letters:

"CITIZENS, REPRESENTATIVES, AND MEMBERS OF THE COMMITTEE OF PUBLIC SAFETY: I address you a copy of a letter which I have to-day written to the Convention. The singular situation in which I find myself determines me to address myself to the whole Convention, of which you are a part.

"THOMAS PAINE.

"Maison d'Arrêt du Luxembourg,
  Le 19 Thermidor, l'an 2 de la République, une et indivisible."

"CITIZEN REPRESENTATIVES: If I should not express myself with the energy I used formerly to do, you will attribute it to the very dangerous illness I have suffered in the prison of the Luxembourg. For several days I was insensible of my own existence; and though I am much recovered, it is with exceeding great difficulty that I find power to write you this letter.

"But before I proceed further, I request the Convention to observe: that this is the first line that has come from me, either to the Convention, or to any of the Committees, since my imprisonment,—which is approaching to Eight months.—Ah, my friends, eight months' loss of Liberty seems almost a life-time to a man who has been, as I have been, the unceasing defender of Liberty for twenty years.

"I have now to inform the Convention of the reason of my not having written before. It is a year ago that I had strong reason to believe that Robespierre was my inveterate enemy, as he was the enemy of every man of virtue and humanity. The address that was sent to the Convention some time about last August from Arras, the native town of Robespierre, I have always been informed was the work of that hypocrite and the partizans he had in the place. The intention of that address was to prepare the way for destroying me, by making the People declare (though without assigning any reason) that I had lost their confidence; the Address, however, failed of success, as it was immediately opposed by a counter-address from St. Omer which declared the direct contrary. But the strange power that Robespierre, by the most consummate hypocrisy and the most hardened cruelties, had obtained rendered any attempt on my part to obtain justice not only useless but even dangerous; for it is the nature of Tyranny always to strike a deeper blow when any attempt has been made to repel a former one. This being my situation I submitted with patience to the hardness of my fate and waited the event of brighter days. I hope they are now arrived to the nation and to me.

"Citizens, when I left the United States in the year 1787, I promised to all my friends that I would return to them the next year; but the hope of seeing a Revolution happily established in France, that might serve as a model to the rest of Europe, and the earnest and disinterested desire of rendering every service in my power to promote it, induced me to defer my return to that country, and to the society of my friends, for more than seven years. This long sacrifice of private tranquillity, especially after having gone through the fatigues and dangers of the American Revolution which continued almost eight years, deserved a better fate than the long imprisonment I have silently suffered. But it is not the nation but a faction that has done me this injustice, and it is to the national representation that I appeal against that injustice. Parties and Factions, various and numerous as they have been, I have always avoided. My heart was devoted to all France, and the object to which I applied myself was the Constitution. The Plan which I proposed to the Committee, of which I was a member, is now in the hands of Barrère, and it will speak for itself.

"It is perhaps proper that I inform you of the cause assigned in the order for my imprisonment. It is that I am 'a Foreigner'; whereas, the *Foreigner* thus imprisoned was invited into France by a decree of the late national Assembly, and that in the hour of her greatest danger, when invaded by Austrians and Prussians. He was, moreover, a citizen of the United States of America, an ally of France, and not a subject of any country in Europe, and consequently not within the intentions of any of the decrees concerning Foreigners. But any excuse can be made to serve the purpose of malignity when it is in power.

"I will not intrude on your time by offering any apology for the broken and imperfect manner in which I have expressed myself. I request you to accept it with the sincerity with which it comes from my heart; and I conclude with wishing Fraternity and prosperity to France, and union and happiness to her representatives.

"Citizens, I have now stated to you my situation, and I can have no doubt but your justice will restore me to the Liberty of which I have been deprived.

"THOMAS PAINE.

"Luxembourg, Thermidor 19th, 2d year of the French Republic, one and indivisible."

No doubt this touching letter would have been effectual had it reached the Convention. But the Committee of Public Safety took care that no whisper even of its existence should be heard. Paine's participation in their fostered dogma, that *Robespierre le veut* explained all crimes, probably cost him three more months in prison. The lamb had confided its appeal to the wolf. Barrère, Billaud-Varennes, and Collot d'Herbois, by skilful use of the dead scapegoat, maintained their places on the Committee until September 1st, and after that influenced its counsels. At the same time Morris, as we have seen, was keeping Monroe out of his place. There might have been a serious reckoning for these men had Paine been set free, or his case inquired into by the Convention. And Thuriot was now on the Committee of Public Safety; he was eager to lay his own crimes on Robespierre, and to conceal those of the Committee. Paine's old friend, Achille Audibert, unsuspicious as himself of the real facts, sent an appeal (August 20th) to "Citizen Thuriot, member of the Committee of Public Safety."

"REPRESENTATIVE :—A friend of mankind is groaning in chains,—Thomas Paine, who was not so politic as to remain silent in regard to a man unlike himself, but dared to say that Robespierre was a monster to be erased from the list of men. From that moment he became a criminal; the despot marked him as his victim, put him into prison, and doubtless prepared the way to the scaffold for him, as for others who knew him and were courageous enough to speak out.[1]

[1] It must be remembered that at this time it seemed the strongest recommendation of any one to public favor to describe him as a victim of Robespierre; and Paine's friends could conceive no other cause for the detention of a man they knew to be innocent.

"Thomas Paine is an acknowledged citizen of the United States. He was the secretary of the Congress for the department of foreign affairs during the Revolution. He has made himself known in Europe by his writings, and especially by his 'Rights of Man.' The electoral assembly of the department of Pas-de-Calais elected him one of its representatives to the Convention, and commissioned me to go to London, inform him of his election, and bring him to France. I hardly escaped being a victim to the English Government with which he was at open war; I performed my mission; and ever since friendship has attached me to Paine. This is my apology for soliciting you for his liberation.

"I can assure you, Representative, that America was by no means satisfied with the imprisonment of a strong column of its Revolution. Please to take my prayer into consideration. But for Robespierre's villainy this friend of man would now be free. Do not permit liberty longer to see in prison a victim of the wretch who lives no more but by his crimes; and you will add to the esteem and veneration I feel for a man who did so much to save the country amidst the most tremendous crisis of our Revolution.

"Greeting, respect, and brotherhood,
"ACHILLE AUDIBERT, of Calais.

"No. 216 Rue de Bellechase, Fauborg St. Germaine."

Audibert's letter, of course, sank under the burden of its Robespierre myth to a century's sleep beside Paine's, in the Committee's closet.

Meanwhile, the regulation against any communication of prisoners with the outside world remaining in force, it was some time before Paine could know that his letter had been suppressed on its way to the Convention. He was thus late in discovering his actual enemies.

An interesting page in the annals of diplomacy remains to be written on the closing weeks of Morris in France. On August 14th he writes to Robert Morris: "I am preparing for my departure, but as yet can take no step, as there is a kind of interregnum in the government and Mr. Monroe is not yet received, at which he grows somewhat impatient." There was no such interregnum, and no such explanation was given to Monroe, who writes:

"I presented my credentials to the commissary of foreign affairs soon after my arrival [August 2d]; but more than a week had elapsed, and I had obtained no answer, when or whether I should be received. A delay beyond a few days surprised me, because I could discern no adequate or rational motive for it."[1]

It is plain that the statement of Paine, who was certainly in communication with the Committees a year later, is true, that Morris was in danger on account of the interception of compromising letters written by him. He needed time to dispose of his house and horses, and ship his wines, and felt it important to retain his protecting credentials. At any moment his friends might be expelled from the Committee, and their papers be examined. While the arrangements for Monroe's reception rested with Morris and this unaltered Committee, there was little prospect of Monroe's being installed at all. The new Minister was therefore compelled, as other Americans had been, to appeal directly to the Convention. That assembly responded at once, and he was received (August 28th) with highest honors. Morris had nothing to do with the arrangement. The historian Frédéric Masson,

[1] "View of the Conduct of the Executive in the Foreign Affairs of the United States," by James Monroe, p. 7.

alluding to the "unprecedented" irregularity of Morris in not delivering or receiving letters of recall, adds that Monroe found it important to state that he had acted without consultation with his predecessor.[1] This was necessary for a cordial reception by the Convention, but it invoked the cordial hatred of Morris, who marked him for his peculiar guillotine set up in Philadelphia.

So completely had America and Congress been left in the dark about Paine that Monroe was surprised to find him a prisoner. When at length the new Minister was in a position to consult the French Minister about Paine, he found the knots so tightly tied around this particular victim—almost the only one left in the Luxembourg of those imprisoned during the Terror—that it was difficult to untie them. The Minister of Foreign Affairs was now M. Bouchot, a weak creature who, as Morris said, would not wipe his nose without permission of the Committee of Public Safety. When Monroe opened Paine's case he was asked whether he had brought instructions. Of course he had none, for the administration had no suspicion that Morris had not, as he said, attended to the case.

When Paine recovered from his fever he heard that Monroe had superseded Morris.

"As soon as I was able to write a note legible enough to be read, I found a way to convey one to him [Monroe] by means of the man who lighted the lamps in the prison, and whose unabated friendship to me, from whom he never received any service, and with difficulty accepted any recompense, puts the character of Mr. Washington to shame. In a few days I re-

---

[1] "Le Départément des Affaires Étrangères," etc., p. 345.

ceived a message from Mr. Monroe, conveyed in a note from an intermediate person, with assurance of his friendship, and expressing a desire that I should rest the case in his hands. After a fortnight or more had passed, and hearing nothing farther, I wrote to a friend [Whiteside], a citizen of Philadelphia, requesting him to inform me what was the true situation of things with respect to me. I was sure that something was the matter; I began to have hard thoughts of Mr. Washington, but I was unwilling to encourage them. In about ten days I received an answer to my letter, in which the writer says: 'Mr. Monroe told me he had no order (meaning from the president, Mr. Washington) respecting you, but that he (Mr. Monroe) will do everything in his power to liberate you, but, from what I learn from the Americans lately arrived in Paris, you are not considered, either by the American government or by individuals, as an American citizen.'"

As the American government did regard Paine as an American citizen, and approved Monroe's demanding him as such, there is no difficulty in recognizing the source from which these statements were diffused among Paine's newly arriving countrymen. Morris was still in Paris.

On the receipt of Whiteside's note, Paine wrote a Memorial to Monroe, of which important parts— amounting to eight printed pages—are omitted from American and English editions of his works. In quoting this Memorial, I select mainly the omitted portions.[1] Paine says that before leaving London for the Convention, he consulted Minister Pinckney, who agreed with him that "it was for the interest of America that the system of European governments should be changed and placed

[1] The whole is published in French: "Mémoire de Thomas Payne, autographé et signé de sa main: addressé à M. Monroe, ministre des États-unis en France, pour réclamer sa mise en liberté comme Citoyen Américain, 10 Septembre, 1794. Villeneuve."

on the same principle with her own"; and adds: "I have wished to see America the mother church of government, and I have done my utmost to exalt her character and her condition." He points out that he had not accepted any title or office under a foreign government, within the meaning of the United States Constitution, because there was no government in France, the Convention being assembled to frame one; that he was a citizen of France only in the honorary sense in which others in Europe and America were declared such; that no oath of allegiance was required or given. The following paragraphs are from various parts of the Memorial.

"They who propagate the report of my not being considered as a citizen of America by government, do it to the prolongation of my imprisonment, and without authority; for Congress, as a government, has neither decided upon it, nor yet taken the matter into consideration; and I request you to caution such persons against spreading such reports. . . .

"I know not what opinions have been circulated in America. It may have been supposed there, that I had voluntarily and intentionally abandoned America, and that my citizenship had ceased by my own choice. I can easily conceive that there are those in that Country who would take such a proceeding on my part somewhat in disgust. The idea of forsaking old friendships for new acquaintances is not agreeable. I am a little warranted in making this supposition by a letter I received some time ago from the wife of one of the Georgia delegates, in which she says, 'your friends on this side the water cannot be reconciled to the idea of your abandoning America.' I have never abandoned America in thought, word, or deed, and I feel it incumbent upon me to give this assurance to the friends I have in that country, and with whom I have always intended, and am determined, if the possibility exists, to close the scene of my life. It is there that I have made myself a home. It is there that I have given the services of my best days. America never saw me flinch from her cause in the most gloomy and perilous of her situations : and I know there are those in that Country who will not flinch from me. If I have Enemies (and every man has some) I leave them to the enjoyment of their ingratitude. . . .

"It is somewhat extraordinary, that the Idea of my not being a Citizen of America should have arisen only at the time that I am imprisoned in France because, or on the pretence that, I am a foreigner. The case involves a strange contradiction of Ideas. None of the Americans who came to France whilst I was in liberty, had conceived any such idea or circulated any such opinion ; and why it should arise now is a matter yet to be explained. However discordant the late American Minister, Gouverneur Morris, and the late French Committee of Public Safety were, it suited the purpose of both that I should be continued in arrestation. The former wished to prevent my return to America, that I should not expose his misconduct ; and the latter, lest I should publish to the world the history of its wickedness. Whilst that Minister and that Committee continued, I had no expectation of liberty. I speak here of the Committee of which Robespierre was a member. . . .

"I here close my Memorial and proceed to offer to you a proposal, that appears to me suited to all the circumstances of the case ; which is, that you reclaim me conditionally, until the opinion of Congress can be obtained upon the subject of my Citizenship of America, and that I remain in liberty under your protection during that time. I found this proposal upon the following grounds :

"First, you say you have no orders respecting me ; consequently you have no orders *not* to reclaim me ; and in this case you are left discretionary judge whether to reclaim or not. My proposal therefore unites a consideration of your situation with my own.

"Secondly, I am put in arrestation because I am a foreigner. It is therefore necessary to determine to what Country I belong. The right of determining this question cannot appertain exclusively to the committee of public safety or general surety ; because I appear to the Minister of the United States, and shew that my citizenship of that Country is good and valid, referring at the same time, through the agency of the

Minister, my claim of Right to the opinion of Congress,—it being a matter between two governments.

"Thirdly, France does not claim me for a citizen; neither do I set up any claim of citizenship in France. The question is simply, whether I am or am not a citizen of America. I am imprisoned here on the decree for imprisoning Foreigners, because, say they, I was born in England. I say in answer, that, though born in England, I am not a subject of the English Government any more than any other American is who was born, as they all were, under the same government, or that the citizens of France are subjects of the French monarchy, under which they were born. I have twice taken the oath of abjuration to the British king and government, and of Allegiance to America. Once as a citizen of the State of Pennsylvania in 1776; and again before Congress, administered to me by the President, Mr. Hancock, when I was appointed Secretary in the office of foreign affairs in 1777. . . .

"Painful as the want of liberty may be, it is a consolation to me to believe that my imprisonment proves to the world that I had no share in the murderous system that then reigned. That I was an enemy to it, both morally and politically, is known to all who had any knowledge of me; and could I have written French as well as I can English, I would publicly have exposed its wickedness, and shown the ruin with which it was pregnant. They who have esteemed me on former occasions, whether in America or England, will, I know, feel no cause to abate that esteem when they reflect, that imprisonment with preservation of character, is preferable to liberty with disgrace."

In a postscript Paine adds that "as Gouverneur Morris could not inform Congress of the cause of my arrestation, as he knew it not himself, it is to be supposed that Congress was not enough acquainted with the case to give any directions respecting me when you left." Which to the reader of the preceding pages will appear sufficiently naïve.

To this Monroe responded (September 18th) with a letter of warm sympathy, worthy of the high-minded gentleman that he was. After ascribing the notion that Paine was not an American to mental confusion, and affirming his determination to maintain his rights as a citizen of the United States, Monroe says:

"It is unnecessary for me to tell you how much all your countrymen, I speak of the great mass of the people, are interested in your welfare. They have not forgotten the history of their own revolution, and the difficult scenes through which they passed; nor do they review its several stages without reviving in their bosoms a due sensibility of the merits of those who served them in that great and arduous conflict. The crime of ingratitude has not yet stained, and I trust never will stain, our national character. You are considered by them, as not only having rendered important services in our own revolution, but as being on a more extensive scale, the friend of human rights, and a distinguished and able advocate in favor of public liberty. To the welfare of Thomas Paine the Americans are not and cannot be indifferent. Of the sense which the President has always entertained of your merits, and of his friendly disposition towards you, you are too well assured to require any declaration of it from me. That I forward his wishes in seeking your safety is what I well know; and this will form an additional obligation on me to perform what I should otherwise consider as a duty.

"You are, in my opinion, menaced by no kind of danger. To liberate you, will be an object of my endeavors, and as soon as possible. But you must, until that event shall be accomplished, face your situation with patience and fortitude; you will likewise have the justice to recollect, that I am placed here upon a difficult theatre, many important objects to attend to, and with few to consult. It becomes me in pursuit of those, to regulate my conduct in respect to each, as to the manner and the time, as will, in my judgment, be best calculated to accomplish the whole.

"With great esteem and respect consider me personally your friend,

"JAMES MONROE."

Monroe was indeed "placed upon a difficult theatre." Morris was showing a fresh letter from the President expressing unabated confidence in him, apologizing for his recall; he still had friends in the Committee of Public Safety, to which Monroe had appealed in vain. The continued dread the conspirators had of Paine's liberation appears in the fact that Monroe's letter, written September 18th, did not reach Paine until October 18th, when Morris had reached the boundary line of Switzerland, which he entered on the 19th. He had left Paris (Sainport) October 14th, when Barrère, Billaud-Varennes, and Collot d'Herbois, no longer on the Committee, were under accusation, and their papers under investigation,—a search that resulted in their exile. Morris got across the line on an irregular passport.

While Monroe's reassuring letter to Paine was taking a month to penetrate his prison walls, he vainly grappled with the subtle obstacles. All manner of delays impeded the correspondence, the principal one being that he could present no instructions from the President concerning Paine. Of course he was fighting in the dark, having no suspicion that the imprisonment was due to his predecessor. At length, however, he received from Secretary Randolph a letter (dated July 30th), from which, though Paine was not among its specifications, he could select a sentence as basis of action: "We have heard with regret that several of our citizens have been thrown into prison in France, from a suspicion of criminal attempts against the government. If they are guilty we are extremely sorry for it; if innocent we must protect them." What Paine had said in his Memorial of collusion between Morris and the Committee of Public Safety probably determined Monroe to apply no more in that quarter; so he wrote (November 2d) to the Committee of General Surety. After stating the general principles and limitations of ministerial protection to an imprisoned countryman, he adds:

"The citizens of the United States cannot look back upon the time of their own revolution without recollecting among the names of their most distinguished patriots that of Thomas Paine; the services he rendered to his country in its struggle for freedom have implanted in the hearts of his countrymen a sense of gratitude never to be effaced as long as they shall deserve the title of a just and generous people.

"The above-named citizen is at this moment languishing in prison, affected with a disease growing more intense from his confinement. I beg, therefore, to call your attention to his condition and to request you to hasten the moment when the law shall decide his fate, in case of any accusation against him, and if none, to restore him to liberty.

"Greeting and fraternity "MONROE."

At this the first positive assertion of Paine's American citizenship the prison door flew open. He had been kept there solely "pour les interêts de l'Amérique," as embodied in Morris, and two days after Monroe undertook, without instructions, to affirm the real interests of America in Paine he was liberated.

"Brumaire, 13th. Third year of the French Republic.—The Committee of General Surety orders that the Citizen Thomas Paine be set at liberty, and the seals taken from his papers, on sight of these presents.

"Members of the Committee (signed): Clauzel, Lesage, Senault, Bentabole, Reverchon, Goupilleau de Fontenai, Rewbell.

"Delivered to Clauzel, as Commissioner."

There are several interesting points about this little decree. It is signed by Bentabole, who had moved Paine's expulsion from the Convention. It orders that the seals be removed from Paine's papers, whereas none had been placed on them, the officers reporting them innocent. This same authority, which had ordered Paine's arrest, now, in ordering his liberation, shows that the imprisonment had never been a subject of French inquiry. It had ordered the seals but did not know whether they were on the papers or not. It was no concern of France, but only of the American Minister. It is thus further evident that when Monroe invited a trial of Paine there was not the least trace of any charge against him. And there was precisely the same absence of any accusation against Paine in the new Committee of Public Safety, to which Monroe's letter was communicated the same day.

Writing to Secretary Randolph (November 7th) Monroe says:

"He was actually a citizen of the United States, and of the United States only; for the Revolution which parted us from Great Britain broke the allegiance which was before due to the Crown, of all who took our side. He was, of course, not a British subject; nor was he strictly a citizen of France, for he came by invitation for the temporary purpose of assisting in the formation of their government only, and meant to withdraw to America when that should be completed. And what confirms this is the act of the Convention itself arresting him, by which he is declared a foreigner. Mr. Paine pressed my interference.

I told him I had hoped getting him enlarged without it ; but, if I did interfere, it could only be by requesting that he be tried, in case there was any charge against him, and liberated in case there was not. This was admitted. His correspondence with me is lengthy and interesting, and I may probably be able hereafter to send you a copy of it. After some time had elapsed, without producing any change in his favor, I finally resolved to address the Committee of General Surety in his behalf, resting my application on the above principle. My letter was delivered by my Secretary in the Committee to the president, who assured him he would communicate its contents immediately to the Committee of Public Safety, and give me an answer as soon as possible. The conference took place accordingly between the two Committees, and, as I presume, on that night, or on the succeeding day ; for on the morning of the day after, which was yesterday, I was presented by the Secretary of the Committee of General Surety with an order for his enlargement. I forwarded it immediately to the Luxembourg, and had it carried into effect ; and have the pleasure now to add that he is not only released to the enjoyment of liberty, but is in good spirits."

In reply, the Secretary of State (Randolph) in a letter to Monroe of March 8, 1795, says: "Your observations on our commercial relations to France, and your conduct as to Mr. Gardoqui's letter, prove your judgment and assiduity. Nor are your measures as to Mr. Paine, and the lady of our friend [Lafayette] less approved."

Thus, after an imprisonment of ten months and nine days, Thomas Paine was liberated from the prison into which he had been cast by a Minister of the United States.

CHAPTER IX.

A RESTORATION.

As in 1792 Paine had left England with the authorities at his heels, so in 1794 escaped Morris from France. The ex-Minister went off to play courtier to George III. and write for Louis XVIII. the despotic proclamation with which monarchy was to be restored in France"[1]; Paine sat in the house of a real American Minister, writing proclamations of republicanism to invade the empires. So passed each to his own place.

While the American Minister in Paris and his wife were nursing their predecessor's victim back into life, a thrill of joy was passing through European courts, on a rumor that the dreaded author had been guillotined. Paine had the satisfaction of reading, at Monroe's fireside, his own last words on the scaffold,[2] and along with it an invitation of

[1] Morris' royal proclamations are printed in full in his biography by Jared Sparks.
[2] "The last dying words of Thomas Paine. Executed at the Guillotine in France on the 1st of September, 1794." The dying speech begins: "Ye numerous spectators gathered around, pray give ear to my last words; I am determined to speak the Truth in these my last moments, altho' I have written and spoke nothing but lies all my life." There is nothing in the witless leaflet worth quoting. When Paine was burnt in effigy, in 1792, it appears to have been with accompaniments of the same kind. Before me is a small placard, which reads thus: "The Dying Speech and Confession of the Arch-Traitor Thomas Paine. Who was executed at Oakham on Thurs-

the Convention to return to its bosom. On December 7, 1794, Thibaudeau had spoken to that assembly in the following terms :

"It yet remains for the Convention to perform an act of justice. I reclaim one of the most zealous defenders of liberty —Thomas Paine. (*Loud applause.*) My reclamation is for a man who has honored his age by his energy in defence of the rights of humanity, and who is so gloriously distinguished by his part in the American revolution. A naturalized Frenchman[1] by a decree of the legislative assembly, he was nominated by the people. It was only by an intrigue that he was driven from the Convention, the pretext being a decree excluding foreigners from representing the French people. There were only two foreigners in the Convention; one [Anacharsis Clootz] is dead, and I speak not of him, but of Thomas Paine, who powerfully contributed to establish liberty in a country allied with the French Republic. I demand that he be recalled to the bosom of the Convention." (*Applause.*)

The *Moniteur*, from which I translate, reports the unanimous adoption of Thibaudeau's motion. But this was not enough. The Committee of Public Instruction, empowered to award pensions for literary services, reported (January 3, 1795) as the first name on their list, Thomas Paine. Chenier, in reading the report, claimed the honor of having originally suggested Paine's name as an honorary citizen of France, and denounced, amid applause, the decree against foreigners under which the great author had suffered.

day the 27th of December 1792. This morning the Officers usually attending on such occasions went in procession on Horseback to the County Gaol, and demanded the Body of the Arch-Traitor, and from thence proceeded with the Criminal drawn in a Cart by an Ass to the usual place of execution with his Pamphlet called the 'Rights of Man' in his right hand."

[1] Here Thibaudeau was inexact. In the next sentence but one he rightly describes Paine as a foreigner. The allusion to "an intrigue" is significant.

"You have revoked that inhospitable decree, and we again see Thomas Paine, the man of genius without fortune, our colleague, dear to all friends of humanity,—a cosmopolitan, persecuted equally by Pitt and by Robespierre. Notable epoch in the life of this philosopher, who opposed the arms of Common Sense to the sword of Tyranny, the Rights of Man to the machiavelism of English politicians; and who, by two immortal works, has deserved well of the human race, and consecrated liberty in the two worlds."

Poor as he was, Paine declined this literary pension. He accepted the honors paid him by the Convention, no doubt with a sorrow at the contrasted silence of those who ruled in America. Monroe, however, encouraged him to believe that he was still beloved there, and, as he got stronger, a great homesickness came upon him. The kindly host made an effort to satisfy him. On January 4th he (Monroe) wrote to the Committee of Public Safety:

" CITIZENS: The Decree just passed, bearing on the execution of Articles 23 and 24 of the Treaty of Friendship and Commerce between the two Republics, is of such great importance to my country, that I think it expedient to send it there officially, by some particularly confidential hand; and no one seems to be better fitted for this errand than Thomas Paine. Having resided a long time in France, and having a perfect knowledge of the many vicissitudes which the Republic has passed, he will be able to explain and compare the happy lot she now enjoys. As he has passed the same himself, remaining faithful to his principles, his reports will be the more trustworthy, and consequently produce a better effect. But as Citizen Paine is a member of the Convention, I thought it better to submit this subject to your consideration. If this affair can be arranged, the Citizen will leave for America immediately, *via* Bordeaux, on an American vessel which will be prepared for him. As he has reason to fear the persecution of the English government, should he be taken prisoner, he desires that his departure may be kept a secret.

"JAS. MONROE."

The Convention alone could give a passport to one of its members, and as an application to it would make Paine's mission known, the Committee returned next day a negative answer.

> "CITIZEN: We see with satisfaction and without surprise, that you attach some interest to sending officially to the United States the Decree which the National Convention has just made, in which are recalled and confirmed the reports of Friendship and Commerce existing between the two Republics.
>
> "As to the design you express of confiding this errand to Citizen Thomas Paine, we must observe to you that the position he holds will not permit him to accept it. Salutation and Friendship.
>
> "CAMBACÉRÈS." [1]

Liberty's great defender gets least of it! The large seal of the Committee—mottoed "Activity, Purity, Attention"—looks like a wheel of fortune; but one year before it had borne from the Convention to prison the man it now cannot do without. France now especially needs the counsel of shrewd and friendly American heads. There are indications that Jay in London is carrying the United States into Pitt's combination against the Republic, just as it is breaking up on the Continent.

Monroe's magnanimity towards Paine found its reward. He brought to his house, and back into life, just the one man in France competent to give him the assistance he needed. Comprehending the history of the Revolution, knowing the record of every actor in it, Paine was able to revise Monroe's impressions, and enable him to check calumnies circulated in America. The despatches of

[1] State Archives of France. États Unis, vol. xliii. Monroe dates his letter, "19th year of the American Republic."

Monroe are of high historic value, largely through knowledge derived from Paine.

Nor was this all. In Monroe's instructions emphasis was laid on the importance to the United States of the free navigation of the Mississippi and its ultimate control.[1] Paine's former enthusiasm in this matter had possibly been utilized by Gouverneur Morris to connect him, as we have seen, with Genêt's proceedings. The Kentuckians consulted Paine at a time when expulsion of the Spaniard was a patriotic American scheme. This is shown in a letter written by the Secretary of State (Randolph) to the President, February 27, 1794.

"Mr. Brown [Senator of Kentucky] has shown me a letter from the famous Dr. O'Fallon to Captain Herron, dated Oct. 18, 1793. It was intercepted, and he has permitted me to take the following extract:—'This plan (an attack on Louisiana) was digested between Gen. Clarke and me last Christmas. I framed the whole of the correspondence in the General's name, and corroborated it by a private letter of my own to Mr. Thomas Paine, of the National Assembly, with whom during the late war I was very intimate. His reply reached me but a few days since, enclosed in the General's despatches from the Ambassador."[2]

[1] "The conduct of Spain towards us is unaccountable and injurious. Mr. Pinckney is by this time gone over to Madrid as our envoy extraordinary to bring matters to a conclusion some way or other. But you will seize any favorable moment to execute what has been entrusted to you respecting the Mississippi."—*Randolph to Monroe*, February 15, 1795.

[2] Two important historical works have recently appeared relating to the famous Senator Brown. The first is a publication of the Filson Club: "The Political Beginnings of Kentucky," by John Mason Brown. The second is: "The Spanish Conspiracy," by Thomas Marshall Green (Cincinnati, Robert Clarke & Co., 1891). The intercepted letter quoted above has some bearing on the controversy between these authors. Apparently, Senator Brown, like many other good patriots, favored independent action in Kentucky when that seemed for the welfare of the United States, but, when the situation had changed, Brown is found co-operating with Washington and Randolph.

That such letters (freely written as they were at the beginning of 1793) were now intercepted indicates the seriousness of the situation time had brought on. The administration had soothed the Kentuckians by pledges of pressing the matter by negotiations. Hence Monroe's instructions, in carrying out which Paine was able to lend a hand.

In the State Archives at Paris (*États Unis*, vol. xliii.) there are two papers marked "Thomas Payne." The first urges the French Ministry to seize the occasion of a treaty with Spain to do a service to the United States : let the free navigation of the Mississippi be made by France a condition of peace. The second paper (endorsed " 3 Ventose, February 21, 1795 ") proposes that, in addition to the condition made to Spain, an effort should be made to include American interests in the negotiation with England, if not too late. The negotiation with England was then finished, but the terms unpublished. Paine recommended that the Convention should pass a resolution that freedom of the Mississippi should be a condition of peace with Spain, which would necessarily accept it ; and that, in case the arrangement with England should prove unsatisfactory, any renewed negotiations should support the just reclamations of their American ally for the surrender of the frontier posts and for depredations on their trade. Paine points out that such a declaration could not prolong the war a day, nor cost France an obole ; whereas it might have a decisive effect in the United States, especially if Jay's treaty with England should be reprehensible, and should be approved in America.

That generosity "would certainly raise the reputation of the French Republic to the most eminent degree of splendour, and lower in proportion that of her enemies." It would undo the bad effects of the depredations of French privateers on American vessels, which rejoiced the British party in the United States and discouraged the friends of liberty and humanity there. It would acquire for France the merit which is her due, supply her American friends with strength against the intrigues of England, and cement the alliance of the Republics.

This able paper might have been acted on, but for the anger in France at the Jay treaty.

While writing in Monroe's house, the invalid, with an abscess in his side and a more painful sore in his heart—for he could not forget that Washington had forgotten him,—receives tidings of new events through cries in the street. In the month of his release they had been resonant with yells as the Jacobins were driven away and their rooms turned to a Normal School. Then came shouts, when, after trial, the murderous committeemen were led to execution or exile. In the early weeks of 1795 the dread sounds of retribution subside, and there is a cry from the street that comes nearer to Paine's heart—"Bread and the Constitution of Ninety-three!" He knows that it is his Constitution for which they are really calling, for they cannot understand the Robespierrian adulteration of it given out, as one said, as an opiate to keep the country asleep. The people are sick of revolutionary rule. These are the people in whom Paine has ever believed,—the honest hearts that summoned him, as author of "The Rights of Man," to help form their Constitution. They, he knows, had to be deceived when cruel deeds were done, and heard of such deeds with as much horror as distant peoples. Over that Constitution for which they were clamoring he and his lost friend Condorcet had spent many a day of honest toil. Of the original Committee of Nine appointed for the work, six had perished by the revolution, one was banished, and two remained—Sieyès and Paine. That original Committee had gradually left the task to Paine and Condorcet,—Sieyès, because he had no real sympathy with republicanism, though he honored Paine.[1] When afterwards asked how he had survived the Terror, Sieyès answered, "I lived." He lived by bending, and now leads a Committee of Eleven on the Constitution, while Paine, who did not bend, is disabled. Paine knows Sieyès well. The people will vainly try for the "Constitution of Ninety-three." They shall have no Constitution but of Sieyès' making, and in it will be some element of monarchy. Sieyès presently seemed to retire from the Committee, but old republicans did not doubt that he was all the more swaying it.

[1] "Mr. Thomas Paine is one of those men who have contributed the most to establish the liberty of America. His ardent love of humanity, and his hatred of every sort of tyranny, have induced him to take up in England the defence of the French revolution, against the amphigorical declamation of Mr. Burke. His work has been translated into our language, and is universally known. What French patriot is there who has not already, from the bottom of his heart, thanked this foreigner for having strengthened our cause by all the powers of his reason and reputation? It is with pleasure that I observe an opportunity of offering him the tribute of my gratitude and my esteem for the truly philosophical application of talents so distinguished as his own."—Sieyès in the *Moniteur*, July 6, 1791.

So once more Paine seizes his pen; his hand is feeble, but his intellect has lost no fibre of force, nor his heart its old faith. His trust in man has passed through the ordeal of seeing his friends— friends of man—murdered by the people's Convention, himself saved by accident; it has survived the apparent relapse of Washington into the arms of George the Third. The ingratitude of his faithfully-served America is represented by an abscess in his side, which may strike into his heart—in a sense has done so—but will never reach his faith in liberty, equality, and humanity.

Early in July the Convention is reading Paine's "Dissertation on First Principles of Government." His old arguments against hereditary right, or investing even an elective individual with extraordinary power, are repeated with illustrations from the passing Revolution.

"Had a Constitution been establishe two years ago, as ought to have been done, the violences that have since desolated France and injured the character of the revolution, would, in my opinion, have been prevented. The nation would hav had a bond of union, and every individual would have known the line of conduct he was to follow. But, instead of this, a revolutionary government, a thing without either principle or authority, was substituted in its place; virtue or crime depended upon accident; and that which was patriotism one day, became treason the next. All these things have followed from the want of a Constitution; for it is the nature and intention of a Constitution to prevent governing by party, by establishing a common principle that shall limit and control the power and impulse of party, and that says to all parties, *Thus far shalt thou go, and no farther*. But in the absence of a Constitution men look entirely to party; and instead of principle governing party, party governs principle.

"An avidity to punish is always dangerous to liberty. It leads men to stretch, to misinterpret and to misapply even the best of laws. He that would make his own liberty secure, must guard even his enemy from oppression ; for if he violates this duty, he establishes a precedent that will reach himself."

Few of Paine's pamphlets better deserve study than this. In writing it, he tells us, he utilized the fragment of a work begun at some time not stated, which he meant to dedicate to the people of Holland, then contemplating a revolution. It is a condensed statement of the principles underlying the Constitution written by himself and Condorcet, now included among Condorcet's works. They who imagine that Paine's political system was that of the democratic demagogues may undeceive themselves by pondering this pamphlet. It has been pointed out, on a previous page of this work, that Paine held the representative to be not the voter's mouthpiece, but his delegated sovereignty. The representatives of a people are therefore its supreme power. The executive, the ministers, are merely as chiefs of the national police engaged in enforcing the laws. They are mere employés, without any authority at all, except of superintendence. "The executive department is official, and is subordinate to the legislative as the body is to the mind." The chief of these official departments is the judicial. In appointing officials the most important rule is, "never to invest any individual with extraordinary power; for besides being tempted to misuse it, it will excite contention and commotion in the nation for the office."

All of this is in logical conformity with the same

author's "Rights of Man," which James Madison declared to be an exposition of the principles on which the United States government is based. It would be entertaining to observe the countenance of a President should our House of Representatives address him as a chief of national police.

Soon after the publication of Paine's "Dissertation" a new French Constitution was textually submitted for popular consideration. Although in many respects it accorded fairly well with Paine's principles, it contained one provision which he believed would prove fatal to the Republic. This was the limitation of citizenship to payers of direct taxes, except soldiers who had fought in one or more campaigns for the Republic, this being a sufficient qualification. This revolutionary disfranchisement of near half the nation brought Paine to the Convention (July 7th) for the first time since the fall of the Brissotins, two years before. The scene at his return was impressive. A special motion was made by Lanthenas and unanimously adopted, "that permission be granted Thomas Paine to deliver his sentiments on the declaration of rights and the Constitution." With feeble step he ascended the tribune, and stood while a secretary read his speech. Of all present this man had suffered most by the confusion of the mob with the people, which caused the reaction on which was floated the device he now challenged. It is an instance of idealism rare in political history. The speech opens with words that caused emotion.

"CITIZENS, The effects of a malignant fever, with which I was afflicted during a rigorous confinement in the Luxembourg, have thus long prevented me from attending at my post in the bosom of the Convention; and the magnitude of the subject under discussion, and no other consideration on earth, could induce me now to repair to my station. A recurrence to the vicissitudes I have experienced, and the critical situations in which I have been placed in consequence of the French Revolution, will throw upon what I now propose to submit to the Convention the most unequivocal proofs of my integrity, and the rectitude of those principles which have uniformly influenced my conduct. In England I was proscribed for having vindicated the French Revolution, and I have suffered a rigorous imprisonment in France for having pursued a similar line of conduct. During the reign of terrorism I was a prisoner for eight long months, and remained so above three months after the era of the 10th Thermidor. I ought, however, to state, that I was not persecuted by the *people*, either of England or France. The proceedings in both countries were the effects of the despotism existing in their respective governments. But, even if my persecution had originated in the people at large, my principles and conduct would still have remained the same. Principles which are influenced and subject to the control of tyranny have not their foundation in the heart."

Though they slay him Paine will trust in the people. There seems a slight slip of memory; his imprisonment, by revolutionary calendar, lasted ten and a half months, or 315 days; but there is no failure of conviction or of thought. He points out the inconsistency of the disfranchisement of indirect tax-payers with the Declaration of Rights, and the opportunity afforded partisan majorities to influence suffrage by legislation on the mode of collecting taxes. The soldier, enfranchised without other qualification, would find his children slaves.

"If you subvert the basis of the Revolution, if you dispense with principles and substitute expedients, you will extinguish that enthusiasm which has hitherto been the life and soul of the revolution; and you will substitute in its place nothing but a cold indifference and self-interest, which will again degenerate into intrigue, cunning, and effeminacy."

There was an educational test of suffrage to which he did not object. "Where knowledge is a duty, ignorance is a crime." But in his appeal to pure principle simple-hearted Paine knew nothing of the real test of the Convention's votes. This white-haired man was the only eminent member of the Convention with nothing in his record to cause shame or fear. He almost alone among them had the honor of having risked his head rather than execute Louis, on whom he had looked as one man upon another. He alone had refused to enter the Convention when it abandoned the work for which it was elected and became a usurping tribunal. During two fearful years the true Republic had been in Paine's house and garden, where he conversed with his disciples; or in Luxembourg prison, where he won all hearts, as did imprisoned George Fox, who reappeared in him, and where, beneath the knife whose fall seemed certain, he criticised consecrated dogmas. With this record Paine spoke that day to men who feared to face the honest sentiment of the harried peasantry. Some of the members had indeed been terrorized, but a majority shared the disgrace of the old Convention. They were jeered at on the streets. The heart of France was throbbing again, and what would become of these "Conventionnels," when their assembly should die in giving birth to a government? They must from potentates become pariahs. Their aim now was to prolong their political existence. The constitutional narrowing of the suffrage was in anticipation of the decree presently appended, that two thirds of the new legislature should be chosen from the Convention.

Paine's speech was delivered against a foregone conclusion. This was his last appearance in the Convention. Out of it he naturally dropped when it ended (October 26, 1795), with the organization of the Directory. Being an American he would not accept candidature in a foreign government.

CHAPTER X.

THE SILENCE OF WASHINGTON.

MONROE, in a letter of September 15th to his relative, Judge Joseph Jones, of Fredericksburg, Virginia, after speaking of the Judge's son and his tutor at St. Germain, adds:

"As well on his account as that of our child, who is likewise at St. Germain, we had taken rooms there, with the intention of occupying for a month or two in the course of the autumn, but fear it will not be in our power to do so, on account of the ill-health of Mr. Paine, who has lived in my house for about ten months past. He was upon my arrival confined in the Luxembourg, and released on my application; after which, being ill, he has remained with me. For some time the prospect of his recovery was good; his malady being an abscess in his side, the consequence of a severe fever in the Luxembourg. Latterly his symptoms have become worse, and the prospect now is that he will not be able to hold out more than a month or two at the furthest. I shall certainly pay the utmost attention to this gentleman, as he is one of those whose merits in our Revolution were most distinguished." [1]

Paine's speech in the Convention told sadly on his health. Again he had to face death. As when, in 1793, the guillotine rising over him, he had set about writing his last bequest, the "Age of Reason," he now devoted himself to its completion. The

[1] I am indebted to Mrs. Gouverneur, of Washington, for this letter, which is among the invaluable papers of her ancestor, President Monroe, which surely should be secured for our national archives.

manuscript of the second part, begun in prison, had been in the printer's hands some time before Monroe wrote of his approaching end. When the book appeared, he was so low that his death was again reported.

So far as France was concerned, there was light about his eventide. "Almost as suddenly," so he wrote, "as the morning light dissipates darkness, did the establishment of the Constitution change the face of affairs in France. Security succeeded to terror, prosperity to distress, plenty to famine, and confidence increased as the days multiplied." This may now seem morbid optimism, but it was shared by the merry youth, and the pretty dames, whose craped arms did not prevent their sandalled feet and Greek-draped forms from dancing in their transient Golden Age. Of all this, we may be sure, the invalid hears many a beguiling story from Madame Monroe.

But there is a grief in his heart more cruel than death. The months have come and gone,—more than eighteen,—since Paine was cast into prison, but as yet no word of kindness or inquiry had come from Washington. Early in the year, on the President's sixty-third birthday, Paine had written him a letter of sorrowful and bitter reproach, which Monroe persuaded him not to send, probably because of its censures on the ministerial failures of Morris, and "the pusillanimous conduct of Jay in England." It now seems a pity that Monroe did not encourage Paine to send Washington, in substance, the personal part of his letter, which was in the following terms :

"As it is always painful to reproach those one would wish to respect, it is not without some difficulty that I have taken the resolution to write to you. The danger to which I have been exposed cannot have been unknown to you, and the guarded silence you have observed upon that circumstance, is what I ought not to have expected from you, either as a friend or as a President of the United States.

"You knew enough of my character to be assured that I could not have deserved imprisonment in France, and, without knowing anything more than this, you had sufficient ground to have taken some interest for my safety. Every motive arising from recollection ought to have suggested to you the consistency of such a measure. But I cannot find that you have so much as directed any enquiry to be made whether I was in prison or at liberty, dead or alive; what the cause of that imprisonment was, or whether there was any service or assistance you could render. Is this what I ought to have expected from America after the part I had acted towards her? Or, will it redound to her honor or to your's that I tell the story?

"I do not hesitate to say that you have not served America with more fidelity, or greater zeal, or greater disinterestedness, than myself, and perhaps with not better effect. After the revolution of America had been established, you rested at home to partake its advantages, and I ventured into new scenes of difficulty to extend the principles which that revolution had produced. In the progress of events you beheld yourself a president in America and me a prisoner in France : you folded your arms, forgot your friend, and became silent.

"As everything I have been doing in Europe was connected with my wishes for the prosperity of America, I ought to be the more surprised at this conduct on the part of her government. It leaves me but one mode of explanation, which is, that everything is not as it ought to be amongst you, and that the presence of a man who might disapprove, and who had credit enough with the country to be heard and believed, was not wished for. This was the operating motive of the despotic faction that imprisoned me in France (though the pretence was, that I was a foreigner) ; and those that have been silent towards me in America, appear to me to have acted from the same motive. It is impossible for me to discover any other."

Unwilling as all are to admit anything disparaging to Washington, justice requires the fair consideration of Paine's complaint. There were in his hands many letters proving Washington's friendship, and his great appreciation of Paine's services. Paine had certainly done nothing to forfeit his esteem. The "Age of Reason" had not appeared in America early enough to affect the matter, even should we suppose it offensive to a deist like Washington. The dry approval, forwarded by the Secretary of State, of Monroe's reclamation of Paine, enhanced the grievance. It admitted Paine's American citizenship. It was not then an old friend unhappily beyond his help, but a fellow-citizen whom he could legally protect, whom the President had left to languish in prison, and in hourly danger of death. During six months he saw no visitor, he heard no word, from the country for which he had fought. To Paine it could appear only as a sort of murder. And, although he kept back the letter, at his friend's desire, he felt that it might yet turn out to be murder. Even so it seemed, six months later, when the effects of his imprisonment, combined with his grief at Washington's continued silence (surely Monroe must have written on the subject), brought him to death's door. One must bear in mind also the disgrace, the humiliation of it, for a man who had been reverenced as a founder of the American Republic, and its apostle in France. This, indeed, had made his last three months in prison, after there had been ample time to hear from Washington, heavier than all the others. After the fall of

Robespierre the prisons were rapidly emptied—from twenty to forty liberations daily,—the one man apparently forgotten being he who wrote, " in the times that tried men's souls," the words that Washington ordered to be read to his dispirited soldiers.

And now death approaches. If there can be any explanation of this long neglect and silence, knowledge of it would soothe the author's dying pillow; and though there be little probability that he can hold out so long, a letter (September 20th) is sent to Washington, under cover to Franklin Bache.

"SIR,—I had written you a letter by Mr. Letombe, French consul, but, at the request of Mr. Monroe, I withdrew it, and the letter is still by me. I was the more easily prevailed upon to do this, as it was then my intention to have returned to America the latter end of the present year (1795;) but the illness I now suffer prevents me. In case I had come, I should have applied to you for such parts of your official letters (and your private ones, if you had chosen to give them) as contained any instructions or directions either to Mr. Monroe, to Mr. Morris, or to any other person, respecting me; for after you were informed of my imprisonment in France it was incumbent on you to make some enquiry into the cause, as you might very well conclude that I had not the opportunity of informing you of it. I cannot understand your silence upon this subject upon any other ground, than as connivance at my imprisonment; and this is the manner in which it is understood here, and will be understood in America, unless you will give me authority for contradicting it. I therefore write you this letter, to propose to you to send me copies of any letters you have written, that I may remove this suspicion. In the Second Part of the "Age of Reason," I have given a memorandum from the handwriting of Robespierre, in which he proposed a decree of accusation against me 'for the interest of America as well as of France.' He could have no cause for putting America in the case, but by interpreting the silence of the American government into connivance and consent. I was imprisoned on the ground of being born in England; and your silence in not inquiring the cause of that imprisonment, and reclaiming me against it, was tacitly giving me up. I ought not to have suspected you of treachery; but whether I recover from the illness I now suffer, or not, I shall continue to think you treacherous, till you give me cause to think otherwise. I am sure you would have found yourself more at your ease had you acted by me as you ought; for whether your desertion of me was intended to gratify the English government, or to let me fall into destruction in France that you might exclaim the louder against the French Revolution; or whether you hoped by my extinction to meet with less opposition in mounting up the American government; either of these will involve you in reproach you will not easily shake off.

"THOMAS PAINE."

This is a bitter letter, but it is still more a sorrowful one. In view of what Washington had written of Paine's services, and for the sake of twelve years of *camaraderie*, Washington should have overlooked the sharpness of a deeply wronged and dying friend, and written to him what his Minister in France had reported. My reader already knows, what the sufferer knew not, that a part of Paine's grievance against Washington was unfounded. Washington could not know that the only charge against Paine was one trumped up by his own Minister in France. But, if he ever saw the letter just quoted, he must have perceived that Paine was laboring under an error in supposing that no inquiry had been made into his case. There are facts antecedent to the letter showing that his complaint had a real basis. For instance, in a letter to Monroe (July 30th), the President's interest was expressed in two other American prisoners in France—Archibald Hunter and Shubael Allen,—but no word was said of Paine. There was certainly a change in Washington towards Paine, and the following may have been its causes.

1. Paine had introduced Genêt to Morris, and probably to public men in America. Genêt had put an affront on Morris, and taken over a demand for his recall, with which Morris connected Paine. In a letter to Washington (private) Morris falsely insinuated that Paine had incited the actions of Genêt which had vexed the President.

2. Morris, perhaps in fear that Jefferson, influenced by Americans in Paris, might appoint Paine to his place, had written to Robert Morris in Philadelphia slanders of Paine, describing him as a sot and an object of contempt. This he knew would reach Washington without passing under the eye of Paine's friend, Jefferson.

3. In a private letter Morris related that Paine had visited him with Colonel Oswald, and treated him insolently. Washington particularly disliked Oswald, an American journalist actively opposing his administration.

4. Morris had described Paine as intriguing against him, both in Europe and America, thus impeding his mission, to which the President attached great importance.

5. The President had set his heart on bribing England with a favorable treaty of commerce to give up its six military posts in America. The most obnoxious man in the world to England was Paine. Any interference in Paine's behalf would

not only have offended England, but appeared as a sort of repudiation of Morris' intimacy with the English court. The (alleged) reclamation of Paine by Morris had been kept secret by Washington even from friends so intimate (at the time) as Madison, who writes of it as having never been done. So carefully was avoided the publication of anything that might vex England.

6. Morris had admonished the Secretary of State that if Paine's imprisonment were much noticed it might endanger his life. So conscience was free to jump with policy.

What else Morris may have conveyed to Washington against Paine can be only matter for conjecture; but what he was capable of saying about those he wished to injure may be gathered from various letters of his. In one (December 19, 1795) he tells Washington that he had heard from a trusted informant that his Minister, Monroe, had told various Frenchmen that "he had no doubt but that, if they would do what was proper here, he and his friends would turn out Washington."

Liability to imposition is the weakness of strong natures. Many an Iago of canine cleverness has made that discovery. But, however Washington's mind may have been poisoned towards Paine, it seems unaccountable that, after receiving the letter of September 20th, he did not mention to Monroe, or to somebody, his understanding that the prisoner had been promptly reclaimed. His silence looks as if he had not received the letter. After Edmund Randolph's resignation his successor, Pickering, suppressed a document that would have exculpated him in Washington's eyes, and it is now among the Pickering papers. Paine had an enemy in Pickering. The letter of Paine was sent under cover to Benjamin Franklin Bache, of the *General Advertiser*, with whom as with other republicans Washington had no intercourse. Pickering may therefore have had official opportunity to intercept it. The President was no longer visited by his old friends, Madison and others, and they could not discuss with him the intelligence they were receiving about Paine. Madison, in a letter to Jefferson (dated at Philadelphia, January 10, 1796), says:

" I have a letter from Thomas Paine which breathes the same sentiments, and contains some keen observations on the administration of the government here. It appears that the neglect to claim him as an American citizen when confined by Robespierre, or even to interfere in any way whatever in his favor, has filled him with an indelible rancor against the President, to whom it appears he has written on the subject [September 20, 1795]. His letter to me is in the style of a dying one, and we hear that he is since dead of the abscess in his side, brought on by his imprisonment. His letter desires that he may be remembered to you."

Whatever the explanation may be, no answer came from Washington. After waiting a year Paine employed his returning strength in embodying the letters of February 22d and September 20th, with large additions, in a printed *Letter to George Washington*. The story of his imprisonment and death sentence here for the first time really reached the American people. His personal case is made preliminary to an attack on Washington's whole career. The most formidable part of the pamphlet was the publication of Washington's letter to the

Committee of Public Safety, which, departing from its rule of secrecy (in anger at the British Treaty), thus delivered a blow not easily answerable. The President's letter was effusive about the "alliance," "closer bonds of friendship," and so forth,—phrases which, just after the virtual transfer of our alliance to the enemy of France, smacked of perfidy. Paine attacks the treaty, which is declared to have put American commerce under foreign dominion. "The sea is not free to her. Her right to navigate is reduced to the right of escaping; that is, until some ship of England or France stops her vessels and carries them into port." The ministerial misconduct of Gouverneur Morris, and his neglect of American interests, are exposed in a sharp paragraph. Washington's military mistakes are relentlessly raked up, with some that he did not commit, and the credit given him for victories won by others heavily discounted.

That Washington smarted under this pamphlet appears by a reference to it in a letter to David Stuart, January 8, 1797. Speaking of himself in the third person, he says: "Although he is soon to become a private citizen, his opinions are to be knocked down, and his character reduced as low as they are capable of sinking it, even by resorting to absolute falsehoods. As an evidence whereof, and of the plan they are pursuing, I send you a letter of Mr. Paine to me, printed in this city [Philadelphia], and disseminated with great industry." In the same letter he says: "Enclosed you will receive also a production of Peter Porcupine, alias William Cobbett. Making allowances for the asperity of an Englishman, for some of his strong and coarse expressions, and a want of official information as to many facts, it is not a bad thing."[1] Cobbett's answer to Paine's personal grievance was really an arraignment of the President. He undertakes to prove that the French Convention was a real government, and that by membership in it Paine had forfeited his American citizenship. But Monroe had formally claimed Paine as an American citizen, and the President had officially endorsed that claim. That this approval was unknown to Cobbett is a remarkable fact, showing that even such small and tardy action in Paine's favor was kept secret from the President's new British and Federalist allies.

For the rest it is a pity that Washington did not specify the "absolute falsehoods" in Paine's pamphlet, if he meant the phrase to apply to that. It might assist us in discovering just how the case stood in his mind. He may have been indignant at the suggestion of his connivance with Paine's imprisonment; but, as a matter of fact, the President had been brought by his Minister into the conspiracy which so nearly cost Paine his life.

On a review of the facts, my own belief is that the heaviest part of Paine's wrong came indirectly from Great Britain. It was probably one more instance of Washington's inability to weigh any injustice against an interest of this country. He ignored compacts of capitulation in the cases of Burgoyne and Asgill, in the Revolution; and when

[1] "Porcupine's Political Censor, for December, 1796. A Letter to the Infamous Tom. Paine, in answer to his letter to General Washington."

convinced that this nation must engage either in war or commercial alliance with England he virtually broke faith with France.[1] To the new alliance he sacrificed his most faithful friends Edmund Randolph and James Monroe; and to it, mainly, was probably due his failure to express any interest in England's outlaw, Paine. For this might gain publicity and offend the government with which Jay was negotiating. Such was George Washington. Let justice add that he included himself in the list of patriotic martyrdoms. By sacrificing France and embracing George III. he lost his old friends, lost the confidence of his own State, incurred denunciations that, in his own words, "could scarcely be applied to a Nero, a notorious defaulter, or even to a common pickpocket." So he wrote before Paine's pamphlet appeared, which, save in the personal matter, added nothing to the general accusations. It is now forgotten that with one exception—Johnson—no President ever went out of office so loaded with odium as Washington. It was the penalty of Paine's power that, of the thousand reproaches, his alone survived to recoil on his memory when the issues and the circumstances that explain if they cannot justify his pam-

[1] In a marginal note on Monroe's "View, etc.," found among his papers, Washington writes: "Did then the situation of our affairs admit of any other alternative than negotiation or war?" (Sparks' "Washington," xi., p. 505). Since writing my "Life of Randolph," in which the history of the British treaty is followed, I found in the French Archives (États-Unis, vol. ii., doc. 12) Minister Fauchet's report of a conversation with Secretary Randolph in which he (Randolph) said: "What would you have us do? We could not end our difficulties with the English but by a war or a friendly treaty. We were not prepared for war; it was necessary to negotiate." It is now tolerably certain that there was "bluff" on the part of the British players, in London and Philadelphia, but it won.

phlet, are forgotten. It is easy for the Washington worshipper of to-day to condemn Paine's pamphlet, especially as he is under no necessity of answering it. But could he imagine himself abandoned to long imprisonment and imminent death by an old friend and comrade, whose letters of friendship he cherished, that friend avowedly able to protect him, with no apparent explanation of the neglect but deference to an enemy against whom they fought as comrades, an unprejudiced reader would hardly consider Paine's letter unpardonable even where unjust. Its tremendous indignation is its apology so far as it needs apology. A man who is stabbed cannot be blamed for crying out. It is only in poetry that dying Desdemonas exonerate even their deluded slayers. Paine, who when he wrote these personal charges felt himself dying of an abscess traceable to Washington's neglect, saw not Iago behind the President. His private demand for explanation, sent through Bache, was answered only with cold silence. "I have long since resolved," wrote Washington to Governor Stone (December 6, 1795), "for the present time at least, to let my calumniators proceed without any notice being taken of their invectives by myself, or by any others with my participation or knowledge." But now, nearly a year later, comes Paine's pamphlet, which is not made up of invectives, but of statements of fact. If, in this case, Washington sent, to one friend at least, Cobbett's answer to Paine, despite its errors which he vaguely mentions, there appears no good reason why he should not have specified those errors, and Paine's also. By his silence, even in the confidence of friendship, the truth which might have come to light was suppressed beyond his grave. For such silence the best excuse to me imaginable is that, in ignorance of the part Morris had acted, the President's mind may have been in bewilderment about the exact facts.

As for Paine's public letter, it was an answer to Washington's unjustifiable refusal to answer his private one. It was the natural outcry of an ill and betrayed man to one whom we now know to have been also betrayed. Its bitterness and wrath measure the greatness of the love that was wounded. The mutual personal services of Washington and Paine had continued from the beginning of the American revolution to the time of Paine's departure for Europe in 1787. Although he recognized, as Washington himself did, the commander's mistakes Paine had magnified his successes; his all-powerful pen defended him against loud charges on account of the retreat to the Delaware, and the failures near Philadelphia. In those days what "Common Sense" wrote was accepted as the People's verdict. It is even doubtful whether the proposal to supersede Washington might not have succeeded but for Paine's fifth *Crisis*.[1] The

[1] "When a party was forming, in the latter end of seventy-seven and beginning of seventy-eight, of which John Adams was one, to remove Mr. Washington from the command of the army, on the complaint that *he did nothing*, I wrote the fifth number of the *Crisis*, and published it at Lancaster (Congress then being at Yorktown, in Pennsylvania), to ward off that meditated blow; for though I well knew that the black times of seventy-six were the natural consequence of his want of military judgment in the choice of positions into which the army was put about New York and New Jersey, I could see no possible advantage, and nothing but mischief, that could arise by distracting the army into parties, which would have been the case had the intended motion gone on."—Paine's Letter iii to the People of the United States (1802).

personal relations between the two had been even affectionate. We find Paine consulting him about his projected publications at little oyster suppers in his own room; and Washington giving him one of his two overcoats, when Paine's had been stolen. Such incidents imply many others never made known; but they are represented in a terrible epigram found among Paine's papers,— " Advice to the statuary who is to execute the statue of Washington.

> "Take from the mine the coldest, hardest stone,
> It needs no fashion: it is Washington.
> But if you chisel, let the stroke be rude,
> And on his heart engrave—Ingratitude."

Paine never published the lines. Washington being dead, old memories may have risen to restrain him; and he had learned more of the treacherous influences around the great man which had poisoned his mind towards other friends besides himself. For his pamphlet he had no apology to make. It was a thing inevitable, volcanic, and belongs to the history of a period prolific in intrigues, of which both Washington and Paine were victims.

CHAPTER XI.

"THE AGE OF REASON."

The reception which the "Age of Reason" met is its sufficient justification. The chief priests and preachers answered it with personal abuse and slander, revealing by such fruits the nature of their tree, and confessing the feebleness of its root, either in reason or human affection.

Lucian, in his "Ζεὺς τραγῳδός," represents the gods as invisibly present at a debate, in Athens, on their existence. Damis, who argues from the evils of the world that there are no gods, is answered by Timocles, a theological professor with large salary. The gods feel doleful, as the argument goes against them, until their champion breaks out against Damis,—"You blasphemous villain, you! Wretch! Accursed monster!" The chief of the gods takes courage, and exclaims: "Well done, Timocles! give him hard words. That is your strong point. Begin to reason and you will be dumb as a fish."

So was it in the age when the Twilight of the Gods was brought on by faith in the Son of Man. Not very different was it when this Son of Man, dehumanized by despotism, made to wield the thunderbolts of Jove, reached in turn his inevitable

Twilight. The man who pointed out the now admitted survivals of Paganism in the despotic system then called Christianity, who said, "the church has set up a religion of pomp and revenue in the pretended imitation of a person whose life was humility and poverty," was denounced as a sot and an adulterer. These accusations, proved in this work unquestionably false, have accumulated for generations, so that a mountain of prejudice must be tunnelled before any reader can approach the "Age of Reason" as the work of an honest and devout mind.

It is only to irrelevant personalities that allusion is here made. Paine was vehement in his arraignment of Church and Priesthood, and it was fair enough for them to strike back with animadversions on Deism and Infidelity. But it was no answer to an argument against the antiquity of Genesis to call Paine a drunkard, had it been true. This kind of reply was heard chiefly in America. In England it was easy for Paine's chief antagonist, the Bishop of Llandaff, to rebuke Paine's strong language, when his lordship could sit serenely in the House of Peers with knowledge that his opponent was answered with handcuffs for every Englishman who sold his book. But in America, slander had to take the place of handcuffs.

Paine is at times too harsh and militant. But in no case does he attack any person's character. Nor is there anything in his language, wherever objectionable, which I have heard censured when uttered on the side of orthodoxy. It is easily forgotten that Luther desired the execution of a rationalist, and that Calvin did burn a Socinian. The furious language of Protestants against Rome, and of Presbyterians against the English Church, is considered even heroic, like the invective ascribed to Christ, "Generation of vipers, how can you escape the damnation of hell!" Although vehement language grates on the ear of an age that understands the real forces of evolution, the historic sense remembers that moral revolutions have been made with words hard as cannon-balls. It was only when soft phrases about the evil of slavery, which "would pass away in God's good time," made way for the abolitionist denunciation of the Constitution as "an agreement with hell," that the fortress began to fall. In other words, reforms are wrought by those who are in earnest.[1] It is difficult in our time to place one's self in the situation of a heretic of Paine's time. Darwin, who is buried in Westminster, remembered the imprisonment of some educated men for opinions far less heretical than his own. George III. egoistic insanity appears (1892) to have been inherited by an imperial descendant, and should Germans be presently punished for their religion, as Paine's early followers were in England, we shall again hear those words that are the "half-battles" preceding victories.

There is even greater difficulty in the appreciation by one generation of the inner sense of the

[1] "In writing upon this, as upon every other subject, I speak a language plain and intelligible. I deal not in hints and intimations. I have several reasons for this : first, that I may be clearly understood ; secondly, that it may be seen I am in earnest ; and thirdly, because it is an affront to truth to treat falsehood with complaisance."—Paine's reply to Bishop Watson.

language of a past one. The common notion that Paine's "Age of Reason" abounds in "vulgarity" is due to the lack of literary culture in those—probably few—who have derived that impression from its perusal. It is the fate of all genius potent enough to survive a century that its language will here and there seem coarse. The thoughts of Boccaccio, Rabelais, Shakespeare,—whose works are commonly expurgated,—are so modern that they are not generally granted the allowances conceded to writers whose ideas are as antiquated as their words. Only the instructed minds can set their classic nudities in the historic perspective that reveals their innocency and value. Paine's book has done as much to modify human belief as any ever written. It is one of the very few religious works of the last century which survives in unsectarian circulation. It requires a scholarly perception to recognize in its occasional expressions, by some called "coarse," the simple Saxon of Norfolkshire. Similar expressions abound in pious books of the time; they are not censured, because they are not read. His refined contemporary antagonists—Dr. Watson and Dr. Priestley—found no fault with Paine's words, though the former twice accuses his assertions as "indecent." In both cases, however, Paine is pointing out some biblical triviality or indecency—or what he conceived such. I have before me original editions of both Parts of the "Age of Reason" printed from Paine's manuscripts. Part First may be read by the most prudish parent to a daughter, without an omission. In Part Second six or seven sentences might be omitted by the parent, where the writer deals, without the least prurience, with biblical narratives that can hardly be daintily touched. Paine would have been astounded at the suggestion of any impropriety in his expressions. He passes over four-fifths of the passages in the Bible whose grossness he might have cited in support of his objection to its immorality. "Obscenity," he says, "in matters of faith, however wrapped up, is always a token of fable and imposture; for it is necessary to our serious belief in God that we do not connect it with stories that run, as this does, into ludicrous interpretations. The story [of the miraculous conception] is, upon the face of it, the same kind of story as that of Jupiter and Leda."

Another fostered prejudice supposes "The Age of Reason" largely made up of scoffs. The Bishop of Llandaff, in his reply to Paine, was impressed by the elevated Theism of the work, to portions of which he ascribed "a philosophical sublimity."[1] Watson apparently tried to constrain his ecclesiastical position into English fair play, so that his actual failures to do so were especially misleading, as many knew Paine only as represented by this eminent antagonist. For instance, the Bishop says, "Moses you term a coxcomb, etc." But Paine, commenting on Numbers xii., 3, "Moses was very meek, above all men," had argued that Moses could not have written the book, for "If Moses said this of himself he was a coxcomb." Again the Bishop says Paine terms Paul "a fool." But Paine had quoted from Paul, "'Thou fool, that

[1] "An Apology for the Bible. By R. Llandaff" [Dr. Richard Watson].

which thou sowest is not quickened except it die.' To which [he says] one might reply in his own language, and say, 'Thou fool, Paul, that which thou sowest is not quickened except it die not.'"

No intellect that knows the law of literature, that deep answers only unto deep, can suppose that the effect of Paine's "Age of Reason," on which book the thirty years' war for religious freedom in England was won, after many martyrdoms, came from a scoffing or scurrilous work. It is never Paine's object to raise a laugh; if he does so it is because of the miserable baldness of the dogmas, and the ignorant literalism, consecrated in the popular mind of his time. Through page after page he peruses the Heavens, to him silently declaring the glory of God, and it is not laughter but awe when he asks, "From whence then could arise the solitary and strange conceit, that the Almighty, who had millions of worlds equally dependent on his protection, should quit the care of all the rest, and come to die in our world, because, they say, one man and one woman had eaten an apple!"

In another work Paine finds allegorical truth in the legend of Eden. The comparative mythologists of to-day, with many sacred books of the East, can find mystical meaning and beauty in many legends of the Bible wherein Paine could see none, but it is because of their liberation by the rebels of last century from bondage to the pettiness of literalism. Paine sometimes exposes an absurdity with a taste easily questionable by a generation not required like his own to take such things under foot of the letter. But his spirit is never flippant, and the sentences that might so seem to a casual reader are such as Browning defended in his "Christmas Eve."

> "If any blames me,
> Thinking that merely to touch in brevity
> The topics I dwell on, were unlawful—
> Or, worse, that I trench, with undue levity,
> On the bounds of the Holy and the awful,
> I praise the heart, and pity the head of him,
> And refer myself to THEE, instead of him;
> Who head and heart alike discernest,
> Looking below light speech we utter,
> When the frothy spume and frequent sputter
> Prove that the soul's depths boil in earnest!"

Even Dr. James Martineau, whose reverential spirit no one can question, once raised a smile in his audience, of which the present writer was one, by saying that the account of the temptation of Jesus, if true, must have been reported by himself, or "by the only other party present." Any allusion to the devil in our day excites a smile. But it was not so in Paine's day, when many crossed themselves while speaking of this dark prince. Paine has "too much respect for the moral character of Christ" to suppose that he told the story of the devil showing him all the kingdoms of the world. "How happened it that he did not discover America; or is it only with *kingdoms* that his sooty highness has any interest?" This is not flippancy; it was by following the inkstand Luther threw at the devil with equally vigorous humor that the grotesque figure was eliminated, leaving the reader of to-day free to appreciate the profound significance of the Temptation.

How free Paine is from any disposition to play to pit or gallery, any more than to dress circle, is shown in his treatment of the Book of Jonah. It is not easy to tell the story without exciting laughter; indeed the proverbial phrases for exaggeration, —"a whale," a "fish story,"—probably came from Jonah. Paine's smile is slight. He says, "it would have approached nearer to the idea of a miracle if Jonah had swallowed the whale"; but this is merely in passing to an argument that miracles, in the early world, would hardly have represented Divinity. Had the fish cast up Jonah in the streets of Nineveh the people would probably have been affrighted, and fancied them both devils. But in the second Part of the work there is a very impressive treatment of the Book of Jonah. This too is introduced with a passing smile—"if credulity could swallow Jonah and the whale it could swallow anything." But it is precisely to this supposed "scoffer" that we owe the first interpretation of the profound and pathetic significance of the book, lost sight of in controversies about its miracle. Paine anticipates Baur in pronouncing it a poetical work of Gentile origin. He finds in it the same lesson against intolerance contained in the story of the reproof of Abraham for piously driving the suffering fire-worshipper from his tent. (This story is told by the Persian Saadi, who also refers to Jonah: "And now the whale swallowed Jonah: the sun set.") In the prophet mourning for his withered gourd, while desiring the destruction of a city, Paine finds a satire; in the divine rebuke he hears the voice of a true God, and one very different from the deity to whom the Jews ascribed massacres. The same critical acumen is shown in his treatment of the Book of Job, which he believes to be also of Gentile origin, and much admires.

The large Paine Mythology cleared aside, he who would learn the truth about this religious teacher will find in his way a misleading literature of uncritical eulogies. Indeed the pious prejudices against Paine have largely disappeared, as one may see by comparing the earlier with the later notices of him in religious encyclopædias. But though he is no longer placed in an infernal triad as in the old hymn—"The world, the devil, and Tom Paine"—and his political services are now candidly recognized, he is still regarded as the propagandist of a bald illiterate deism. This, which is absurdly unhistorical, Paine having been dealt with by eminent critics of his time as an influence among the educated, is a sequel to his long persecution. For he was relegated to the guardianship of an unlearned and undiscriminating radicalism, little able to appreciate the niceties of his definitions, and was gilded by its defensive commonplaces into a figurehead. Paine therefore has now to be saved from his friends more perhaps than from his enemies. It has been shown on a former page that his governmental theories were of a type peculiar in his time. Though such writers as Spencer, Frederic Harrison, Bagehot, and Dicey have familiarized us with his ideas, few of them have the historic perception which enables Sir George Trevelyan to recognize Paine's connection with them. It must now be added that Paine's religion was of a still more peculiar type. He cannot be classed with deists of the past or theists of the present. Instead of being the mere iconoclast, the militant assailant of Christian beliefs, the "infidel" of pious slang, which even men who should know better suppose, he was an exact thinker, a slow and careful writer, and his religious ideas, developed through long years, require and repay study.

The dedication of "The Age of Reason" places the work under the "protection" of its author's fellow-citizens of the United States. To-day the trust comes to many who really are such as Paine supposed all of his countrymen to be,—just and independent lovers of truth and right. We shall see that his trust was not left altogether unfulfilled by a multitude of his contemporaries, though they did not venture to do justice to the man. Paine had idealized his countrymen, looking from his prison across three thousand miles. But, to that vista of space, a century of time had to be added before the book which fanatical Couthon suppressed, and the man whom murderous Barrère sentenced to death, could both be fairly judged by educated America.

"The Age of Reason" is in two Parts, published in successive years. These divisions are interesting as memorials of the circumstances under which they were written and published,—in both cases with death evidently at hand. But taking the two Parts as one work, there appears to my own mind a more real division: a part written by Paine's century, and another originating from himself. Each of these has an important and traceable evolution.

I. The first of these divisions may be considered, fundamentally, as a continuation of the old revolution against arbitrary authority. Carlyle's humor covers a profound insight when he remarks that Paine, having freed America with his "Common Sense," was resolved to free this whole world, and perhaps the other! All the authorities were and are interdependent. "If thou release this man thou art not Cæsar's friend," cried the Priest to Pilate. The proconsul must face the fact that in Judea Cæsarism rests on the same foundation with Jahvism. Authority leans on authority; none can stand alone. It is still a question whether political revolutions cause or are caused by religious revolutions. Buckle maintained that the French Revolution was chiefly due to the previous overthrow of spiritual authority; Rocquain, that the political *régime* was shaken before the philosophers arose.[1] In England religious changes seem to have usually followed those of a political character, not only in order of time, but in character. In beginning the "Age of Reason," Paine says:

" Soon after I had published the pamphlet 'Common Sense' in America I saw the exceeding probability that a revolution in the system of government would be followed by a revolution in the system of religion. The adulterous connection of church and state, wherever it had taken place, whether Jewish, Christian, or Turkish, had so effectually prohibited by pains and penalties every discussion upon established creeds, and upon first principles of religion, that until the system of government should be changed those subjects could not be

[1] Felix Rocquain's fine work, "L'Esprit révolutionnaire avant la Révolution," has lately been well condensed and translated by Miss Hunting, of London, with an excellent introduction by Professor Huxley.

brought fairly and openly before the world; but that whenever this should be done a revolution in the system of religion would follow. Human inventions and priestcraft would be detected; and man would return to the pure, unmixed, and unadulterated belief of one God and no more."

The historical continuity of the critical negations of Paine with the past is represented in his title. The Revolution of 1688,—the secular arm transferring the throne from one family to another,—brought the monarchical superstition into doubt; straightway the Christian authority was shaken. One hundred years before Paine's book, appeared Charles Blount's "Oracles of Reason." Macaulay describes Blount as the head of a small school of "infidels," troubled with a desire to make converts; his delight was to worry the priests by asking them how light existed before the sun was made, and where Eve found thread to stitch her fig-leaves. But to this same Blount, Macaulay is constrained to attribute emanicipation of the press in England.

Blount's title was taken up in America by Ethan Allen, leader of the "Green Mountain Boys." Allen's "Oracles of Reason" is forgotten; he is remembered by his demand (1775) for the surrender of Fort Ticonderoga, "in the name of Jehovah and the Continental Congress." The last five words of this famous demand would have been a better title for the book. It introduces the nation to a Jehovah qualified by the Continental Congress. Ethan Allen's deity is no longer a King of kings: arbitrariness has disappeared; men are summoned to belief in a governor administering laws inherent in the constitution of a universe co-eternal with himself, and with which he is interdependent. His administration is not for any divine glory, but, in anticipation of our constitutional preamble, to "promote the general welfare." The old Puritan alteration in the Lord's Prayer, "Thy Commonwealth come!" would in Allen's church have been "Thy Republic come!" That is, had he admitted prayer, which to an Executive is of course out of place. It must not, however, be supposed that Ethan Allen is conscious that his system is inspired by the Revolution. His book is a calm, philosophical analysis of New England theology and metaphysics; an attempt to clear away the ancient biblical science and set Newtonian science in its place; to found what he conceives "Natural Religion."

In editing his "Account of Arnold's Campaign in Quebec," John Joseph Henry says in a footnote that Paine borrowed from Allen. But the aged man was, in his horror of Paine's religion, betrayed by his memory. The only connection between the books runs above the consciousness of either writer. There was necessarily some resemblance between negations dealing with the same narratives, but a careful comparison of the books leaves me doubtful whether Paine ever read Allen. His title may have been suggested by Blount, whose "Oracles of Reason" was in the library of his assistant at Bordentown, John Hall. The works are distinct in aim, products of different religious climes. Allen is occupied mainly with the metaphysical, Paine with quite other, aspects of their common subject. There is indeed a conscientious originality in the freethinkers who successively availed themselves of the era of liberty secured by Blount. Collins, Bolingbroke, Hume, Toland, Chubb, Woolston, Tindal, Middleton, Annet, Gibbon,—each made an examination for himself, and represents a distinct chapter in the religious history of England. Annet's "Free Inquirer," aimed at enlightenment of the lower classes, proved that free thought was tolerated only as an aristocratic privilege; the author was pilloried, just thirty years before the cheapening of the "Rights of Man" led to Paine's prosecution. Probably Morgan did more than any of the deists to prepare English ground for Paine's sowing, by severely criticising the Bible by a standard of civilized ethics, so far as ethics were civilized in the early eighteenth century. But none of these writers touched the deep chord of religious feeling in the people. The English-speaking people were timid about venturing too much on questions which divided the learned, and were content to express their protest against the worldliness of the Church, and faithlessness to the lowly Saviour, by following pietists and enthusiasts. The learned clergy, generally of the wealthy classes, were largely deistical, but conservative. They gradually perceived that the political and the theological authority rested on the same foundation. So between the deists and the Christians there was, as Leslie Stephen says, a "comfortable compromise, which held together till Wesley from one side, and Thomas Paine from another, forced more serious thoughts on the age."[1]

While "The Age of Reason" is thus, in one aspect, the product of its time, the renewal of an

[1] "History of English Thought in the Eighteenth Century."

old siege—begun far back indeed as Celsus,—its intellectual originality is none the less remarkable. Paine is more complete master of the comparative method than Tindal in his "Christianity as old as the Creation." In his studies of "Christian Mythology" (his phrase), one is surprised by anticipations of Baur and Strauss. These are all the more striking by reason of his homely illustrations. Thus, in discussing the liabilities of ancient manuscripts to manipulation, he mentions in his second Part that in the first, printed less than two years before, there was already a sentence he never wrote; and contrasts this with the book of nature wherein no blade of grass can be imitated or altered.[1] He distinguishes the historical Jesus from the mythical Christ with nicety, though none had previously done this. He is more discriminating than the early deists in his explanations of the scriptural marvels which he discredits. There was not the invariable alternative of imposture with which the orthodoxy of his time had been accustomed to deal. He does indeed suspect Moses with his rod of conjuring, and thinks no better of those who pretended knowledge of future events; but the incredible narratives are traditions, fables, and occasionally "downright lies."

[1] The sentence imported into Paine's Part First is: "The book of Luke was carried by one voice only." I find the words added as a footnote in the Philadelphia edition, 1794, p. 33. While Paine in Paris was utilizing the ascent of the footnote to his text, Dr. Priestley in Pennsylvania was using it to show Paine's untrustworthiness. ("Letters to a Philosophical Unbeliever," p. 73.) But it would appear, though neither discovered it, that Paine's critic was the real offender. In quoting the page, before answering it, Priestley incorporated in the text the footnote of an American editor. Priestley could not of course imagine such editorial folly, but all the same the reader may here see the myth-insect already building the Paine Mythology.

"It is not difficult to discover the progress by which even simple supposition, with the aid of credulity, will in time grow into a lie, and at last be told as a fact; and wherever we can find a charitable reason for a thing of this kind we ought not to indulge a severe one." Paine's use of the word "lies" in this connection is an archaism. Carlyle told me that his father always spoke of such tales as "The Arabian Nights" as "downright lies"; by which he no doubt meant fables without any indication of being such, and without any moral. Elsewhere Paine uses "lie" as synonymous with "fabulous"; when he means by the word what it would now imply, "wilful" is prefixed. In the Gospels he finds "inventions" of Christian Mythologists—tales founded on vague rumors, relics of primitive works of imagination mistaken for history,—fathered upon disciples who did not write them.

His treatment of the narrative of Christ's resurrection may be selected as an example of his method. He rejects Paul's testimony, and his five hundred witnesses to Christ's reappearance, because the evidence did not convince Paul himself, until he was struck by lightning, or otherwise converted. He finds disagreements in the narratives of the gospels, concerning the resurrection, which, while proving there was no concerted imposture, show that the accounts were not written by witnesses of the events; for in this case they would agree more nearly. He finds in the narratives of Christ's reappearances,—"suddenly coming in and going out when doors are shut, vanishing out of sight and appearing again,"—and the lack of details, as to his dress, etc., the familiar signs of a ghost-story, which is apt to be told in different ways. "Stories of this kind had been told of the assassination of Julius Cæsar, not many years before, and they generally have their origin in violent deaths, or in the execution of innocent persons. In cases of this kind compassion lends its aid, and benevolently stretches the story. It goes on a little and a little further, till it becomes a most certain truth. Once start a ghost, and credulity fills up its life and assigns the cause of its appearance." The moral and religious importance of the resurrection would thus be an afterthought. The secrecy and privacy of the alleged appearances of Christ after death are, he remarks, repugnant to the supposed end of convincing the world.[1]

Paine admits the power of the deity to make a revelation. He therefore deals with each of the more notable miracles on its own evidence, adhering to his plan of bringing the Bible to judge the Bible. Such an investigation, written with lucid style and quaint illustration, without one timid or uncandid sentence, coming from a man whose services and sacrifices for humanity were great, could not have failed to give the "Age of Reason" long life, even had these been its only qualities. Four years

[1] In 1778 Lessing set forth his "New Hypothesis of the Evangelists," that they had independently built on a basis derived from some earlier Gospel of the Hebrews,—a theory now confirmed by the recovered fragments of that lost Memoir, collected by Dr. Nicholson of the Bodleian Library. It is tolerably certain that Paine was unacquainted with Lessing's work, when he became convinced, by variations in the accounts of the resurrection, that some earlier narrative "became afterwards the foundation of the four books ascribed to Matthew, Mark, Luke, and John,"—these being, traditionally, eye-witnesses.

before the book appeared, Burke said in Parliament: "Who, born within the last forty years, has read one word of Collins, and Toland, and Tindal, and Chubb, and Morgan, and the whole race who call themselves freethinkers?" Paine was, in one sense, of this intellectual pedigree; and had his book been only a digest and expansion of previous negative criticisms, and a more thorough restatement of theism, these could have given it but a somewhat longer life; the "Age of Reason" must have swelled Burke's list of forgotten freethinking books. But there was an immortal soul in Paine's book. It is to the consideration of this its unique life, which has defied the darts of criticism for a century, and survived its own faults and limitations, that we now turn.

II. Paine's book is the uprising of the human HEART against the Religion of Inhumanity.

This assertion may be met with a chorus of denials that there was, or is, in Christendom any Religion of Inhumanity. And, if Thomas Paine is enjoying the existence for which he hoped, no heavenly anthem would be such music in his ears as a chorus of stormiest denials from earth reporting that the Religion of Inhumanity is so extinct as to be incredible. Nevertheless, the Religion of Inhumanity did exist, and it defended against Paine a god of battles, of pomp, of wrath; an instigator of race hatreds and exterminations; an establisher of slavery; a commander of massacres in punishment of theological beliefs; a sender of lying spirits to deceive men, and of destroying angels to afflict them with plagues;

a creator of millions of human beings under a certainty of their eternal torture by devils and fires of his own creation. This apotheosis of Inhumanity is here called a religion, because it managed to survive from the ages of savagery by violence of superstition, to gain a throne in the Bible by killing off all who did not accept its authority to the letter, and because it was represented by actual inhumanities. The great obstruction of Science and Civilization was that the Bible was quoted in sanction of war, crusades against alien religions, murders for witchcraft, divine right of despots, degradation of reason, exaltation of credulity, punishment of opinion and unbiblical discovery, contempt of human virtues and human nature, and costly ceremonies before an invisible majesty, which, exacted from the means of the people, were virtually the offering of human sacrifices.

There had been murmurs against this consecrated Inhumanity through the ages, dissentients here and there; but the Revolution began with Paine. Nor was this accidental. He was just the one man in the world who had undergone the training necessary for this particular work.

The higher clergy, occupied with the old textual controversy, proudly instructing Paine in Hebrew or Greek idioms, little realized their ignorance in the matter now at issue. Their ignorance had been too carefully educated to even imagine the University in which words are things, and things the word, and the many graduations passed between Thetford Quaker meeting and the French

Convention. What to scholastics, for whom humanities meant ancient classics, were the murders and massacres of primitive tribes, declared to be the word and work of God? Words, mere words. They never saw these things. But Paine had seen that war-god at his work. In childhood he had seen the hosts of the Defender of the Faith as, dripping with the blood of Culloden and Inverness, they marched through Thetford; in manhood he had seen the desolations wrought "by the grace of" that deity to the royal invader of America; he had seen the massacres ascribed to Jahve repeated in France, while Robespierre and Couthon were establishing worship of an infrahuman deity. By sorrow, poverty, wrong, through long years, amid revolutions and death-agonies, the stay-maker's needle had been forged into a pen of lightning. No Oxonian conductor could avert that stroke, which was not at mere irrationalities, but at a huge idol worshipped with human sacrifices.

The creation of the heart of Paine, historically traceable, is so wonderful, its outcome seems so supernatural, that in earlier ages he might have been invested with fable, like some Avatar. Of some such man, no doubt, the Hindu poets dreamed in their picture of young Arguna (in the *Bhagavatgîtâ*). The warrior, borne to the battlefield in his chariot, finds arrayed against him his kinsmen, friends, preceptors. He bids his charioteer pause; he cannot fight those he loves. His charioteer turns: 't is the radiant face of divine Chrishna, his Saviour! Even He has led him to this grievous contention with kinsmen, and those to whose welfare he was devoted. Chrishna instructs his disciple that the war is an illusion; it is the conflict by which, from age to age, the divine life in the world is preserved. " This imperishable devotion I declared to the sun, the sun delivered it to Manu, Manu to Ikshâku; handed down from one to another it was studied by the royal sages. In the lapse of time that devotion was lost. It is even the same discipline which I this day communicate to thee, for thou art my servant and my friend. Both thou and I have passed through many births. Mine are known to me; thou knowest not of thine. I am made evident by my own power: as often as there is a decline of virtue, and an insurrection of wrong and injustice in the world, I appear."

Paine could not indeed know his former births; and, indeed, each former self of his—Wycliffe, Fox, Roger Williams—was sectarianized beyond recognition. He could hardly see kinsmen in the Unitarians, who were especially eager to disown the heretic affiliated on them by opponents; nor in the Wesleyans, though in him was the blood of their apostle, who declared salvation a present life, free to all. In a profounder sense, Paine was George Fox. Here was George Fox disowned, freed from his accidents, naturalized in the earth and humanized in the world of men. Paine is explicable only by the intensity of his Quakerism, consuming its own traditions as once the church's ceremonies and sacraments. On him, in Thetford meeting-house, rolled the burden of that Light that enlighteneth every man, effacing distinctions of rank, race, sex, making all equal, clearing away privilege, whether of priest or mediator, subjecting all scriptures to its immediate illumination.

This faith was a fearful heritage to carry, even in childhood, away from the Quaker environment which, by mixture with modifying "survivals," in habit and doctrine, cooled the fiery gospel for the average tongue. The intermarriage of Paine's father with a family in the English Church brought the precocious boy's Light into early conflict with his kindred, his little lamp being still fed in the meeting-house. A child brought up without respect for the conventional symbols of religion, or even with pious antipathy to them, is as if born with only one spiritual skin; he will bleed at a touch.

> "I well remember, when about seven or eight years of age, hearing a sermon read by a relation of mine, who was a great devotee of the Church, upon the subject of what is called *redemption by the death of the Son of God*. After the sermon was ended I went into the garden, and as I was going down the garden steps, (for I perfectly remember the spot), I revolted at the recollection of what I had heard, and thought to myself that it was making God Almighty act like a passionate man, that killed his son when he could not revenge himself in any other way; and, as I was sure a man would be hanged that did such a thing, I could not see for what purpose they preached such sermons. This was not one of that kind of thoughts that had anything in it of childish levity; it was to me a serious reflection, arising from the idea I had, that God was too good to do such an action, and also too almighty to be under any necessity of doing it. I believe in the same manner at this moment; and I moreover believe that any system of religion that has anything in it which shocks the mind of a child, cannot be a true system."

The child took his misgivings out into the garden; he would not by a denial shock his aunt Cocke's faith as his own had been shocked. For many years he remained silent in his inner garden, nor ever was drawn out of it until he found the abstract dogma of the death of God's Son an altar for sacrificing men, whom he reverenced as all God's sons. What he used to preach at Dover and Sandwich cannot now be known. His ignorance of Greek and Latin, the scholastic "humanities," had prevented his becoming a clergyman, and introduced him to humanities of another kind. His mission was then among the poor and ignorant.[1] Sixteen years later he is in Philadelphia, attending the English Church, in which he had been confirmed. There were many deists in that Church, whose laws then as now were sufficiently liberal to include them. In his "Common Sense" (published January 10, 1776) Paine used the reproof of Israel (I. Samuel) for desiring a King. John Adams, a Unitarian and monarchist, asked him if he really believed in the inspiration of the Old Testament. Paine said he did not, and intended at a later period to publish his opinions on the subject. There was nothing inconsistent in Paine's believing that a passage confirmed by his own Light was a divine direction, though contained in a book whose alleged inspiration throughout he did not accept. Such was the Quaker principle. Before that, soon after his arrival in the country, when he found African Slavery supported by the Old Testament, Paine had repudiated the authority of that book; he declares it abolished by "Gospel light,"

[1] " Old John Berry, the late Col. Hay's servant, told me he knew Paine very well when he was at Dover—had heard him preach there—thought him a staymaker by trade."—W. Weedon, of Glynde, quoted in *Notes and Queries* (London), December 29, 1866.

which includes man-stealing among the greatest crimes. When, a year later, on the eve of the Revolution, he writes "Common Sense," he has another word to say about religion, and it is strictly what the human need of the hour demands. Whatever his disbeliefs, he could never sacrifice human welfare to them, any more than he would suffer dogmas to sacrifice the same. It would have been a grievous sacrifice of the great cause of republican independence, consequently of religious liberty, had he introduced a theological controversy at the moment when it was of vital importance that the sects should rise above their partition-walls and unite for a great common end. The Quakers, deistical as they were, preserved religiously the "separatism" once compulsory; and Paine proved himself the truest Friend among them when he was "moved" by the Spirit of Humanity, for him at length the Holy Spirit, to utter (1776) his brave cheer for Catholicity.

"As to religion, I hold it to be the indispensable duty of all governments to protect all conscientious professors thereof, and I know of no other business which government hath to do therewith. Let a man throw aside that narrowness of soul, that selfishness of principle, which the niggards of all professions are so unwilling to part with, and he will be at once delivered of his fears on that head. Suspicion is the companion of mean souls, and the bane of all good society. For myself, I fully and conscientiously believe, that it is the will of the Almighty that there should be a diversity of religious opinions amongst us: it affords a larger field for our Christian kindness. Were we all of one way of thinking, our religious dispositions would want matter for probation; and, on this liberal principle, I look on the various denominations among us to be like children of the same family, differing only in what is called their Christian names."

There was no pedantry whatever about Paine, this obedient son of Humanity. He would defend Man against men, against sects and parties; he would never quarrel about the botanical label of a tree bearing such fruits as the Declaration of Independence. But no man better knew the power of words, and that a botanical error may sometimes result in destructive treatment of the tree. For this reason he censured the Quakers for opposing the Revolution on the ground that, in the words of their testimony (1776), "the setting up and putting down kings and governments is God's peculiar prerogative." Kings, he answers, are not removed by miracles, but by just such means as the Americans were using. "Oliver Cromwell thanks you. Charles, then, died not by the hands of man; and should the present proud imitator of him come to the same untimely end, the writers and publishers of the Testimony are bound, by the doctrine it contains, to applaud the fact."

Paine was a Christian. In his "Epistle to Quakers" he speaks of the dispersion of the Jews as "foretold by our Saviour." In his famous first *Crisis* he exhorts the Americans not to throw "the burden of the day upon Providence, but show your faith by your works,' that God may bless you." For in those days there was visible to such eyes as his, as to anti-slavery eyes in our civil war,

"A fiery Gospel writ in burnished rows of steel."

The Republic, not American but Human, became Paine's religion. "Divine Providence intends this country to be the asylum of persecuted virtue from every quarter of the globe." So he had written before the Declaration of Independence. In 1778 he finds that there still survives some obstructive superstition among English churchmen in America about the connection of Protestant Christianity with the King. In his seventh *Crisis* (November 21, 1778) he wrote sentences inspired by his new conception of religion.

> "In a Christian and philosophical sense, mankind seem to have stood still at individual civilization, and to retain as nations all the original rudeness of nature. . . . As individuals we profess ourselves Christians, but as nations we are heathens, Romans, and what not. I remember the late Admiral Saunders declaring in the House of Commons, and that in the time of peace, 'That the city of Madrid laid in ashes was not a sufficient atonement for the Spaniards taking off the rudder of an English sloop of war.' . . . The arm of Britain has been spoken of as the arm of the Almighty, and she has lived of late as if she thought the whole world created for her diversion. Her politics, instead of civilizing, has tended to brutalize mankind, and under the vain unmeaning title of 'Defender of the Faith,' she has made war like an Indian on the Religion of Humanity."[1]

Thus, forty years before Auguste Comte sat, a youth of twenty, at the feet of Saint Simon, learning the principles now known as "The Religion of Humanity," Thomas Paine had not only minted the name, but with it the idea of international civilization, in which nations are to treat each other as gentlemen in private life. National honor was, he said, confused with "bullying"; but "that which is the best character for an indi-

[1] Mr. Thaddeus B. Wakeman, an eminent representative of the "Religion of Humanity," writes me that he has not found this phrase in any work earlier than Paine's *Crisis*, vii.

vidual is the best character for a nation." The great and pregnant idea was, as in the previous instances, occasional. It was a sentence passed upon the "Defender-of-the-Faith" superstition, which detached faith from humanity, and had pressed the Indian's tomahawk into the hands of Jesus.

At the close of the American Revolution there appeared little need for a religious reformation. The people were happy, prosperous, and, there being no favoritism toward any sect under the new state constitutions, but perfect equality and freedom, the Religion of Humanity meant sheathing of controversial swords also. It summoned every man to lend a hand in repairing the damages of war, and building the new nationality. Paine therefore set about constructing his iron bridge of thirteen symbolic ribs, to overleap the ice-floods and quicksands of rivers. His assistant in this work, at Bordentown, New Jersey, John Hall, gives us in his journal, glimpses of the religious ignorance and fanaticism of that region. But Paine showed no aggressive spirit towards them. "My employer," writes Hall (1786), has *Common Sense* enough to disbelieve most of the common systematic theories of Divinity, but does not seem to establish any for himself." In all of his intercourse with Hall (a Unitarian just from England), and his neighbors, there is no trace of any disposition to deprive any one of a belief, or to excite any controversy. Humanity did not demand it, and by that direction he left the people to their weekly toils and Sunday sermons.

But when (1787) he was in England, Humanity gave another command. It was obeyed in the eloquent pages on religious liberty and equality in "The Rights of Man." Burke had alarmed the nation by pointing out that the Revolution in France had laid its hand on religion. The cry was raised that religion was in danger. Paine then uttered his impressive paradox:

> "Toleration is not the opposite of intoleration, but the counterfeit of it. Both are despotisms. The one assumes the right of withholding liberty of conscience, and the other of granting it. The one is the pope armed with fire and faggot, the other is the pope selling or granting indulgences. . . . Toleration by the same assumed authority by which it tolerates a man to pay his worship, presumptuously and blasphemously sets itself up to tolerate the Almighty to receive it. . . . Who then art thou, vain dust and ashes, by whatever name thou art called, whether a king, a bishop, a church or a state, a parliament or anything else, that obtrudest thine insignificance between the soul of man and his maker? Mind thine own concerns. If he believes not as thou believest, it is a proof that thou believest not as he believeth, and there is no earthly power can determine between you. . . . Religion, without regard to names, as directing itself from the universal family of mankind to the divine object of all adoration, is man bringing to his maker the fruits of his heart; and though these fruits may differ like the fruits of the earth, the grateful tribute of every one is accepted.

This, which I condense with reluctance, was the affirmation which the Religion of Humanity needed in England. But when he came to sit in the French Convention a new burden rolled upon him. There was Marat with the Bible always before him, picking out texts that justified his murders; there were Robespierre and Couthon invoking the God of Nature to sanction just such massacres as Marat found in his Bible ; and there were crude "atheists" consecrating the ferocities of nature more dangerously than if they had named them Siva, Typhon, or Satan. Paine had published the rights of man for men ; but here human hearts and minds had been buried under the superstitions of ages. The great mischief had ensued, to use his own words, "by the possession of power before they understood principles: they earned liberty in words but not in fact." Exhumed suddenly, as if from some Nineveh, resuscitated into semi-conscious strength, they remembered only the methods of the allied inquisitors and tyrants they were overthrowing; they knew no justice but vengeance; and when on crumbled idols they raised forms called "Nature" and "Reason," old idols gained life in the new forms. These were the gods which had but too literally created, by the slow evolutionary force of human sacrifices, the new revolutionary priesthood. Their massacres could not be questioned by those who acknowledged the divine hand in the slaughter of Canaanites.[1]

[1] On August 10, 1793, there was a sort of communion of the Convention around the statue of Nature, whose breasts were fountains of water. Hérault de Séchelles, at that time president, addressed the statue : "Sovereign of the savage and of the enlightened nations, O Nature, this great people, gathered at the first beam of day before thee, is free ! It is in thy bosom, it is in thy sacred sources, that it has recovered its rights, that it has regenerated itself after traversing so many ages of error and servitude : it must return to the simplicity of thy ways to rediscover liberty and equality. O Nature ! receive the expression of the eternal attachment of the French people for thy laws ; and may the teeming waters gushing from thy breasts, may this pure beverage which refreshed the first human beings, consecrate in this Cup of Fraternity and Equality the vows that France makes thee this day,—the most beautiful that the sun has illumined since it was suspended in the immensity of space." The cup passed around from lip to lip, amid fervent ejaculations. Next year Nature's breasts issued Hérault's blood.

The Religion of Humanity again issued its command to its minister. The "Age of Reason" was written, in its first form, and printed in French. "Couthon," says Lanthenas, "to whom I sent it, seemed offended with me for having translated it."[1] Couthon raged against the priesthood, but could not tolerate a work which showed vengeance to be atheism, and compassion—not merely for men, but for animals—true worship of God. On the other hand, Paine's opposition to atheism would appear to have brought him into danger from another quarter, in which religion could not be distinguished from priestcraft. In a letter to Samuel Adams Paine says that he endangered his life by opposing the king's execution, and "a second time by opposing atheism." Those who denounce the "Age of Reason" may thus learn that red-handed Couthon, who hewed men to pieces before his Lord, and those who acknowledged no Lord, agreed with them. Under these menaces the original work was as I have inferred, suppressed. But the demand of Humanity was peremptory, and Paine re-wrote it all, and more. When it appeared he was a prisoner; his life was in Couthon's hands. He had personally nothing to gain by its publication—neither wife, child, nor relative to reap benefit by its sale. It was published as purely for the good of mankind as any work ever written. Nothing could be more simply true than his declaration, near the close of life:

---

[1] The letter of Lanthenas to Merlin de Thionville, of which the original French is before me, is quoted in an article in *Scribner*, September, 1880, by Hon. E. B. Washburne (former Minister to France); it is reprinted in Remsburg's compilation of testimonies: "Thomas Paine, the Apostle of Religious and Political Liberty" (1880). See also p. 135 of this volume.

"As in my political works my motive and object have been to give man an elevated sense of his own character, and free him from the slavish and superstitious absurdity of monarchy and hereditary government, so, in my publications on religious subjects, my endeavors have been directed to bring man to a right use of the reason that God has given him ; to inpress on him the great principles of divine morality, justice, and mercy, and a benevolent disposition to all men, and to all creatures ; and to inspire in him a spirit of trust, confidence and consolation, in his Creator, unshackled by the fables of books pretending to be the word of God."

It is misleading at the present day to speak of Paine as an opponent of Christianity. This would be true were Christianity judged by the authorized formulas of any church ; but nothing now acknowledged as Christianity by enlightened Christians of any denomination was known to him. In our time, when the humanizing wave, passing through all churches, drowns old controversies, floats the dogmas, till it seems ungenerous to quote creeds and confessions in the presence of our "orthodox" lovers of man—even "totally depraved" and divinely doomed man—the theological eighteenth century is inconceivable. Could one wander from any of our churches, unless of the Christian Pagans or remote villagers *(pagani)*, into those of the last century, he would find himself moving in a wilderness of cinders, with only the plaintive song of John and Charles Wesley to break the solitude. If he would hear recognition of the human Jesus, on whose credit the crowned Christ is now maintained, he would be sharply told that it were a sin to "know Christ after the flesh," and must seek such recognition among those stoned as infidels. Three noble and pathetic tributes to the Man of Nazareth are audible from the last century—those of Rousseau, Voltaire, and Paine. From its theologians and its pulpits not one! Should the tribute of Paine be to-day submitted, without his name, to our most eminent divines, even to leading American and English Bishops, beside any theological estimate of Christ from the same century, the Jesus of Paine would be surely preferred.

Should our cultured Christian of to-day press beyond those sectarian, miserable controversies of the eighteenth century, known to him now as cold ashes, into the seventeenth century, he would find himself in a comparatively embowered land; that is, in England, and in a few oases in America—like that of Roger Williams in Rhode Island. In England he would find brain and heart still in harmony, as in Tillotson and South; still more in Bishop Jeremy Taylor, "Shakespeare of divines." He would hear this Jeremy reject the notions of original sin and transmitted guilt, maintain the "liberty of prophesying," and that none should suffer for conclusions concerning a book so difficult of interpretation as the Bible. In those unsophisticated years Jesus and the disciples and the Marys still wore about them the reality gained in miracle-plays. What Paine need arise where poets wrote the creed, and men knew the Jesus of whom Thomas Dekker wrote:

> " The best of men
> That e'er wore earth about him was a sufferer;
> A soft, meek, patient, humble, tranquil spirit,
> The first true gentleman that ever breathed."

Dean Swift, whose youth was nourished in that living age, passed into the era of dismal disputes, where he found the churches "dormitories of the living as well as of the dead." Some ten years before Paine's birth the Dean wrote: "Since the union of Divinity and Humanity is the great Article of our Religion, 't is odd to see some clergymen, in their writings of Divinity, wholly devoid of Humanity." Men have, he said, enough religion to hate, but not to love. Had the Dean lived to the middle of the eighteenth century he might have discovered exceptions to this holy heartlessness, chiefly among those he had traditionally feared—the Socinians. These, like the Magdalene, were seeking the lost humanity of Jesus. He would have sympathized with Wesley, who escaped from "dormitories of the living" far enough to publish the Life of a Socinian (Firmin), with the brave apology, "I am sick of opinions, give me the life." But Socianism, in eagerness to disown its bolder children, presently lost the heart of Jesus, and when Paine was recovering it the best of them could not comprehend his separation of the man from the myth. So came on the desiccated Christianity of which Emerson said, even among the Unitarians of fifty years ago, "The prayers and even the dogmas of our church are like the zodiac of Denderah, wholly insulated from anything now extant in the life and business of the people." Emerson may have been reading Paine's idea that Christ and the Twelve were mythically connected with Sun and Zodiac, this speculation being an indication of their distance from the Jesus he tenderly revered. If Paine rent the temple-veils of his time, and revealed the stony images behind them, albeit with rudeness, let it not be supposed that those forms were akin to the Jesus and the Marys whom skeptical criticism is re-incarnating, so that they dwell with us. Outside Paine's heart the Christ of his time was not more like the Jesus of our time than Jupiter was like the Prometheus he bound on a rock. The English Christ was then not a Son of Man, but a Prince of Dogma, bearing handcuffs for all who reasoned about him; a potent phantasm that tore honest thinkers from their families and cast them into outer darkness, because they circulated the works of Paine, which reminded the clergy that the Jesus even of their own Bible sentenced those only who ministered not to the hungry and naked. the sick and in prison. Paine's religious culture was English. There the brain had retreated to deistic caves, the heart had gone off to "Salvationism" of the time; the churches were given over to the formalist and the politician, who carried divine sanction to the repetition of biblical oppressions and massacres by Burke and Pitt. And in all the world there had not been one to cry *Sursum Corda* against the consecrated tyranny until that throb of Paine's heart which brought on it the vulture. But to-day, were we not swayed by names and prejudices, it would bring on that prophet of the divine humanity, even the Christian dove.

Soon after the appearance of Part First of the "Age of Reason" it was expurgated of its negative criticisms, probably by some English Unitarians, and published as a sermon, with text from Job xi., 7: "Canst thou by searching find out God? Canst thou find out the Almighty to perfection?" It was printed anonymously; and were its sixteen pages read in any orthodox church to-day it would be regarded as admirable. It might be criticised by left wings as somewhat old-fashioned in the warmth of its theism. It is fortunate that Paine's name was not appended to this doubtful use of his work, for it would have been a serious misrepresentation.[1] That his Religion of Humanity took the deistical form was an evolutionary necessity. English deism was not a religion, but at first a philosophy, and afterwards a scientific generalization. Its founder, as a philosophy, Herbert of Cherbury, had created the matrix in which was formed the Quaker religion of the "inner light," by which Paine's childhood was nurtured; its founder as a scientific theory of creation, Sir Isaac Newton, had determined the matrix in which all unorthodox systems should originate. The real issue was between a sanctified ancient science and a modern science. The utilitarian English race, always the stronghold of science, had established the freedom of the new deism, which thus became the mould into which all unorthodoxies ran. From the time of Newton, English and American thought

[1] "A Lecture on the Existence and Attributes of the Deity, as Deduced from a Contemplation of His Works. M,DCC,XCV." The copy in my possession is inscribed with pen: "This was J. Joyce's copy, and noticed by him as Paine's work." Mr. Joyce was a Unitarian minister. It is probable that the suppression of Paine's name was in deference to his outlawry, and to the dread, by a sect whose legal position was precarious, of any suspicion of connection with "Painite" principles.

and belief have steadily become Unitarian. The dualism of Jesus, the thousand years of faith which gave every soul its post in a great war between God and Satan, without which there would have been no church, has steadily receded before a monotheism which, under whatever verbal disguises, makes the deity author of all evil. English Deism prevailed only to be reconquered into alliance with a tribal god of antiquity, developed into the tutelar deity of Christendom. And this evolution involved the transformation of Jesus into Jehovah, deity of a "chosen" or "elect" people. It was impossible for an apostle of the international republic, of the human brotherhood, whose Father was degraded by any notion of favoritism to a race, or to a "first-born son," to accept a name in which foreign religions had been harried, and Christendom established on a throne of thinkers' skulls. The philosophical and scientific deism of Herbert and Newton had grown cold in Paine's time, but it was detached from all the internecine figure-heads called gods; it appealed to the reason of all mankind; and in that manger, amid the beasts, royal and revolutionary, was cradled anew the divine humanity.

Paine wrote "Deism" on his banner in a militant rather than an affirmative way. He was aiming to rescue the divine Idea from traditional degradations in order that he might with it confront a revolutionary Atheism defying the celestial monarchy. In a later work, speaking of a theological book, "An Antidote to Deism," he remarks: "An antidote to Deism must be Atheism." So far as it is theological, the "Age of Reason" was meant to combat Infidelity. It raised before the French the pure deity of Herbert, of Newton, and other English deists whose works were unknown in France. But when we scrutinize Paine's positive Theism we find a distinctive nucleus forming within the nebulous mass of deistical speculations. Paine recognizes a deity only in the astronomic laws and intelligible order of the universe, and in the corresponding reason and moral nature of man. Like Kant, he was filled with awe by the starry heavens and man's sense of right.[1] The first part of the "Age of Reason" is chiefly astronomical; with those celestial wonders he contrasts such stories as that of Samson and the foxes. "When we contemplate the immensity of that Being who directs and governs the incomprehensible Whole, of which the utmost ken of human sight can discover but a part, we ought to feel shame at calling such paltry stories the word of God." Then turning to the Atheist he says: "We did not make ourselves; we did not make the principles of science, which we discover and apply but cannot alter." The only revelation of God in which he believes is "the universal display of himself in the works of creation, and that repugnance we feel in ourselves to bad actions, and disposition to do good ones." "The only idea we can have of serving God, is that of

[1] Astronomy, as we know, he had studied profoundly. In early life he had studied astronomic globes, purchased at the cost of many a dinner, and the orrery, and attended lectures at the Royal Society. In the "Age of Reason" he writes, twenty-one years before Herschel's famous paper on the Nebulæ: "The probability is that each of those fixed stars is also a sun, round which another system of worlds or planets, though too remote for us to discover, performs its revolutions."

contributing to the happiness of the living creation that God has made."

It thus appears that in Paine's Theism the deity is made manifest, not by omnipotence, a word I do not remember in his theories, but in this correspondence of universal order and bounty with reason and conscience, and the humane heart. In later works this speculative side of his Theism presented a remarkable Zoroastrian variation. When pressed with Bishop Butler's terrible argument against previous Deism,—that the God of the Bible is no more cruel than the God of Nature,—Paine declared his preference for the Persian religion, which exonerated the deity from responsibility for natural evils, above the Hebrew which attributed such things to God. He was willing to sacrifice God's omnipotence to his humanity. He repudiates every notion of a devil, but was evidently unwilling to ascribe the unconquered realms of chaos to the divine Being in whom he believed.

Thus, while theology was lowering Jesus to a mere King, glorying in baubles of crown and throne, pleased with adulation, and developing him into an authorizor of all the ills and agonies of the world, so depriving him of his humanity, Paine was recovering from the universe something like the religion of Jesus himself. " Why even of yourselves judge ye not what is right." In affirming the Religion of Humanity, Paine did not mean what Comte meant, a personification of the continuous life of our race[1]; nor did he merely mean

[1] Paine's friend and fellow-prisoner, Anacharsis Clootz, was the first to describe Humanity as " L'Être Suprême."

benevolence towards all living creatures. He affirmed a Religion based on the authentic divinity of that which is supreme in human nature and distinctive of it. The sense of right, justice, love, mercy, is God himself in man; this spirit judges all things,—all alleged revelations, all gods. In affirming a deity too good, loving, just, to do what is ascribed to Jahve, Paine was animated by the same spirit that led the early believer to turn from heartless elemental gods to one born of woman, bearing in his breast a human heart. Pauline theology took away this human divinity, and effected a restoration, by making the Son of Man Jehovah, and commanding the heart back from its seat of judgment, where Jesus had set it. "Shall the clay say to the potter, why hast thou formed me thus?" "Yes," answered Paine, "if the thing felt itself hurt, and could speak." He knew as did Emerson, whom he often anticipates, that "no god dare wrong a worm."

The force of the "Age of Reason" is not in its theology, though this ethical variation of Deism in the direction of humanity is of exceeding interest to students who would trace the evolution of avatars and incarnations. Paine's theology was but gradually developed, and in this work is visible only as a tide beginning to rise under the fiery orb of his religious passion. For abstract theology he cares little. "If the belief of errors not morally bad did no mischief, it would make no part of the moral duty of man to oppose and remove them." He evinces regret that the New Testament, containing so many elevated moral precepts, should, by leaning on supposed prophecies in the Old Testament, have been burdened with its barbarities. "It must follow the fate of its foundation." This fatal connection, he knows, is not the work of Jesus; he ascribes it to the church which evoked from the Old Testament a crushing system of priestly and imperial power reversing the benign principles of Jesus. It is this oppression, the throne of all oppressions, that he assails. His affirmations of the human deity are thus mainly expressed in his vehement denials.

This long chapter must now draw to a close. It would need a volume to follow thoroughly the argument of this epoch-making book, to which I have here written only an introduction, calling attention to its evolutionary factors, historical and spiritual. Such then was the new Pilgrim's Progress. As in that earlier prison, at Bedford, there shone in Paine's cell in the Luxembourg a great and imperishable vision, which multitudes are still following. The book is accessible in many editions. The Christian teacher of to-day may well ponder this fact. The atheists and secularists of our time are printing, reading, revering a work that opposes their opinions. For above its arguments and criticisms they see the faithful heart contending with a mighty Apollyon, girt with all the forces of revolutionary and royal Terrorism. Just this one Englishman, born again in America, confronting George III. and Robespierre on earth and tearing the like of them from the throne of the universe! Were it only for the grandeur of this spectacle in the past Paine would maintain his hold on thoughtful minds.

But in America the hold is deeper than that. In this self-forgetting insurrection of the human heart against deified Inhumanity there is an expression of the inarticulate wrath of humanity against continuance of the same wrong. In the circulation throughout the earth of the Bible as the Word of God, even after its thousand serious errors of translation are turned, by exposure, into falsehoods; in the deliverance to savages of a scriptural sanction of their tomahawks and poisoned arrows; in the diffusion among cruel tribes of a religion based on human sacrifice, after intelligence has abandoned it; in the preservation of costly services to a deity who "needs nothing at men's hands," beside hovels of the poor who need much; in an exemption of sectarian property from taxation which taxes every man to support the sects, and continues the alliance of church and state; in these things, and others—the list is long—there is still visible, however refined, the sting and claw of the Apollyon against whom Paine hurled his far-reaching dart. The "Age of Reason" was at first published in America by a religious house, and as a religious book. It was circulated in Virginia by Washington's old friend, Parson Weems. It is still circulated, though by supposed unbelievers, as a religious book, and such it is.

Its religion is expressed largely in those same denunciations which theologians resent. I have explained them; polite agnostics apologize for them, or cast Paine over as a Jonah of the rationalistic ship. But to make one expression more gentle would mar the work. As it stands, with all its violences and faults, it represents, as no elaborate or polite treatise could, the agony and bloody sweat of a heart breaking in the presence of crucified Humanity. What dear heads, what noble hearts had that man seen laid low; what shrieks had he heard in the desolate homes of the Condorcets, the Brissots; what Canaanite and Midianite massacres had he seen before the altar of Brotherhood, erected by himself! And all because every human being had been taught from his cradle that there is something more sacred than humanity, and to which man should be sacrificed. Of all those massacred thinkers not one voice remains: they have gone silent: over their reeking guillotine sits the gloating Apollyon of Inhumanity. But here is one man, a prisoner, preparing for his long silence. He alone can speak for those slain between the throne and the altar. In these outbursts of laughter and tears, these outcries that think not of literary style, these appeals from surrounding chaos to the starry realm of order, from the tribune of vengeance to the sun shining for all, this passionate horror of cruelty in the powerful which will brave a heartless heaven or hell with its immortal indignation,—in all these the unfettered mind may hear the wail of enthralled Europe, sinking back choked with its blood, under the chain it tried to break. So long as a link remains of the same chain, binding reason or heart, Paine's "Age of Reason" will live. It is not a mere book—it is a man's heart.

CHAPTER XII.

FRIENDSHIPS.

BARON PICHON, who had been a sinuous Secretary of Legation in America under Genêt and Fauchet, and attached to the Foreign Office in France under the Directory, told George Ticknor, in 1837, that "Tom Paine, who lived in Monroe's house at Paris, had a great deal too much influence over Monroe."[1] The Baron, apart from his prejudice against republicanism (Talleyrand was his master), knew more about American than French politics at the time of Monroe's mission in France. The agitation caused in France by Jay's negotiations in England, and rumors set afloat by their secrecy,—such secrecy being itself felt as a violation of good faith—rendered Monroe's position unhappy and difficult. After Paine's release from prison, his generous devotion to France, undiminished by his wrongs, added to the painful illness that reproached the Convention's negligence, excited a chivalrous enthusiasm for him. The tender care of Mr. and Mrs. Monroe for him, the fact that this faithful friend of France was in their house, were circumstances of international importance. Of Paine's fidelity to republican principles,

---

[1] "Life of George Ticknor," ii., p. 113.

and his indignation at their probable betrayal in England, there could be no doubt in any mind. He was consulted by the French Executive, and was virtually the most important *attaché* of the United States Legation. The "intrigue" of which Thibaudeau had spoken, in Convention, as having driven Paine from that body, was not given to the public, but it was well understood to involve the American President. If Paine's suffering represented in London Washington's deference to England, all the more did he stand to France as a representative of those who in America were battling for the Alliance. He was therefore a tower of strength to Monroe. It will be seen by the subjoined letter that while he was Monroe's guest it was to him rather than the Minister that the Foreign Office applied for an introduction of a new Consul to Samuel Adams, Governor of Massachusetts—a Consul with whom Paine was not personally acquainted. The general feeling and situation in France at the date of this letter (March 6th), and the anger at Jay's secret negotiations in England, are reflected in it:

"MY DEAR FRIEND,—Mr. Mozard, who is appointed Consul, will present you this letter. He is spoken of here as a good sort of man, and I can have no doubt that you will find him the same at Boston. When I came from America it was my intention to return the next year, and I have intended the same every year since. The case I believe is, that as I am embarked in the revolution, I do not like to leave it till it is finished, notwithstanding the dangers I have run. I am now almost the only survivor of those who began this revolution, and I know not how it is that I have escaped. I know however that I owe nothing to the government of America. The executive department has never directed either the former or the present Minister to enquire whether I was dead or alive, in prison or in liberty, what the cause of the imprisonment was, and whether there was any service or assistance it could render. Mr. Monroe acted voluntarily in the case, and reclaimed me as an American citizen; for the pretence for my imprisonment was that I was a foreigner, born in England.

"The internal scene here from the 31 of May 1793 to the fall of Robespierre has been terrible. I was shut up in the prison of the Luxembourg eleven months, and I find by the papers of Robespierre that have been published by the Convention since his death, that I was designed for a worse fate. The following memorandum is in his own handwriting: 'Démander que Thomas Paine soit décrété d'accusation pour les interêts de l'Amérique autant que de la France.'

"You will see by the public papers that the successes of the French arms have been and continue to be astonishing, more especially since the fall of Robespierre, and the suppression of the system of Terror. They have fairly beaten all the armies of Austria, Prussia, England, Spain, Sardignia, and Holland. Holland is entirely conquered, and there is now a revolution in that country.

"I know not how matters are going on your side the water, but I think everything is not as it ought to be. The appointment of G. Morris to be Minister here was the most unfortunate and the most injudicious appointment that could be made. I wrote this opinion to Mr. Jefferson at the time, and I said the same to Morris. Had he not been removed at the time he was I think the two countries would have been involved in a quarrel, for it is a fact, that he would either have been ordered away or put in arrestation; for he gave every reason to suspect that he was secretly a British Emissary.

"What Mr. Jay is about in England I know not; but is it possible that any man who has contributed to the Independence of America, and to free her from the tyranny of the British Government, can read without shame and indignation the note of Jay to Grenville? That the *United States has no other resource than in the justice and magnanimity of his Majesty*, is a satire upon the Declaration of Independence, and exhibits [such] a spirit of meanness on the part of America, that, were it true, I should be ashamed of her. Such a declaration may suit the spaniel character of Aristocracy, but it cannot agree with manly character of a Republican.

"Mr. Mozard is this moment come for this letter, and he sets off directly.—God bless you, remember me among the circle of our friends, and tell them how much I wish to be once more among them.

"THOMAS PAINE."[1]

There are indications of physical feebleness as well as haste in this letter. The spring and summer brought some vigor, but, as we have seen by Monroe's letter to Judge Jones, he sank again, and in the autumn seemed nearing his end. Once more the announcement of his death appeared in England, this time bringing joy to the orthodox. From the same quarter, probably, whence issued, in 1793, " Intercepted Correspondence from Satan to Citizen Paine," came now (1795) a folio sheet: "Glorious News for Old England. The British Lyon rous'd; or John Bull for ever.

> "The Fox has lost his Tail
> The Ass has done his Braying,
> The Devil has got Tom Paine."

Good-hearted as Paine was, it must be admitted that he was cruelly persistent in disappointing these British obituaries. Despite anguish, fever, and abscess—this for more than a year eating into his side,—he did not gratify those prayerful expectations by becoming a monument of divine retribution. Nay, amid all these sufferings he had managed to finish Part Second of the "Age of Reason," write the "Dissertation on Government," and give

[1] Mr. Spofford, Librarian of Congress, has kindly copied this letter for me from the original, among the papers of George Bancroft.

the Address before the Convention. Nevertheless when, in November, he was near death's door, there came from England tidings grievous enough to crush a less powerful constitution. It was reported that many of his staunchest old friends had turned against him on account of his heretical book. This report seemed to find confirmation in the successive volumes of Gilbert Wakefield in reply to the two Parts of Paine's book. Wakefield held Unitarian opinions, and did not defend the real fortress besieged by Paine. He was enraged that Paine should deal with the authority of the Bible, and the orthodox dogmas, as if they were Christianity, ignoring unorthodox versions altogether. This, however, hardly explains the extreme and coarse vituperation of these replies, which shocked Wakefield's friends.[1] Although in his thirty-eighth year at this time, Wakefield was not old enough to escape the *sequelæ* of his former clericalism. He had been a Fellow of Jesus College, Cambridge, afterwards had a congregation, and had continued his connection with the English Church after he was led, by textual criticism, to adopt Unitarian opinions. He had great reputation as a linguist, and wrote Scriptural expositions and retranslations. But few read his books, and he became a tutor in a dissenting college at Hackney, mainly under influence of the Unitarian leaders,

---

[1] "The office of 'castigation' was unworthy of our friend's talents, and detrimental to his purpose of persuading others. Such a contemptuous treatment, even of an unfair disputant, was also too well calculated to depreciate in the public estimation that benevolence of character by which Mr. Wakefield was so justly distinguished."—"Life of Gilbert Wakefield," 1804, ii., p. 33.

Price and Priestley. Wakefield would not condescend to any connection with a dissenting society, and his career at Hackney was marked by arrogant airs towards Unitarians, on account of a university training, then not open to dissenters. He attacked Price and Priestley, his superiors in every respect, apart from their venerable position and services, in a contemptuous way; and, in fact, might be brevetted a prig, with a fondness for coarse phrases, sometimes printed with blanks. He flew at Paine as if he had been waiting for him; his replies, not affecting any vital issue, were displays of linguistic and textual learning, set forth on the background of Paine's page, which he blackened. He exhausts his large vocabulary of vilification on a book whose substantial affirmations he concedes; and it is done in the mean way of appropriating the credit of Paine's arguments.

Gilbert Wakefield was indebted to the excitement raised by Paine for the first notice taken by the general public of anything he ever wrote. Paine, however, seems to have been acquainted with a sort of autobiography which he had published in 1792. In this book Wakefield admitted with shame that he had subscribed the Church formulas when he did not believe them, while indulging in flings at Price, Priestley, and others, who had suffered for their principles. At the same time there were some things in Wakefield's autobiography which could not fail to attract Paine: it severely attacked slavery, and also the whole course of Pitt towards France. This was done with talent and courage. It was consequently a shock when Gilbert Wakefield's outrageous abuse of himself came to the invalid in his sick-room. It appeared to be an indication of the extent to which he was abandoned by the Englishmen who had sympathized with his political principles, and to a large extent with his religious views. This acrimonious repudiation added groans to Paine's sick and sinking heart, some of which were returned upon his Socinian assailant, and in kind. This private letter my reader must see, though it was meant for no eye but that of Gilbert Wakefield. It is dated at Paris, November 19, 1795.

"DEAR SIR,—When you prudently chose, like a starved apothecary, to offer your eighteenpenny antidote to those who had taken my two-and-sixpenny Bible-purge,[1] you forgot that although my dose was rather of the roughest, it might not be the less wholesome for possessing that drastick quality; and if I am to judge of its salutary effects on your infuriate polemic stomach, by the nasty things it has made you bring away, I think you should be the last man alive to take your own panacea. As to the collection of words of which you boast the possession, nobody, I believe, will dispute their amount, but every one who reads your answer to my 'Age of Reason' will wish there were not so many scurrilous ones among them; for though they may be very usefull in emptying your gall-bladder they are too apt to move the bile of other people.

"Those of Greek and Latin are rather foolishly thrown away, I think, on a man like me, who, you are pleased to say, is *'the greatest ignoramus in nature'*: yet I must take the liberty to tell you, that wisdom does not consist in the mere knowledge of language, but of things.

"You recommend me to *know myself*,—a thing very easy to advise, but very difficult to practice, as I learn from your own book; for you take yourself to be a meek disciple of Christ, and yet give way to passion and pride in every page of its composition.

These were the actual prices of the books.

"You have raised an ant-hill about the roots of my sturdy oak, and it may amuse idlers to see your work ; but neither its body nor its branches are injured by you ; and I hope the shade of my Civic Crown may be able to preserve your little contrivance, at least for the season.

"When you have done as much service to the world by your writings, and suffered as much for them, as I have done, you will be better entitled to dictate : but although I know you to be a keener politician than Paul, I can assure you, from my experience of mankind, that you do not much commend the Christian doctrines to them by announcing that it requires the labour of a learned life to make them understood.

"May I be permitted, after all, to suggest that your truly vigorous talents would be best employed in teaching men to preserve their liberties exclusively,—leaving to that God who made their immortal souls the care of their eternal welfare.

"I am, dear Sir,
"Your true well-wisher,
"THO. PAINE.
"To GILBERT WAKEFIELD, A. B."

After a first perusal of this letter has made its unpleasant impression, the reader will do well to read it again. Paine has repaired to his earliest Norfolkshire for language appropriate to the coarser tongue of his Nottinghamshire assailant; but it should be said that the offensive paragraph, the first, is a travesty of one written by Wakefield. In his autobiography, after groaning over his books that found no buyers, a veritable "starved apothecary," Wakefield describes the uneasiness caused by his pamphlet on "Religious Worship" as proof that the disease was yielding to his "potion." He says that "as a physician of spiritual maladies" he had seconded "the favourable operation of the first prescription,"—and so forth. Paine, in using the simile, certainly allows the drugs and phials of his sick-room to enter it to a disagreeable extent, but we must bear in mind that we are looking over his shoulder. We must also, by the same consideration of its privacy, mitigate the letter's egotism. Wakefield's ant-hill protected by the foliage, the "civic crown," of Paine's oak which it has attacked,—gaining notice by the importance of the work it belittles,—were admirable if written by another; and the egotism is not without some warrant. It is the rebuke of a scarred veteran of the liberal army to the insults of a subaltern near twenty years his junior. It was no doubt taken to heart. For when the agitation which Gilbert Wakefield had contributed to swell, and to lower, presently culminated in handcuffs for the circulators of Paine's works, he was filled with anguish. He vainly tried to resist the oppression, and to call back the Unitarians, who for twenty-five years continued to draw attention from their own heresies by hounding on the prosecution of Paine's adherents.[1] The prig perished; in his place stood

[1] "But I would not forcibly suppress this book ["Age of Reason"]; much less would I punish (O my God, be such wickedness far from me, or leave me destitute of thy favour in the midst of this perjured and sanguinary generation!) much less would I punish, by fine or imprisonment, from any possible consideration, the publisher or author of these pages."—Letter of Gilbert Wakefield to Sir John Scott, Attorney General, 1798. For evidence of Unitarian intolerance see the discourse of W. J. Fox on "The Duties of Christians towards Deists" (Collected Works, vol. i.). In this discourse, October 24, 1819, on the prosecution of Carlile for publishing the "Age of Reason," Mr. Fox expresses his regret that the first prosecution should have been conducted by a Unitarian. "Goaded," he says, "by the calumny which would identify them with those who yet reject the Saviour, they have, in repelling so unjust an accusation, caught too much of the tone of their opponents, and given the most undesirable proof of their affinity to other Christians by that unfairness towards the disbeliever which does not become any Christian." Ultimately Mr. Fox became the champion of all the principles of "The Age of Reason" and "The Rights of Man."

a martyr of the freedom bound up with the work he had assailed. Paine's other assailant, the Bishop of Llandaff, having bent before Pitt, and episcopally censured the humane side he once espoused, Gilbert Wakefield answered him with a boldness that brought on him two years' imprisonment. When he came out of prison (1801) he was received with enthusiasm by all of Paine's friends, who had forgotten the wrong so bravely atoned for. Had he not died in the same year, at the age of forty-five, Gilbert Wakefield might have become a standard-bearer of the freethinkers.

Paine's recovery after such prolonged and perilous suffering was a sort of resurrection. In April (1796) he leaves Monroe's house for the country, and with the returning life of nature his strength is steadily recovered. What to the man whose years of anguish, imprisonment, disease, at last pass away, must have been the paths and hedgerows of Versailles, where he now meets the springtide, and the more healing sunshine of affection! Risen from his thorny bed of pain—

> "The meanest floweret of the vale,
> The simplest note that swells the gale,
> The common sun, the air, the skies,
> To him are opening paradise."

So had it been even if nature alone had surrounded him. But Paine had been restored by the tenderness and devotion of friends. Had it not been for friendship he could hardly have been saved. We are little able, in the present day, to appreciate the reverence and affection with which Thomas Paine was regarded by those who saw in him the greatest apostle of liberty in the world. Elihu Palmer spoke a very general belief when he declared Paine " probably the most useful man that ever existed upon the face of the earth." This may sound wild enough on the ears of those to whom Liberty has become a familiar drudge. There was a time when she was an ideal Rachel, to win whom many years of terrible service were not too much ; but now in the garish day she is our prosaic Leah,—a serviceable creature in her way, but quite unromantic. In Paris there were ladies and gentlemen who had known something of the cost of Liberty,—Colonel and Mrs. Monroe, Sir Robert and Lady Smith, Madame Lafayette, Mr. and Mrs. Barlow, M. and Madame De Bonneville. They had known what it was to watch through anxious nights with terrors surrounding them. He who had suffered most was to them a sacred person. He had come out of the succession of ordeals, so weak in body, so wounded by American ingratitude, so sore at heart, that no delicate child needed more tender care. Set those ladies and their charge a thousand years back in the poetic past, and they become Morgan le Fay, and the Lady Nimue, who bear the wounded warrior away to their Avalon, there to be healed of his grievous hurts. Men say their Arthur is dead, but their love is stronger than death. And though the service of these friends might at first have been reverential, it had ended with attachment, so great was Paine's power, so wonderful and pathetic his memories, so charming the play of his wit, so full his response to kindness.

One especially great happiness awaited him when he became convalescent. Sir Robert Smith, a wealthy banker in Paris, made his acquaintance, and he discovered that Lady Smith was no other than "The Little Corner of the World," whose letters had carried sunbeams into his prison.[1] An intimate friendship was at once established with Sir Robert and his lady, in whose house, probably at Versailles, Paine was a guest after leaving the Monroes. To Lady Smith, on discovering her, Paine addressed a poem,—"The Castle in the Air to the Little Corner of the World":

> "In the region of clouds, where the whirlwinds arise,
>   My Castle of Fancy was built;
> The turrets reflected the blue from the skies,
>   And the windows with sunbeams were gilt.
>
> "The rainbow sometimes, in its beautiful state,
>   Enamelled the mansion around;
> And the figures that fancy in clouds can create
>   Supplied me with gardens and ground.
>
> "I had grottos, and fountains, and orange-tree groves,
>   I had all that enchantment has told;
> I had sweet shady walks for the gods and their loves,
>   I had mountains of coral and gold.
>
> "But a storm that I felt not had risen and rolled,
>   While wrapped in a slumber I lay;
> And when I looked out in the morning, behold,
>   My Castle was carried away.

---

[1] Sir Robert Smith (Smythe in the Peerage List) was born in 1744, and married, first, Miss Blake of London (1776). The name of the second Lady Smith, Paine's friend, before her marriage I have not ascertained.

"It passed over rivers and valleys and groves,
    The world it was all in my view ;
  I thought of my friends, of their fates, of their loves,
    And often, full often, of YOU.

"At length it came over a beautiful scene,
    That nature in silence had made ;
  The place was but small, but 't was sweetly serene,
    And chequered with sunshine and shade.

"I gazed and I envied with painful good will,
    And grew tired of my seat in the air ;
  When all of a sudden my Castle stood still,
    As if some attraction were there.

"Like a lark from the sky it came fluttering down,
    And placed me exactly in view,
  When whom should I meet in this charming retreat,
    This corner of calmness, but—YOU.

"Delighted to find you in honour and ease,
    I felt no more sorrow nor pain ;
  But the wind coming fair, I ascended the breeze,
    And went back with my Castle again."

Paine was now a happy man. The kindness that rescued him from death was followed by the friendship that beguiled him from horrors of the past. From gentle ladies he learned that beyond the Age of Reason lay the forces that defeat Giant Despair.

"To reason [so he writes to Lady Smith] against feelings is as vain as to reason against fire : it serves only to torture the torture, by adding reproach to horror. All reasoning with ourselves in such cases acts upon us like the reasoning of another person, which, however kindly done, serves but to insult the misery we suffer. If Reason could remove the pain, Reason would have prevented it. If she could not do the one, how is she to perform the other? In all such cases we must look upon Reason as dispossessed of her empire, by a revolt of the mind. She retires to a distance to weep, and the ebony sceptre of Despair rules alone. All that Reason can do is to suggest, to hint a thought, to signify a wish, to cast now and then a kind of bewailing look, to hold up, when she can catch the eye, the miniature shaded portrait of Hope; and though dethroned, and can dictate no more, to wait upon us in the humble station of a handmaid."

The mouth of the rescued and restored captive was filled with song. Several little poems were circulated among his friends, but not printed; among them the following:

"CONTENTMENT; OR, IF YOU PLEASE, CONFESSION. *To Mrs. Barlow, on her pleasantly telling the author that, after writing against the superstition of the Scripture religion, he was setting up a religion capable of more bigotry and enthusiasm, and more dangerous to its votaries—that of making a religion of Love.*

"O could we always live and love,
    And always be sincere,
I would not wish for heaven above,
    My heaven would be here.

"Though many countries I have seen,
    And more may chance to see,
My *Little Corner of the World*
    Is half the world to me.

"The other half, as you may guess,
    America contains;
And thus, between them, I possess
    The whole world for my pains.

"I'm then contented with my lot,
    I can no happier be;
For neither world I'm sure has got
    So rich a man as me.

"Then send no fiery chariot down
    To take me off from hence,
But leave me on my heavenly ground—
    This prayer is *common sense*.

"Let others choose another plan,
    I mean no fault to find ;
The true theology of man
    Is happiness of mind."

Paine gained great favor with the French government and fame throughout Europe by his pamphlet, "The Decline and Fall of the English System of Finance," in which he predicted the suspension of the Bank of England, which followed the next year. He dated the pamphlet April 8th, and the Minister of Foreign Affairs is shown, in the Archives of that office, to have ordered, on April 27th, a thousand copies. It was translated in all the languages of Europe, and was a terrible retribution for the forged assignats whose distribution in France the English government had considered a fair mode of warfare. This translation "into all the languages of the continent" is mentioned by Ralph Broome, to whom the British government entrusted the task of answering the pamphlet.[1] As Broome's answer is dated June 4th, this circulation in six or seven weeks is remarkable. The proceeds were devoted by Paine to the relief of prisoners for debt in Newgate, London.[2]

---

[1] "Observations on Mr. Paine's Pamphlet," etc. Broome escapes the charge of prejudice by speaking of "Mr. Paine, whose abilities I admire and deprecate in a breath." Paine's pamphlet was also replied to by George Chalmers ("Oldys") who had written the slanderous biography.

[2] Richard Carlile's sketch of Paine, p. 20. This large generosity to English sufferers appears the more characteristic beside the closing paragraph of

The concentration of this pamphlet on its immediate subject, which made it so effective, renders it of too little intrinsic interest in the present day to delay us long, especially as it is included in all editions of Paine's works. It possesses, however, much biographical interest as proving the intellectual power of Paine while still but a convalescent. He never wrote any work involving more study and mastery of difficult details. It was this pamphlet, written in Paris, while "Peter Porcupine," in America, was rewriting the slanders of "Oldys," which revolutionized Cobbett's opinion of Paine, and led him to try and undo the injustice he had wrought.

It now so turned out that Paine was able to repay all the kindnesses he had received. The relations between the French government and Monroe, already strained, as we have seen, became in the spring of 1796 almost intolerable. The Jay treaty seemed to the French so incredible that, even after it was ratified, they believed that the Representatives would refuse the appropriation needed for its execution. But when tidings came that this effort of the House of Representatives had been crushed by a menaced *coup d'état*, the ideal America fell in France, and was broken in

---

Paine's pamphlet, "As an individual citizen of America, and as far as an individual can go, I have revenged (if I may use the expression without any immoral meaning) the piratical depredations committed on American commerce by the English government. I have retaliated for France on the subject of finance: and I conclude with retorting on Mr. Pitt the expression he used against France, and say, that the English system of finance 'is on the verge, nay even in the gulf of bankruptcy.'"

Concerning the false French assignats forged in England, see Louis Blanc's "History of the Revolution," vol. xii., p. 101.

fragments. Monroe could now hardly have remained save on the credit of Paine with the French. There was, of course, a fresh accession of wrath towards England for this appropriation of the French alliance. Paine had been only the first sacrifice on the altar of the new alliance; now all English families and all Americans in Paris except himself were likely to become its victims. The English-speaking residents there made one little colony, and Paine was sponsor for them all. His fatal blow at English credit proved the formidable power of the man whom Washington had delivered up to Robespierre in the interest of Pitt. So Paine's popularity reached its climax; the American Legation found through him a *modus vivendi* with the French government; the families which had received and nursed him in his weakness found in his intimacy their best credential. Mrs. Joel Barlow especially, while her husband was in Algeria, on the service of the American government, might have found her stay in Paris unpleasant but for Paine's friendship. The importance of his guarantee to the banker, Sir Robert Smith, appears by the following note, written at Versailles, August 13th:

"CITIZEN MINISTER: The citizen Robert Smith, a very particular friend of mine, wishes to obtain a passport to go to Hamburg, and I will be obliged to you to do him that favor. Himself and family have lived several years in France, for he likes neither the government nor the climate of England. He has large property in England, but his Banker in that country has refused sending him remittances. This makes it necessary for him to go to Hamburg, because from there he can draw his money out of his Banker's hands, which he cannot do whilst in France. His family remains in France.—*Salut et fraternité*.

"THOMAS PAINE."[1]

Amid his circle of cultured and kindly friends Paine had dreamed of a lifting of the last cloud from his life, so long overcast. His eyes were strained to greet that shining sail that should bring him a response to his letter of September to Washington, in his heart being a great hope that his apparent wrong would be explained as a miserable mistake, and that old friendship restored. As the reader knows, the hope was grievously disappointed. The famous public letter to Washington (August 3d), which was not published in France, has already been considered, in advance of its chronological place. It will be found, however, of more significance if read in connection with the unhappy situation, in which all of Paine's friends, and all Americans in Paris, had been brought by the Jay treaty. From their point of view the deliverance of Paine to prison and the guillotine was only one incident in a long-planned and systematic treason, aimed at the life of the French republic. Jefferson in America, and Paine in France, represented the faith and hope of republicans that the treason would be overtaken by retribution and reversal.

[1] Soon after Jefferson became President Paine wrote to him, suggesting that Sir Robert's firm might be safely depended on as the medium of American financial transactions in Europe.

CHAPTER XIII.

THEOPHILANTHROPY.

In the ever-recurring controversies concerning Paine and his "Age of Reason" we have heard many triumphal claims. Christianity and the Church, it is said, have advanced and expanded, unharmed by such criticisms. This is true. But there are several fallacies implied in this mode of dealing with the religious movement caused by Paine's work. It assumes that Paine was an enemy of all that now passes under the name of Christianity—a title claimed by nearly a hundred and fifty different organizations, with some of which (as the Unitarians, Universalists, Broad Church, and Hicksite Friends) he would largely sympathize. It further assumes that he was hostile to all churches, and desired or anticipated their destruction. Such is not the fact. Paine desired and anticipated their reformation, which has steadily progressed. At the close of the "Age of Reason" he exhorts the clergy to "preach something that is edifying, and from texts that are known to be true."

"The Bible of the creation is inexhaustible in texts. Every part of science, whether connected with the geometry of the universe, with the systems of animal and vegetable life, or with the properties of inanimate matter, is a text for devotion as well as for philosophy—for gratitude as for human improvement. It will perhaps be said, that, if such a revolution in the system of religion takes place, every preacher ought to be a philosopher. *Most certainly.* And every house of devotion a school of science. It has been by wandering from the immutable laws of science, and the right use of reason, and setting up an invented thing called revealed religion, that so many wild and blasphemous conceits nave been formed of the Almighty. The Jews have made him the assassin of the human species, to make room for the religion of the Jews. The Christians have made him the murderer of himself, and the founder of a new religion, to supersede and expel the Jewish religion. And to find pretence and admission for these things they must have supposed his power and his wisdom imperfect, or his will changeable ; and the changeableness of the will is the imperfection of the judgment. The philosopher knows that the laws of the Creator have never changed with respect either to the principles of science, or the properties of matter. Why then is it to be supposed they have changed with respect to man ? "

To the statement that Christianity has not been impeded by the "Age of Reason," it should be added that its advance has been largely due to modifications rendered necessary by that work. The unmodified dogmas are represented in small and eccentric communities. The advance has been under the Christian name, with which Paine had no concern ; but to confuse the word "Christianity" with the substance it labels is inadmissible. England wears the device of St. George and the Dragon ; but English culture has reduced the saint and dragon to a fable.

The special wrath with which Paine is still visited, above all other deists put together, or even atheists, is a tradition from a so-called Christianity which his work compelled to capitulate. That system is now nearly extinct, and the *vendetta* it bequeathed should now end. The capitulation began immediately with the publication of the Bishop of Llandaff's "Apology for the Bible," a title that did not fail to attract notice when it appeared (1796). There were more than thirty replies to Paine, but they are mainly taken out of the Bishop's "Apology," to which they add nothing. It is said in religious encyclopedias that Paine was "answered" by one and another writer, but in a strict sense Paine was never answered, unless by the successive surrenders referred to. As Bishop Watson's "Apology" is adopted by most authorities as the sufficient "answer," it may be here accepted as a representative of the rest. Whether Paine's points dealt with by the Bishop are answerable or not, the following facts will prove how uncritical is the prevalent opinion that they were really answered.

Dr. Watson concedes generally to Paine the discovery of some "real difficulties" in the Old Testament, and the exposure, in the Christian grove, of "a few unsightly shrubs, which good men had wisely concealed from public view" (p. 44).[1] It is not Paine that here calls some "sacred" things unsightly, and charges the clergy with concealing them—it is the Bishop. Among the particular and direct concessions made by the Bishop are the following:

1. That Moses may not have written every part of the Pentateuch. Some passages were probably written by later hands, transcribers or editors (pp.

[1] Carey's edition, Philadelphia, 1796.

9-11, 15). [If human reason and scholarship are admitted to detach any portions, by what authority can they be denied the right to bring all parts of the Pentateuch, or even the whole Bible, under their human judgment?]

2. The law in Deuteronomy giving parents the right, under certain circumstances, to have their children stoned to death, is excused only as a "humane restriction of a power improper to be lodged with any parent" (p. 13). [Granting the Bishop's untrue assertion, that the same "improper" power was arbitrary among the Romans, Gauls, and Persians, why should it not have been abolished in Israel? And if Dr. Watson possessed the right to call any law established in the Bible "improper," how can Paine be denounced for subjecting other things in the book to moral condemnation? The moral sentiment is not an episcopal prerogative.]

3. The Bishop agrees that it is "the opinion of many learned men and good Christians" that the Bible, though authoritative in religion, is fallible in other respects, "relating the ordinary history of the times" (p. 23). [What but human reason, in the absence of papal authority, is to draw the line between the historical and religious elements in the Bible?]

4. It is conceded that "Samuel did not write any part of the second book bearing his name, and only a part of the first" (p. 24). [One of many blows dealt by this prelate at confidence in the Bible.]

5. It is admitted that Ezra contains a contradiction in the estimate of the numbers who returned from Babylon; it is attributed to a transcriber's

mistake of one Hebrew figure for another (p. 30). [Paine's question here had been: "What certainty then can there be in the Bible for anything"? It is no answer to tell him how an error involving a difference of 12,542 people may perhaps have occurred.]

5. It is admitted that David did not write some of the Psalms ascribed to him (p. 131).

7. "It is acknowledged that the order of time is not everywhere observed" [in Jeremiah]; also that this prophet, fearing for his life, suppressed the truth [as directed by King Zedekiah]. "He was under no obligation to tell the whole [truth] to men who were certainly his enemies and no good subjects of the king" (pp. 36, 37). [But how can it be determined how much in Jeremiah is the "word of God," and how much uttered for the casual advantage of himself or his king?]

8. It is admitted that there was no actual fulfilment of Ezekiel's prophecy, "No foot of man shall pass through it [Egypt], nor foot of beast shall pass through it, for forty years" (p. 42).

9. The discrepancies between the genealogies of Christ, in Matthew and Luke, are admitted: they are explained by saying that Matthew gives the genealogy of Joseph, and Luke that of Mary; and that Matthew commits "an error" in omitting three generations between Joram and Ozias (p. 48.) [Paine had asked, why might not writers mistaken in the natural genealogy of Christ be mistaken also in his celestial genealogy? To this no answer was attempted.]

Such are some of the Bishop's direct admissions.

There are other admissions in his silences and evasions. For instance, having elaborated a theory as to how the error in Ezra might occur, by the close resemblance of Hebrew letters representing widely different numbers, he does not notice Nehemiah's error in the same matter, pointed out by Paine,— a self-contradiction, and also a discrepancy with Ezra, which could not be explained by his theory. He says nothing about several other contradictions alluded to by Paine. The Bishop's evasions are sometimes painful, as when he tries to escape the force of Paine's argument, that Paul himself was not convinced by the evidences of the resurrection which he adduces for others. The Bishop says: "That Paul had so far resisted the evidence which the apostles had given of the resurrection and ascension of Jesus, as to be a persecutor of the disciples of Christ, is certain; but I do not remember the place where he declares that he had not believed them." But when Paul says, "I verily thought with myself that I ought to do many things contrary to the name of Jesus of Nazareth," surely this is inconsistent with his belief in the resurrection and ascension. Paul declares that when it was the good pleasure of God "to reveal his Son in me," immediately he entered on his mission. He "was not disobedient to the heavenly vision." Clearly then Paul had not been convinced of the resurrection and ascension until he saw Christ in a vision.

In dealing with Paine's moral charges against the Bible the Bishop has left a confirmation of all that I have said concerning the Christianity of his time. An "infidel" of to-day could need no better moral arguments against the Bible than those framed by the Bishop in its defence. He justifies the massacre of the Canaanites on the ground that they were sacrificers of their own children to idols, cannibals, addicted to unnatural lust. Were this true it would be no justification; but as no particle of evidence is adduced in support of these utterly unwarranted and entirely fictitious accusations, the argument now leaves the massacre without any excuse at all. The extermination is not in the Bible based on any such considerations, but simply on a divine command to seize the land and slay its inhabitants. No legal right to the land is suggested in the record; and, as for morality, the only persons spared in Joshua's expedition were a harlot and her household, she having betrayed her country to the invaders, to be afterwards exalted into an ancestress of Christ. Of the cities destroyed by Joshua it is said: "It was of Jehovah to harden their hearts, to come against Israel in battle, that he might utterly destroy them, that they might have no favor, but that he might destroy them, as Jehovah commanded Moses" (Joshua xi., 20). As their hearts were thus in Jehovah's power for hardening, it may be inferred that they were equally in his power for reformation, had they been guilty of the things alleged by the Bishop. With these things before him, and the selection of Rahab for mercy above all the women in Jericho—every woman slain save the harlot who delivered them up to slaughter—the Bishop says: "The destruction of the Canaanites exhibits to all nations, in all ages, a signal proof of God's displeasure against sin."

The Bishop rages against Paine for supposing that the commanded preservation of the Midianite maidens, when all males and married women were slain, was for their " debauchery."

> "Prove this, and I will allow that Moses was the horrid monster you make him—prove this, and I will allow that the Bible is what you call it—'a book of lies, wickedness, and blasphemy'—prove this, or excuse my warmth if I say to you, as Paul said to Elymas the sorcerer, who sought to turn away Sergius Paulus from the faith, ' O full of all subtilty, and of all mischief, thou child of the devil, thou enemy of all righteousness, wilt thou not cease to pervert the right ways of the Lord?'—I did not, when I began these letters, think that I should have been moved to this severity of rebuke, by anything you could have written; but when so gross a misrepresentation is made of God's proceedings, coolness would be a crime."

And what does my reader suppose is the alternative claimed by the prelate's foaming mouth? The maidens, he declares, were not reserved for debauchery, but for slavery!

Little did the Bishop foresee a time when, of the two suppositions, Paine's might be deemed the more lenient. The subject of slavery was then under discussion in England, and the Bishop is constrained to add, concerning this enslavement of thirty-two thousand maidens, from the massacred families, that slavery is "a custom abhorrent from our manners, but everywhere practised in former times, and still practised in countries where the benignity of the Christian religion has not softened the ferocity of human nature." Thus, Jehovah is represented as not only ordering the wholesale murder of the worshippers of another deity, but an adoption of their "abhorrent" and inhuman customs.

This connection of the deity of the Bible with "the ferocity of human nature" in one place, and its softening in another, justified Paine's solemn rebuke to the clergy of his time.

"Had the cruel and murderous orders with which the Bible is filled, and the numberless torturing executions of men, women, and children, in consequence of those orders, been ascribed to some friend whose memory you revered, you would have glowed with satisfaction at detecting the falsehood of the charge, and gloried in defending his injured fame. It is because ye are sunk in the cruelty of superstition, or feel no interest in the honor of your Creator, that ye listen to the horrid tales of the Bible, or hear them with callous indifference."

This is fundamentally what the Bishop has to answer, and of course he must resort to the terrible *Tu quoque* of Bishop Butler. Dr. Watson says he is astonished that "so acute a reasoner" should reproduce the argument.

"You profess yourself to be a deist, and to believe that there is a God, who created the universe, and established the laws of nature, by which it is sustained in existence. You profess that from a contemplation of the works of God you derive a knowledge of his attributes; and you reject the Bible because it ascribes to God things inconsistent (as you suppose) with the attributes which you have discovered to belong to him; in particular, you think it repugnant to his moral justice that he should doom to destruction the crying and smiling infants of the Canaanites. Why do you not maintain it to be repugnant to his moral justice that he should suffer crying or smiling infants to be swallowed up by an earthquake, drowned by an inundation, consumed by fire, starved by a famine, or destroyed by a pestilence?"

Dr. Watson did not, of course, know that he was following Bishop Butler in laying the foundations of atheism, though such was the case. As was said in my chapter on the "Age of Reason," this dilemma did not really apply to Paine. His deity was inferred, despite all the disorders in nature, exclusively from its apprehensible order without, and from the reason and moral nature of man. He had not dealt with the problem of evil, except implicitly, in his defence of the divine goodness, which is inconsistent with the responsibility of his deity for natural evils, or for anything that would be condemned by reason and conscience if done by man. It was thus the Christian prelate who had abandoned the primitive faith in the divine humanity for a natural deism, while the man he calls a "child of the devil" was defending the divine humanity.

This then was the way in which Paine was "answered," for I am not aware of any important addition to the Bishop's "Apology" by other opponents. I cannot see how any Christian of the present time can regard it otherwise than as a capitulation of the system it was supposed to defend, however secure he may regard the Christianity of to-day. It subjects the Bible to the judgment of human reason for the determination of its authorship, the integrity of its text, and the correction of admitted errors in authorship, chronology, and genealogy; it admits the fallibility of the writers in matters of fact; it admits that some of the moral laws of the Old Testament are "improper" and others, like slavery, belonging to "the ferocity of human nature"; it admits the non-fulfilment of one prophet's prediction, and the self-interested suppression of truth by another; and it admits that "good men" were engaged in concealing these "unsightly" things. Here are gates thrown open for the whole "Age of Reason."

The unorthodoxy of the Bishop's "Apology" does not rest on the judgment of the present writer alone. If Gilbert Wakefield presently had to reflect on his denunciations of Paine from the inside of a prison, the Bishop of Llandaff had occasion to appreciate Paine's ideas on "mental lying" as the Christian infidelity. The Bishop, born in the same year (1737) with the two heretics he attacked—Gibbon and Paine—began his career as a professor of chemistry at Cambridge (1764), but seven years later became Regius professor of divinity there. His posthumous papers present a remarkable picture of the church in his time. In replying to Gibbon he studied first principles, and assumed a brave stand against all intellectual and religious coercion. On the episcopal bench he advocated a liberal policy toward France. In undertaking to answer Paine he became himself unsettled; and at the very moment when unsophisticated orthodoxy was hailing him as its champion, the sagacious magnates of Church and State proscribed him. He learned that the king had described him as "impracticable"; with bitterness of soul he saw prelates of inferior rank and ability promoted over his head. He tried the effect of a political recantation, in one of his charges; and when Williams was imprisoned for publishing the "Age of Reason," and Gilbert Wakefield for rebuking his "Charge," this former champion of free speech dared not utter a protest. But by this servility he gained nothing. He seems to have at length made up his mind that if he was to be punished for his liberalism he would enjoy it. While preaching on "Revealed Religion" he saw the Bishop of London shaking his head. In 1811, five years before his death, he writes this significant note: "I have treated my divinity as I, twenty-five years ago, treated my chemical papers: I have lighted my fire with the labour of a great portion of my life."[1]

Next to the "Age of Reason," the book that did most to advance Paine's principles in England was, as I believe, Dr. Watson's "Apology for the Bible." Dean Swift had warned the clergy that if they began to reason with objectors to the creeds they would awaken skepticism. Dr. Watson fulfilled this prediction. He pointed out, as Gilbert Wakefield did, some exegetical and verbal errors in Paine's book, but they no more affected its main purpose and argument than the grammatical mistakes in "Common Sense" diminished its force in the American Revolution. David Dale, the great manu-

[1] Patrick Henry's Answer to the "Age of Reason" shared the like fate. "When, during the first two years of his retirement, Thomas Paine's 'Age of Reason' made its appearance, the old statesman was moved to write out a somewhat elaborate treatise in defence of the truth of Christianity. This treatise it was his purpose to have published. 'He read the manuscript to his family as he progressed with it, and completed it a short time before his death' [1799]. When it was finished, however, 'being diffident about his own work,' and impressed also by the great ability of the replies to Paine which were then appearing in England, 'he directed his wife to destroy' what he had written. She 'complied literally with his directions,' and thus put beyond the chance of publication a work which seemed, to some who heard it, 'the most eloquent and unanswerable argument in defence of the Bible which was ever written.'"—Fontaine MS. quoted in Tyler's "Patrick Henry."

facturer at Paisley, distributed three thousand copies of the "Apology" among his workmen. The books carried among them extracts from Paine, and the Bishop's admissions. Robert Owen married Dale's daughter, and presently found the Paisley workmen a ripe harvest for his rationalism and radicalism.

Thus, in the person of its first clerical assailant, began the march of the "Age of Reason" in England. In the Bishop's humiliations for his concessions to truth, were illustrated what Paine had said of his system's falsity and fraudulence. After the Bishop had observed the Bishop of London manifesting disapproval of his sermon on "Revealed Religion" he went home and wrote: "What is this thing called Orthodoxy, which mars the fortunes of honest men? It is a sacred thing to which every denomination of Christians lays exclusive claim, but to which no man, no assembly of men, since the apostolic age, can prove a title." There is now a Bishop of London who might not acknowledge the claim even for the apostolic age. The principles, apart from the particular criticisms, of Paine's book have established themselves in the English Church. They were affirmed by Bishop Wilson in clear language: "Christian duties are founded on reason, not on the sovereignty of God commanding what he pleases: God cannot command us what is not fit to be believed or done, all his commands being founded in the necessities of our nature." It was on this principle that Paine declared that things in the Bible, "not fit to be believed or done," could not be divine commands.

His book, like its author, was outlawed, but men more heretical are now buried in Westminster Abbey, and the lost bones of Thomas Paine are really reposing in those tombs. It was he who compelled the hard and heartless Bibliolatry of his time to repair to illiterate conventicles, and the lovers of humanity, true followers of the man of Nazareth, to abandon the crumbling castle of dogma, preserving its creeds as archaic bric-a-brac. As his " Rights of Man " is now the political constitution of England, his " Age of Reason " is in the growing constitution of its Church,—the most powerful organization in Christendom because the freest and most inclusive.

The excitement caused in England by the "Age of Reason," and the large number of attempted replies to it, were duly remarked by the *Moniteur* and other French journals. The book awakened much attention in France, and its principles were reproduced in a little French book entitled " A Manual of the Theoantropophiles." This appeared in September, 1796. In January, 1797, Paine, with five families, founded in Paris the church of Theophilanthropy,—a word, as he stated in a letter to Erskine " compounded of three Greek words, signifying God, Love, and Man. The explanation given to this word is *Lovers of God and Man*, or *Adorers of God and Friends of Man.*" The society opened "in the street Denis, No. 34, corner of Lombard Street." " The Theophilanthropists believe in the existence of God, and the immortality of the soul." The inaugural discourse was given by Paine. It opens with these words : " Religion has two principal enemies, Fanaticism and Infidelity, or that which is called atheism. The first requires to be combated by reason and morality, the other by natural philosophy." The discourse is chiefly an argument for a divine existence based on motion, which, he maintains, is not a property of matter. It proves a Being "at the summit of all things." At the close he says:

"The society is at present in its infancy, and its means are small; but I wish to hold in view the subject I allude to, and instead of teaching the philosophical branches of learning as ornamental branches only, as they have hitherto been taught, to teach them in a manner that shall combine theological knowledge with scientific instruction. To do this to the best advantage, some instruments will be necessary for the purpose of explanation, of which the society is not yet possessed. But as the views of the Society extend to public good, as well as to that of the individual, and as its principles can have no enemies, means may be devised to procure them. If we unite to the present instruction a series of lectures on the ground I have mentioned, we shall, in the first place, render theology the most entertaining of all studies. In the next place, we shall give scientific instruction to those who could not otherwise obtain it. The mechanic of every profession will there be taught the mathematical principles necessary to render him proficient in his art. The cultivator will there see developed the principles of vegetation; while, at the same time, they will be led to see the hand of God in all these things."

A volume of 214 pages put forth at the close of the year shows that the Theophilanthropists sang theistic and humanitarian hymns, and read Odes; also that ethical readings were introduced from the Bible, and from the Chinese, Hindu, and Greek authors. A library was established ("rue Neuve-Etienne-l'Estrapade, No. 25) at which was issued (1797), "Instruction Élémentaire sur la

Morale religieuse,"—this being declared to be morality based on religion.

Thus Paine, pioneer in many things, helped to found the first theistic and ethical society.

It may now be recognized as a foundation of the Religion of Humanity. It was a great point with Paine that belief in the divine existence was the one doctrine common to all religions. On this rock the Church of Man was to be built. Having vainly endeavored to found the international Republic he must repair to an ideal moral and human world. Robespierre and Pitt being unfraternal he will bring into harmony the sages of all races. It is a notable instance of Paine's unwillingness to bring a personal grievance into the sacred presence of Humanity that one of the four festivals of Theophilanthropy was in honor of Washington, while its catholicity was represented in a like honor to St. Vincent de Paul. The others so honored were Socrates and Rousseau. These selections were no doubt mainly due to the French members, but they could hardly have been made without Paine's agreement. It is creditable to them all that, at a time when France believed itself wronged by Washington, his services to liberty should alone have been remembered. The flowers of all races, as represented in literature or in history, found emblematic association with the divine life in nature through the flowers that were heaped on a simple altar, as they now are in many churches and chapels. The walls were decorated with ethical mottoes, enjoining domestic kindness and public benevolence.

Paine's pamphlet of this year (1797) on "Agrarian Justice" should be considered part of the theophilanthropic movement. It was written as a proposal to the French government, at a time when readjustment of landed property had been rendered necessary by the Revolution.[1] It was suggested by a sermon printed by the Bishop of Llandaff, on "The wisdom and goodness of God in having made both rich and poor." Paine denies that God made rich and poor: "he made only male and female, and gave them the earth for their inheritance." The earth, though naturally the equal possession of all, has been necessarily appropriated by individuals, because their improvements, which alone render its productiveness adequate to human needs, cannot be detached from the soil. Paine maintains that these private owners do nevertheless owe mankind ground-rent. He therefore proposes a tithe,—not for God, but for man. He advises that at the time when the owner will feel it least,—when property is passing by inheritance from one to another,—the tithe shall be taken from it. Personal property also owes a debt to society, without which wealth could not exist,—as in the case of one alone on an island. By a careful estimate he estimates that a tithe on inheritances would give every person, on reaching majority, fifteen pounds, and after the age of fifty an annuity of ten pounds, leaving a substantial surplus for charity. The practical scheme submitted is enforced by practical rather than theoretical con-

[1] "Thomas Payne à la Législature et au Directoire : ou la Justice Agraire Opposée à la Loi et aux Privilèges Agraires."

siderations. Property is always imperilled by poverty, especially where wealth and splendor have lost their old fascinations, and awaken emotions of disgust.

"To remove the danger it is necessary to remove the antipathies, and this can only be done by making property productive of a national blessing, extending to every individual. When the riches of one man above another shall increase the national fund in the same proportion; when it shall be seen that the prosperity of that fund depends on the prosperity of individuals; when the more riches a man acquires, the better it shall be for the general mass; it is then that antipathies will cease, and property be placed on the permanent basis of national interest and protection.

"I have no property in France to become subject to the plan I propose. What I have, which is not much, is in the United States of America. But I will pay one hundred pounds sterling towards this fund in France, the instant it shall be established; and I will pay the same sum in England, whenever a similar establishment shall take place in that country."

The tithe was to be given to rich and poor alike, including owners of the property tithed, in order that there should be no association of alms with this "agrarian justice."

About this time the priesthood began to raise their heads again. A report favorable to a restoration to them of the churches, the raising of bells, and some national recognition of public worship, was made by Camille Jordan for a committee on the subject. The jesuitical report was especially poetical about church bells, which Paine knew would ring the knell of the Republic. He wrote a theophilanthropic letter to Camille Jordan, from which I quote some paragraphs.

"You claim a privilege incompatible with the Constitution, and with Rights. The Constitution protects equally, as it ought to do, every profession of religion ; it gives no exclusive privilege to any. The churches are the common property of all the people ; they are national goods, and cannot be given exclusively to any one profession, because the right does not exist of giving to any one that which appertains to all. It would be consistent with right that the churches should be sold, and the money arising therefrom be invested as a fund for the education of children of poor parents of every profession, and, if more than sufficient for this purpose, that the surplus be appropriated to the support of the aged poor. After this every profession can erect its own place of worship, if it choose—support its own priests, if it choose to have any— or perform its worship without priests, as the Quakers do."

"It is a want of feeling to talk of priests and bells whilst so many infants are perishing in the hospitals, and aged and infirm poor in the streets. The abundance that France possesses is sufficient for every want, if rightly applied ; but priests and bells, like articles of luxury, ought to be the least articles of consideration."

"No man ought to make a living by religion. It is dishonest to do so. Religion is not an act that can be performed by proxy. One person cannot act religion for another. Every person must perform it for himself ; and all that a priest can do is to take from him ; he wants nothing but his money, and then to riot in the spoil and laugh at his credulity. The only people who, as a professional sect of Christians, provide for the poor of their society, are people known by the name of Quakers. These men have no priests. They assemble quietly in their places of worship, and do not disturb their neighbors with shows and noise of bells. Religion does not unite itself to show and noise. True religion is without either.'

"One good schoolmaster is of more use than a hundred priests. If we look back at what was the condition of France under the *ancien régime*, we cannot acquit the priests of corrupting the morals of the nation."

"Why has the Revolution of France been stained with crimes, while the Revolution of the United States of America was not? Men are physically the same in all countries; it is education that makes them different. Accustom a people to believe that priests, or any other class of men, can forgive sins, and you will have sins in abundance."

While Thomas Paine was thus founding in Paris a religion of love to God expressed in love to man, his enemies in England were illustrating by characteristic fruits the dogmas based on a human sacrifice. The ascendency of the priesthood of one church over others, which he was resisting in France, was exemplified across the channel in the prosecution of his publisher, and the confiscation of a thousand pounds which had somehow fallen due to Paine.[1] The "Age of Reason," amply advertised by its opponents, had reached a vast circulation, and a prosecution of its publisher, Thomas Williams, for blasphemy, was instituted in the King's Bench. Williams being a poor man, the defence was sustained by a subscription.[2] The trial occurred June 24th. The extent to which the English reign of terror had gone was shown in the fact that Erskine was now the prosecutor; he who five years before had defended the "Rights of Man," who had left the court in a carriage drawn by the people, now stood in the same room to assail the most sacred of rights. He began with a menace to the

[1] This loss, mentioned by Paine in a private note, occurred about the time when he had devoted the proceeds of his pamphlet on English Finance, a very large sum, to prisoners held for debt in Newgate. I suppose the thousand pounds were the proceeds of the "Age of Reason."

[2] "Subscriptions (says his circular) will be received by J. Ashley, Shoemaker, No. 6 High Holborn; C. Cooper, Grocer, New Compton-st., Soho; G. Wilkinson, Printer, No. 115 Shoreditch; J. Rhynd, Printer, Ray-st., Clerkenwell; R. Hodgson, Hatter, No. 29 Brook-st., Holborn." It will be observed that the defence of free printing had fallen to humble people.

defendant's counsel (S. Kyd) on account of a notice served on the prosecution, foreshadowing a search into the Scriptures.[1] "No man," he cried, "deserves to be upon the Rolls of the Court who dares, as an Attorney, to put his name to such a notice. It is an insult to the authority and dignity of the Court of which he is an officer; since it seems to call in question the very foundations of its jurisdiction." So soon did Erskine point the satire of the fable he quoted from Lucian, in Paine's defence, of Jupiter answering arguments with thunderbolts. Erskine's argument was that the King had taken a solemn oath "to maintain the Christian Religion as it is promulgated by God in the Holy Scriptures." "Every man has a right to investigate, with modesty and decency, controversial points of the Christian religion; but no man, consistently with a law which only exists under its sanction, has a right not only broadly to deny its very existence, but to pour forth a shocking and insulting invective, etc." The law, he said, permits, by a like principle, the intercourse between the sexes to be set forth in plays and novels, but punishes such as "address the imagination in a manner to lead the passions into dangerous excesses." Erskine read several passages from the "Age of Reason," which, their main point being omitted, seemed mere aimless abuse. In his speech, he quoted as Paine's words of his own collocation,

[1] "The King v. Thomas Williams for Blasphemy.—Take notice that the Prosecutors of the Indictment against the above named Defendant will upon the Trial of this cause be required to produce a certain Book described in the said Indictment to be the Holy Bible.—John Martin, Solicitor for the Defendant. Dated the 17th day of June 1797."

representing the author as saying, "The Bible teaches nothing but 'lies, obscenity, cruelty, and injustice.'" This is his entire and inaccurate rendering of what Paine,—who always distinguishes the "Bible" from the "New Testament,"—says at the close of his comment on the massacre of the Midianites and appropriation of their maidens:

"People in general know not what wickedness there is in this pretended word of God. Brought up in habits of superstition, they take it for granted that the Bible [Old Testament] is true, and that it is good; they permit themselves not to doubt it; and they carry the ideas they form of the benevolence of the Almighty to the book they have been taught to believe was written by his authority. Good heavens! it is quite another thing! it is a book of lies, wickedness, and blasphemy; for what can be greater blasphemy than to ascribe the wickedness of man to the orders of the Almighty?"

Erskine argued that the sanction of Law was the oath by which judges, juries, witnesses administered law and justice under a belief in "the revelation of the unutterable blessings which shall attend their observances, and the awful punishments which shall await upon their transgressions." The rest of his opening argument was, mainly, that great men had believed in Christianity.

Mr. Kyd, in replying, quoted from the Bishop of Llandaff's "Answer to Gibbon": "I look upon the right of private judgment, in every respect concerning God and ourselves, as superior to the control of human authority"; and his claim that the Church of England is distinguished from Mahometanism and Romanism by its permission of every man to utter his opinion freely. He also cites Dr. Lardner, and

Dr. Waddington, the Bishop of Chichester, who declared that Woolston "ought not to be punished for being an infidel, nor for writing against the Christian religion." He quoted Paine's profession of faith on the first page of the incriminated book: "I believe in one God and no more; I hope for happiness, beyond this life; I believe in the equality of men, and I believe that religious duties consist in doing justice, loving mercy, and endeavouring to make our fellow creatures happy." He also quoted Paine's homage to the character of Jesus. He defied the prosecution to find in the "Age of Reason" a single passage "inconsistent with the most chaste, the most correct system of morals," and declared the very passages selected for indictment pleas against obscenity and cruelty. Mr. Kyd pointed out fourteen narratives in the Bible (such as Sarah giving Hagar to Abraham, Lot and his daughters, etc.) which, if found in any other book, would be pronounced obscene. He was about to enumerate instances of cruelty when the judge, Lord Kenyon, indignantly interrupted him, and with consent of the jury said he could only allow him to cite such passages without reading them. (Mr. Kyd gratefully acknowledged this release from the "painful task" of reading such horrors from the "Word of God"!) One of the interesting things about this trial was the disclosure of the general reliance on Butler's "Analogy," used by Bishop Watson in his reply to Paine,—namely, that the cruelties objected to in the God of the Bible are equally found in nature, through which deists look up to their God. When Kyd, after quoting from Bishop Watson, said, "Gentlemen, observe the weakness of this answer," Lord Kenyon exclaimed: "I cannot sit in this place and hear this kind of discussion." Kyd said: "My Lord, I stand here on the privilege of an advocate in an English Court of Justice: this man has applied to me to defend him; I have undertaken his defence; and I have often heard your Lordship declare, that every man had a right to be defended. I know no other mode by which I can seriously defend him against this charge, than that which I am now pursuing; if your Lordship wish to prevent me from pursuing it, you may as well tell me to abandon my duty to my client at once." Lord Kenyon said: "Go on, Sir." Returning to the analogy of the divinely ordered massacres in the Bible with the like in nature, Kyd said:

"Gentlemen, this is reasoning by comparison; and reasoning by comparison is often fallacious. On the present occasion the fallacy is this: that, in the first case, the persons perish by the operation of the general laws of nature, not suffering punishment for a crime; whereas, in the latter, the general laws of nature are suspended or transgressed, and God commands the slaughter to avenge his offended will. Is this then a satisfactory answer to the objection? I think it is not; another may think so too; which it may be fairly supposed the Author did; and then the objection, as to him, remains in full force, and he cannot, from insisting upon it, be fairly accused of malevolent intention."

In his answer Erskine said: "The history of man is the history of man's vices and passions, which could not be censured without adverting to their existence; many of the instances that have been referred to were recorded as memorable warnings and examples for the instruction of mankind." But for this argument Erskine was indebted to his old client, Paine, who did not argue against the things being recorded, but against the belief "that the inhuman and horrid butcheries of men, women, and children, told of in those books, were done, as those books say they were done, at the command of God." Paine says: "Those accounts are nothing to us, nor to any other persons, unless it be to the Jews, as a part of the history of their nation; and there is just as much of the word of God in those books as there is in any of the histories of France, or Rapin's 'History of England,' or the history of any other country."

As in Paine's own trial in 1792, the infallible scheme of a special jury was used against Williams. Lord Kenyon closed his charge with the words: "Unless it was for the most malignant purposes, I cannot conceive how it was published. It is, however, for you to judge of it, and to do justice between the Public and the Defendant."

"The jury instantly found the Defendant—Guilty."

Paine at once wrote a letter to Erskine, which was first printed in Paris. He calls attention to the injustice of the special jury system, in which all the jurymen are nominated by the crown. In London a special jury generally consists of merchants. "Talk to some London merchants about scripture, and they will understand you mean scrip, and tell you how much it is worth at the Stock Exchange. Ask them about Theology, and they will say they know no such gentleman upon 'Change." He also declares that Lord Kenyon's course in preventing Mr. Kyd from reading passages from the Bible was irregular, and contrary to words, which he cites, used by the same judge in another case.

This Letter to Erskine contains some effective passages. In one of these he points out the sophistical character of the indictment in declaring the "Age of Reason" a blasphemous work, tending to bring in contempt the holy scriptures. The charge should have stated that the work was intended to prove certain books not the holy scriptures. "It is one thing if I ridicule a work as being written by a certain person; but it is quite a different thing if I write to prove that such a work was not written by such person. In the first case I attack the person through the work; in the other case I defend the honour of the person against the work." After alluding to the two accounts in Genesis of the creation of man, according to one of which there was no Garden of Eden and no forbidden tree, Paine says :

"Perhaps I shall be told in the cant language of the day, as I have often been told by the Bishop of Llandaff and others, of the great and laudable pains that many pious and learned men have taken to explain the obscure, and reconcile the contradictory, or, as they say, the seemingly contradictory passages of the Bible. It is because the Bible needs such an undertaking, that is one of the first causes to suspect it is *not* the word of God : this single reflection, when carried home to the mind, is in itself a volume. What ! does not the Creator of the Universe, the Fountain of all Wisdom, the Origin of all Science, the Author of all Knowledge, the God of Order and of Harmony, know how to write ? When we contemplate the vast economy of the creation, when we behold the unerring regularity of the visible solar system, the perfection with which all its several parts revolve, and by corresponding assemblage form a whole;—when we launch our eye into the boundless ocean of space, and see ourselves surrounded by innumerable worlds, not one of which varies from its appointed place—when we trace the power of a Creator, from a mite to an elephant, from an atom to an universe, can we suppose that the mind [which] could conceive such a design, and the power that executed it with incomparable perfection, cannot write without inconsistence; or that a book so written can be the work of such a power? The writings of Thomas Paine, even of Thomas Paine, need no commentator to explain, compound, arrange, and re-arrange their several parts, to render them intelligible—he can relate a fact, or write an essay, without forgetting in one page what he has written in another; certainly then, did the God of all perfection condescend to write or dictate a book, that book would be as perfect as himself is perfect: The Bible is not so, and it is confessedly not so, by the attempts to mend it."

Paine admonishes Erskine that a prosecution to preserve God's word, were it really God's word, would be like a prosecution to prevent the sun from falling out of heaven; also that he should be able to comprehend that the motives of those who declare the Bible not God's word are religious. He then gives him an account of the new church of Theophilanthropists in Paris, and appends his discourse before that society.

In the following year, Paine's discourse to the Theophilanthropists was separately printed by Clio Rickman, with a sentence from Shakespeare in the title-page: "I had as lief have the foppery of freedom as the morality of imprisonment." There was also the following dedication:

"The following little Discourse is dedicated to the enemies of Thomas Paine, by one who has known him long and intimately, and who is convinced that he is the enemy of no man. It is printed to do good, by a well wisher to the world. By one who thinks that discussion should be unlimited, that all coercion is error; and that human beings should adopt no other conduct towards each other but an appeal to truth and reason."

Paine wrote privately, in the same sense as to Erskine, to his remonstrating friends. In one such letter (May 12th) he goes again partly over the ground. "You," he says, "believe in the Bible from the accident of birth, and the Turks believe in the Koran from the same accident, and each calls the other *infidel*. This answer to your letter is not written for the purpose of changing your opinion. It is written to satisfy you, and some other friends whom I esteem, that my disbelief of the Bible is founded on a pure and religious belief in God." "All are infidels who believe falsely of God." "Belief in a cruel God makes a cruel man."

Paine had for some time been attaining unique fame in England. Some publisher had found it worth while to issue a book, entitled "Tom Paine's Jests: Being an entirely new and select Collection of Patriotic Bon Mots, Repartees, Anecdotes, Epigrams, &c., on Political Subjects. By Thomas Paine." There are hardly a half dozen items by Paine in the book (72 pages), which shows that his name was considered marketable. The government had made the author a cause. Erskine, who had lost his office as Attorney-General for the Prince of Wales by becoming Paine's counsel in 1792, was at once taken back into favor after prosecuting the "Age of Reason," and put on his way to become Lord Erskine. The imprisonment of Williams caused a reaction in the minds of those who had turned against Paine. Christianity suffered under royal patronage. The terror manifested at the name of Paine—some were arrested even for showing his portrait—was felt to be political. None of the aristocratic deists, who wrote for the upper classes, were dealt with in the same way. Paine had proclaimed from the housetops what, as Dr. Watson confessed, scholars were whispering in the ear. There were lampoons of Paine, such as those of Peter Pindar (Rev. John Wolcott), but they only served to whet popular curiosity concerning him.[1] The "Age of Reason" had passed through several editions before it was outlawed, and every copy of it passed through many hands. From the prosecution and imprisonment of Williams may be dated the consolidation of the movement for the "Rights of Man," with antagonism to the kind of Christianity which that injustice illustrated. Political liberalism and heresy thenceforth progressed in England, hand in hand.

[1] "I have preserved," says Royall Tyler, "an epigram of Peter Pindar's, written originally in a blank leaf of a copy of Paine's 'Age of Reason,' and not inserted in any of his works.

> "'Tommy Paine wrote this book to prove that the bible
> Was an old woman's dream of fancies most idle;
> That Solomon's proverbs were made by low livers,
> That prophets were fellows who sang semiquavers;
> That religion and miracles all were a jest,
> And the devil in torment a tale of the priest.
> Though Beelzebub's absence from hell I'll maintain,
> Yet we all must allow that the Devil's in Paine.'"

CHAPTER XIV.

THE REPUBLICAN ABDIEL.

THE sight of James Monroe and Thomas Paine in France, representing Republican America, was more than Gouverneur Morris could stand. He sent to Washington the abominable slander of Monroe already quoted (ii., p. 173), and the Minister's recall came at the close of 1796.[1] Monroe could not sail in midwinter with his family, so they remained until the following spring. Paine made preparations to return to America with them, and accompanied them to Havre; but he found so many "british frigates cruising in sight" (so he writes Jefferson) that he did not "trust [himself] to their discretion, and the more so as [he] had no confidence in the Captain of the Dublin Packet." Sure enough this Captain Clay was friendly enough

[1] This sudden recall involved Monroe in heavy expenses, which Congress afterwards repaid. I am indebted to Mr. Frederick McGuire, of Washington, for the manuscript of Monroe's statement of his expenses and annoyances caused by his recall, which he declares due to "the representations which were made to him [Washington] by those in whom he confided." He states that Paine remained in his house a year and a half, and that he advanced him 250 louis d'or. For these services to Paine, he adds, "no claims were ever presented on my part, nor is any indemnity now desired." This money was repaid ($1,188) to Monroe by an Act of Congress, April 7, 1831. The advances are stated in the Act to have been made "from time to time," and were no doubt regarded by both Paine and Monroe as compensated by the many services rendered by the author to the Legation.

with the British cruiser which lay in wait to catch Paine, but only succeeded in finding his letter to Jefferson. Before returning from Havre to Paris he wrote another letter to Vice-President Jefferson.

"HAVRE, May 14th, 1797.

"DEAR SIR,—I wrote to you by the Ship Dublin Packet, Captain Clay, mentioning my intention to have returned to America by that Vessel, and to have suggested to some Member of the House of Representatives the propriety of calling Mr. Monroe before them to have enquired into the state of their affairs in France. This might have laid the foundation for some resolves on their part that might have led to an accomodation with France, for that House is the only part of the American Government that have any reputation here. I apprised Mr. Monroe of my design, and he wishes to be called up.

"You will have heard before this reaches you that the Emperor has been obliged to sue for peace, and to consent to the establishment of the new republic in Lombardy. How France will proceed with respect to England, I am not, at this distance from Paris, in the way of knowing, but am inclined to think she meditates a descent upon that Country, and a revolution in its Government. If this should be the plan, it will keep me in Europe at least another year.

"As the british party has thrown the American commerce into wretched confusion, it is necessary to pay more attention to the appointment of Consuls in the ports of france, than there was occasion to do in time of peace; especially as there is now no Minister, and Mr. Skipwith, who stood well with the Government here, has resigned. Mr. Cutting, the Consul for Havre, does not reside at it, and the business is altogether in the hands of De la Motte, the Vice Consul, who is a frenchman, [and] cannot have the full authority proper for the office in the difficult state matters are now in. I do not mention this to the disadvantage of Mr. Cutting, for no man is more proper than himself if he thought it an object to attend to.

"I know not if you are acquainted with Captain Johnson of Massachusetts—he is a staunch man and one of the oldest

American Captains in the American employ. He is now settled at Havre and is a more proper man for a Vice Consul than La Motte. You can learn his character from Mr. Monroe. He has written to some of his friends to have the appointment and if you can see an opportunity of throwing in a little service for him, you will do a good thing. We have had several reports of Mr. Madison's coming. He would be well received as an individual, but as an Envoy of John Adams he could do nothing.

"THOMAS PAINE."

The following, in Paine's handwriting, is copied from the original in the Morrison papers, at the British Museum. It was written in the summer of 1797, when Lord Malmsbury was at Lille in negotiation for peace. The negotiations were broken off because the English commissioners were unauthorized to make the demanded restorations to Holland and Spain. Paine's essay was no doubt sent to the Directory in the interests of peace, suggesting as it does a compromise, as regards the Cape of Good Hope.

"CAPE OF GOOD HOPE.—It is very well known that Dundas, the English Minister for Indian affairs, is tenacious of holding the Cape of Good Hope, because it will give to the English East India Company a monopoly of the commerce of India; and this, on the other hand, is the very reason that such a claim is inadmissible by France, and by all the nations trading in India and to Canton, and would also be injurious to Canton itself.—We pretend not to know anything of the negociations at Lille, but it is very easy to see, from the nature of the case, what ought to be the condition of the Cape. It ought to be a free port open to the vessels of all nations trading to any part of the East Indias. It ought also to be a neutral port at all times, under the guarantee of all nations; the expense of keeping the port in constant repair to be defrayed by a tonnage tax to be paid by every vessel, whether of commerce or of war, and in proportion to the time of their stay.—Nothing then remains but with respect to the nation who shall be the portmaster; and this ought to be the Dutch, because they understand the business best. As the Cape is a half-way stage between Europe and India, it ought to be considered as a tavern, where travellers on a long journey put up for rest and refreshment.—T. P."

The suspension of peace negotiations,[1] and the bloodless defeat of Pichigru's conspiracy of 18 Fructidor (September 4th) were followed by a pamphlet addressed to "The People of France and the French Armies." This little work is of historical value, in connection with 18 Fructidor, but it was evidently written to carry two practical points. The first was, that if the war with England must continue it should be directed to the end of breaking the Anglo-Germanic compact. England has the right to her internal arrangements, but this is an external matter. While "with respect to England it has been the cause of her immense national debt, the ruin of her finances, and the insolvency of her bank," English intrigues on the continent "are generated by, and act through, the medium of this Anglo-Germanic compound. It will be necessary to dissolve it. Let the elector retire to his electorate, and the world will have peace." Paine's other

[1] In a letter to Duane, many years later, Paine relates the following story concerning the British Union: "When Lord Malmsbury arrived in Paris, in the time of the Directory Government, to open a negociation for a peace, his credentials ran in the old style of 'George, by the grace of God, of Great Britain, *France*, and Ireland, king.' Malmsbury was informed that although the assumed title of king of France, in his credentials, would not prevent France opening a negociation, yet that no treaty of peace could be concluded until that assumed title was removed. Pitt then hit on the Union Bill, under which the assumed title of king of France was discontinued."

main point is, that the neutral nations should secure, in time of war, an unarmed neutrality.

"Were the neutral nations to associate, under an honorable injunction of fidelity to each other, and publickly declare to the world, that if any belligerent power shall seize or molest any ship or vessel belonging to the citizens or subjects of any of the powers composing that association, that the whole association will shut its ports against the flag of the offending nation, and will not permit any goods, wares, or merchandize, produced or manufactured in the offending nation, or appertaining thereto, to be imported into any of the ports included in the association, until reparation be made to the injured party; the reparation to be three times the value of the vessel and cargo ; and moreover that all remittances in money, goods, and bills of exchange, do cease to be made to the offending nation, until the said reparation be made. Were the neutral nations only to do this, which it is their direct interest to do, England, as a nation depending on the commerce of neutral nations in time of war, dare not molest them, and France would not. But whilst, from want of a common system, they individually permit England to do it, because individually they cannot resist it, they put France under the necessity of doing the same thing. The supreme of all laws, in all cases, is that of self-preservation."

It is a notable illustration of the wayward course of political evolution, that the English republic—for it is such—grew largely out of the very parts of its constitution once so oppressive. The foreign origin of the royal family helped to form its wholesome timidity about meddling with politics, allowing thus a development of ministerial government. The hereditary character of the throne, which George III.'s half-insane condition associated with the recklessness of irresponsibility, was by his complete insanity made to serve ministerial independence. Regency is timid about claiming power, and childhood cannot exercise it. The decline of royal and aristocratic authority in England secured freedom to commerce, which necessarily gave hostages to peace. The protection of neutral commerce at sea, concerning which Paine wrote so much, ultimately resulted from English naval strength, which formerly scourged the world.

To Paine, England, at the close of 1797, could appear only as a dragon-guarded prison of fair Humanity. The press was paralyzed, thinkers and publishers were in prison, some of the old orators like Erskine were bought up, and the forlorn hope of liberty rested only with Fox and his fifty in Parliament, overborne by a majority made brutal by strength. The groans of imprisoned thought in his native land reached its outlawed representative in Paris. And at the same time the inhuman decree went forth from that country that there should be no peace with France. It had long been his conviction that the readiness of Great Britain to go to war was due to an insular position that kept the horrors at a distance. War never came home to her. This conviction, which we have several times met in these pages, returned to him with new force when England now insisted on more bloodshed. He was convinced that the right course of France would be to make a descent on England, ship the royal family to Hanover, open the political prisons, and secure the people freedom to make a Constitution. These views, freely expressed to his friends of the Directory and Legislature, reached the ears of Napoleon on his triumphal return from Italy.

The great man called upon Paine in his little room, and invited him to dinner. He made the eloquent professions of republicanism so characteristic of Napoleons until they became pretenders. He told Paine that he slept with the "Rights of Man" under his pillow, and that its author ought to have a statue of gold.[1] He consulted Paine about a descent on England, and adopted the plan. He invited the author to accompany the expedition, which was to consist of a thousand gun-boats, with a hundred men each. Paine consented, "as [so he wrote Jefferson] the intention of the expedition was to give the people of England an opportunity of forming a government for themselves, and thereby bring about peace." One of the points to be aimed at was Norfolk, and no doubt Paine indulged a happy vision of standing once more in Thetford and proclaiming liberty throughout the land !

The following letter (December 29, 1797) from Paine to Barras is in the archives of the Directory, with a French translation :

"CITIZEN PRESIDENT,—A very particular friend of mine, who had a passport to go to London upon some family affairs and to return in three months, and whom I had commissioned upon some affairs of my own (for I find that the English government has seized upon a thousand pounds sterling which I had in the hands of a friend), returned two days ago and gave me the memorandum which I enclose :—the first part relates only to my publication on the event of the 18 Fructidor, and to a letter to Erskine (who had been counsel for the prosecution against a former work of mine the 'Age of Reason') both of which I desired my friend to publish in London. The other part of the memorandum respects the state of affairs in that country, by which I see they have little

[1] Rickman, p. 164.

or no idea of a descent being made upon them; tant mieux—but they will be guarded in Ireland, as they expect a descent there.

"I expect a printed copy of the letter to Erskine in a day or two. As this is in English, and on a subject that will be amusing to the Citizen Revellière Le Peaux, I will send it to him. The friend of whom I speak was a pupil of Dessault the surgeon, and whom I once introduced to you at a public audience in company with Captain Cooper on his plan respecting the Island of Bermuda.—Salut et Respect."

Thus once again did the great hope of a liberated, peaceful, and republican Europe shine before simple-hearted Paine. He was rather poor now, but gathered up all the money he had, and sent it to the Council of Five Hundred. The accompanying letter was read by Coupè at the sitting of January 28, 1798:

"CITIZENS REPRESENTATIVES,—Though it is not convenient to me, in the present situation of my affairs, to subscribe to the loan towards the descent upon England, my economy permits me to make a small patriotic donation. I send a hundred livres, and with it all the wishes of my heart for the success of the descent, and a voluntary offer of any service I can render to promote it.

"There will be no lasting peace for France, nor for the world, until the tyranny and corruption of the English government be abolished, and England, like Italy, become a sister republic. As to those men, whether in England, Scotland, or Ireland, who, like Robespierre in France, are covered with crimes, they, like him, have no other resource than in committing more. But the mass of the people are the friends of liberty: tyranny and taxation oppress them, but they deserve to be free.

"Accept, Citizens Representatives, the congratulations of an old colleague in the dangers we have passed, and on the happy prospect before us. Salut et respect.

"THOMAS PAINE."

Coupè added: "The gift which Thomas Paine offers you appears very trifling, when it is compared with the revolting injustice which this faithful friend of liberty has experienced from the English government; but compare it with the state of poverty in which our former colleague finds himself, and you will then think it considerable." He moved that the notice of this gift and Thomas Paine's letter be printed. "Mention honorable et impression," adds the *Moniteur*.

The President of the Directory at this time was Larevélliére-Lépeaux, a friend of the Theophilanthropic Society. To him Paine gave, in English, which the president understood, a plan for the descent, which was translated into French, and adopted by the Directory. Two hundred and fifty gun-boats were built, and the expedition abandoned. To Jefferson, Paine intimates his suspicion that it was all "only a feint to cover the expedition to Egypt, which was then preparing." He also states that the British descent on Ostend, where some two thousand of them were made prisoners, "was in search of the gun-boats, and to cut the dykes, to prevent their being assembled." This he was told by Vanhuile, of Bruges, who heard it from the British officers.

After the failure of his attempt to return to America with the Monroes, Paine was for a time the guest of Nicolas de Bonneville, in Paris, and the visit ended in an arrangement for his abode with that family. Bonneville was an editor, thirty-seven years of age, and had been one of the five members of Paine's Republican Club, which placarded Paris with its manifesto after the king's flight in 1791. An enthusiastic devotee of Paine's principles from youth, he had advocated them in his successive journals, *Le Tribun du Peuple*, *Bouche de Fer*, and *Bien Informé*. He had resisted Marat and Robespierre, and suffered imprisonment during the Terror. He spoke English fluently, and was well known in the world of letters by some striking poems, also by his translation into French of German tales, and parts of Shakespeare. He had set up a printing office at No. 4 Rue du Théâtre-Français, where he published liberal pamphlets, also his *Bien Informé*. Then, in 1794, he printed in French the "Age of Reason." He also published, and probably translated into French, Paine's letter to the now exiled Camille Jordan,— "Lettre de Thomas Paine, sur les Cultes." Paine, unable to converse in French, found with the Bonnevilles a home he needed. M. and Madame Bonneville had been married three years, and their second child had been named after Thomas Paine, who stood as his godfather. Paine, as we learn from Rickman, who knew the Bonnevilles, paid board, but no doubt he aided Bonneville more by his pen.

With public affairs, either in France or America, Paine now mingled but little. The election of John Adams to the presidency he heard of with dismay. He wrote to Jefferson that since he was not president, he was glad he had accepted the vice-presidency, "for John Adams has such a talent for blundering and offending, it will be necessary to keep an eye over him." Finding, by the abandonment of a descent on England for one on Egypt, that Napoleon was by no means his ideal missionary of republicanism, he withdrew into his little study, and now remained so quiet that some English papers announced his arrival and cool reception in America. He was, however, fairly bored with visitors from all parts of the world, curious to see the one international republican left. It became necessary for Madame Bonneville, armed with polite prevarications, to defend him from such sight-seers. For what with his visits to and from the Barlows, the Smiths, and his friends of the Directory, Paine had too little time for the inventions in which he was again absorbed,—his "Saints." Among his intimate friends at this time was Robert Fulton, then residing in Paris. Paine's extensive studies of the steam-engine, and his early discovery of its adaptability to navigation, had caused Rumsey to seek him in England, and Fitch to consult him both in America and Paris. Paine's connection with the invention of the steamboat was recognized by Fulton, as indeed by all of his scientific contemporaries.[1] To Fulton he freely gave his ideas, and may perhaps have had some hope that the steamboat might prove a missionary of international republicanism, though Napoleon had failed.

[1] Sir Richard Phillips says: "In 1778 Thomas Paine proposed, in America, this application of steam." ("Million of Facts," p. 776.) As Sir Richard assisted Fulton in his experiments on the Thames, he probably heard from him the fact about Paine, though, indeed, in the controversy between Rumsey and Fitch, Paine's priority to both was conceded. In America, however, the priority really belonged to the eminent mechanician William Henry, of Lancaster, Pa. When Fitch visited Henry, in 1785, he was told by him that he was not the first to devise steam-navigation; that

It will not be forgotten that in the same year in which Paine startled William Henry with a plan for steam-navigation, namely in 1778, he wrote his sublime sentence about the "Religion of Humanity." The steamships, which Emerson described as enormous shuttles weaving the races of men into the woof of humanity, have at length rendered possible that universal human religion which Paine foresaw. In that old Lancaster mansion of the Henrys, which still stands, Paine left his spectacles, now in our National Museum; they are strong and far-seeing; through them looked eyes held by visions that the world is still steadily following. One cannot suppress some transcendental sentiment in view of the mystical harmony of this man's inventions for human welfare,—mechanical, political, religious. Of his gunpowder motor, mention has already been made (i., p. 240). On this he was engaged about the time that he was answering Bishop Watson's book on the "Age of Reason." The two occupations are related. He could not believe, he said, that the qualities of gunpowder— the small and light grain with maximum of force— were meant only for murder, and his faith in the divine humanity is in the sentence. To supersede

he himself had thought of it in 1776, and mentioned it to Andrew Ellicott; and that Thomas Paine, while a guest at his house in 1778, had spoken to him on the subject. I am indebted to Mr. John W. Jordan, of the Historical Society of Pennsylvania, for notes from the papers of Henry, his ancestor, showing that Paine's scheme was formed without knowledge of others, and that it contemplated a turbine application of steam to a wheel. Both he and Henry, as they had not published their plans, agreed to leave Fitch the whole credit. Fitch publicly expressed his gratitude to Paine. Thurston adds that Paine, in 1788, proposed that Congress should adopt the whole matter for the national benefit. ("History of the Growth of the Steam Engine," pp. 252, 253.)

destroying gunpowder with beneficent gunpowder, and to supersede the god of battles with the God of Love, were kindred aims in Paine's heart. Through the fiery furnaces of his time he had come forth with every part of his being welded and beaten and shaped together for this Human Service. Patriotism, in the conventional sense, race-pride, sectarianism, partizanship, had been burnt out of his nature. The universe could not have wrung from his tongue approval of a wrong because it was done by his own country.

It might be supposed that there were no heavier trials awaiting Paine's political faith than those it had undergone. But it was becoming evident that liberty had not the advantage he once ascribed to truth over error,—"it cannot be unlearned." The United States had unlearned it as far as to put into the President's hands a power of arbitrarily crushing political opponents, such as even George III. hardly aspired to. The British Treaty had begun to bear its natural fruits. Washington signed the Treaty to avoid war, and rendered war inevitable with both France and England. The affair with France was happily a transient squall, but it was sufficient to again bring on Paine the offices of an American Minister in France. Many an American in that country had occasion to appreciate his powerful aid and unfailing kindness. Among these was Captain Rowland Crocker of Massachusetts, who had sailed with a letter of marque. His vessel was captured by the French, and its wounded commander brought to Paris, where he was more agreeably conquered by kindness. Freeman's

"History of Cape Cod" (of which region Crocker was a native) has the following:

"His [Captain Crocker's] reminiscences of his residence in that country, during the most extraordinary period of its history, were of a highly interesting character. He had taken the great Napoleon by the hand; he had familiarly known Paine, at a time when his society was sought for and was valuable. Of this noted individual, we may in passing say, with his uniform and characteristic kindness, he always spoke in terms which sounded strange to the ears of a generation which has been taught, with or without justice, to regard the author of 'The Age of Reason' with loathing and abhorrence. He remembered Paine as a well-dressed and most gentlemanly man, of sound and orthodox republican principles, of a good heart, a strong intellect, and a fascinating address."

The *coup d'état* in America, which made President Adams virtual emperor, pretended constitutionality, and was reversible. That which Napoleon and Sieyès—who had his way at last—effected in France (November 9, 1799) was lawless and fatal. The peaceful Bonneville home was broken up. Bonneville, in his *Bien Informé*, described Napoleon as "a Cromwell," and was promptly imprisoned. Paine, either before or soon after this catastrophe, went to Belgium, on a visit to his old friend Vanhuile, who had shared his cell in the Luxembourg prison. Vanhuile was now president of the municipality of Bruges, and Paine got from him information about European affairs. On his return he found Bonneville released from prison, but under severe surveillance, his journal being suppressed. The family was thus reduced to penury and anxiety, but there was all the more reason that Paine should stand by them. He continued his abode in their house, now probably supported by drafts on his resources in America, to which country they turned their thoughts.

The European Republic on land having become hopeless, Paine turned his attention to the seas. He wrote a pamphlet on "Maritime Compact," including in it ten articles for the security of neutral commerce, to be signed by the nations entering the "Unarmed Association," which he proposed. This scheme was substantially the same as that already quoted from his letter "To the People of France, and to the French Armies." It was translated by Bonneville, and widely circulated in Europe. Paine sent it in manuscript to Jefferson, who at once had it printed. His accompanying letter to Jefferson (October 1, 1800) is of too much biographical interest to be abridged.

"DEAR SIR,—I wrote to you from Havre by the ship Dublin Packet in the year 1797. It was then my intention to return to America; but there were so many British frigates cruising in sight of the port, and which after a few days knew that I was at Havre waiting to go to America, that I did not think it best to trust myself to their discretion, and the more so, as I had no confidence in the Captain of the Dublin Packet (Clay). I mentioned to you in that letter, which I believe you received thro' the hands of Colonel [Aaron] Burr, that I was glad since you were not President that you had accepted the nomination of Vice President.

"The Commissioners Ellsworth & Co.[1] have been here about eight months, and three more useless mortals never came upon

[1] Oliver Ellsworth, William V. Murray, and William R. Davie, were sent by President Adams to France to negotiate a treaty. There is little doubt that the famous letter of Joel Barlow to Washington, October 2, 1798, written in the interest of peace, was composed after consultation with Paine. Adams, on reading the letter, abused Barlow. "Tom Paine," he said, "is

public business. Their presence appears to me to have been rather an injury than a benefit. They set themselves up for a faction as soon as they arrived. I was then in Belgia. Upon my return to Paris I learned they had made a point of not returning the visits of Mr. Skipwith and Barlow, because, they said, they had not the confidence of the executive. Every known republican was treated in the same manner. I learned from Mr. Miller of Philadelphia, who had occasion to see them upon business, that they did not intend to return my visit, if I made one. This I supposed it was intended I should know, that I might not make one. It had the contrary effect. I went to see Mr. Ellsworth. I told him, I did not come to see him as a commissioner, nor to congratulate him upon his mission; that I came to see him because I had formerly known him in Congress. I mean not, said I, to press you with any questions, or to engage you in any conversation upon the business you are come upon, but I will nevertheless candidly say that I know not what expectations the Government or the people of America may have of your mission, or what expectations you may have yourselves, but I believe you will find you can do but little. The treaty with England lies at the threshold of all your business. The American Government never did two more foolish things than when it signed that Treaty and recalled Mr. Monroe, who was the only man could do them any service. Mr. Ellsworth put on the dull gravity of a Judge, and was silent. I added, you may perhaps make a treaty like that you have made with England, which is a surrender of the rights of the American flag; for the principle that neutral ships make neutral property must be general or not at all. I then changed the subject, for I had all the talk to myself upon this topic, and enquired after Sam. Adams, (I asked nothing about John,) Mr. Jefferson, Mr. Monroe, and others of my friends, and the melancholy case of the yellow fever,—of which he gave me as circumstantial an account as if he had been summing up a case to a Jury. Here my visit ended, and had Mr. Ellsworth been

not a more worthless fellow." But he obeyed the letter. The Commissioners he sent were associated with the anti-French and British party in America, but peace with America was of too much importance to the new despot of France for the opportunity to be missed of forming a Treaty.

as cunning as a statesman, or as wise as a Judge, he would have returned my visit that he might appear insensible of the intention of mine.

"I now come to the affairs of this country and of Europe. You will, I suppose, have heard before this arrives to you, of the battle of Marengo in Italy, where the Austrians were defeated—of the armistice in consequence thereof, and the surrender of Milan, Genoa, etc., to the french—of the successes of the french army in Germany—and the extension of the armistice in that quarter—of the preliminaries of peace signed at Paris—of the refusal of the Emperor [of Austria] to ratify these preliminaries—of the breaking of the armistice by the french Government in consequence of that refusal—of the 'gallant' expedition of the Emperor to put himself at the head of his Army—of his pompous arrival there—of his having made his will—of prayers being put in all his churches for the preservation of the life of this Hero—of General Moreau announcing to him, immediately on his arrival at the Army, that hostilities would commence the day after the next at sunrise, unless he signed the treaty or gave security that he would sign within 45 days—of his surrendering up three of the principal keys of Germany (Ulm, Philipsbourg, and Ingolstad), as security that he would sign them. This is the state things [they] are now in, at the time of writing this letter; but it is proper to add that the refusal of the Emperor to sign the preliminaries was motived upon a note from the King of England to be admitted to the Congress for negociating Peace, which was consented to by the french upon the condition of an armistice at Sea, which England, before knowing of the surrender the Emperor had made, had refused. From all which it appears to me, judging from circumstances, that the Emperor is now so compleatly in the hands of the french, that he has no way of getting out but by a peace. The Congress for the peace is to be held at Luneville, a town in france. Since the affair of Rastadt the french commissioners will not trust themselves within the Emperor's territory.

"I now come to domestic affairs. I know not what the Commissioners have done, but from a paper I enclose to you, which appears to have some authority, it is not much. The paper as you will perceive is considerably prior to this letter. I knew that the Commissioners before this piece appeared intended setting off. It is therefore probable that what they have done is conformable to what this paper mentions, which certainly will not atone for the expence their mission has incurred, neither are they, by all the accounts I hear of them, men fitted for the business.

"But independently of these matters there appears to be a state of circumstances rising, which if it goes on, will render all partial treaties unnecessary. In the first place I doubt if any peace will be made with England; and in the second place, I should not wonder to see a coalition formed against her, to compel her to abandon her insolence on the seas. This brings me to speak of the manuscripts I send you.

"The piece No. 1, without any title, was written in consequence of a question put to me by Bonaparte. As he supposed I knew England and English Politics he sent a person to me to ask, that in case of negociating a Peace with Austria, whether it would be proper to include England. This was when Count St. Julian was in Paris, on the part of the Emperor negociating the preliminaries:—which as I have before said the Emperor refused to sign on the pretence of admitting England.

"The piece No. 2, entitled *On the Jacobinism of the English at Sea*, was written when the English made their insolent and impolitic expedition to Denmark, and is also an auxiliary to the politic of No. 1. I shewed it to a friend [Bonneville] who had it translated into french, and printed in the form of a Pamphlet, and distributed gratis among the foreign Ministers, and persons in the Government. It was immediately copied into several of the french Journals, and into the official Paper, the Moniteur. It appeared in this paper one day before the last dispatch arrived from Egypt; which agreed perfectly with what I had said respecting Egypt. It hit the two cases of Denmark and Egypt in the exact proper moment.

"The piece No. 3, entitled *Compact Maritime*, is the sequel of No. 2 digested in form. It is translating at the time I write this letter, and I am to have a meeting with the Senator Garat upon the subject. The pieces 2 and 3 go off in manuscript to England, by a confidential person, where they will be published.

"By all the news we get from the North there appears to be something meditating against England. It is now given for certain that Paul has embargoed all the English vessels and English property in Russia till some principle be established for protecting the Rights of neutral Nations, and securing the liberty of the Seas. The preparations in Denmark continue, notwithstanding the convention that she has made with England, which leaves the question with respect to the right set up by England to stop and search Neutral vessels undecided. I send you the paragraphs upon the subject.

"The tumults are great in all parts of England on account of the excessive price of corn and bread, which has risen since the harvest. I attribute it more to the abundant increase of paper, and the non-circulation of cash, than to any other cause. People in trade can push the paper off as fast as they receive it, as they did by continental money in America; but as farmers have not this opportunity they endeavor to secure themselves by going considerably in advance.

"I have now given you all the great articles of intelligence, for I trouble not myself with little ones, and consequently not with the Commissioners, nor any thing they are about, nor with John Adams, otherwise than to wish him safe home, and a better and wiser man in his place.

"In the present state of circumstances and the prospects arising from them, it may be proper for America to consider whether it is worth her while to enter into any treaty at this moment, or to wait the event of those circumstances which, if they go on will render partial treaties useless by deranging them. But if, in the mean time, she enters into any treaty it ought to be with a condition to the following purpose : Reserving to herself the right of joining in an association of Nations for the protection of the Rights of Neutral Commerce and the security of the liberty of the Seas.

"The pieces 2, 3, may go to the press. They will make a small pamphlet and the printers are welcome to put my name to it. It is best it should be put from thence; they will get into the newspapers. I know that the faction of John Adams abuses me pretty heartily. They are welcome. It does not disturb me, and they lose their labour ; and in return for it I am doing America more service, as a neutral nation, than their expensive Commissioners can do, and she has that service from me for nothing. The piece No. 1 is only for your own amusement and that of your friends.

"I come now to speak confidentially to you on a private subject. When Mr. Ellsworth and Davie return to America, Murray will return to Holland, and in that case there will be nobody in Paris but Mr. Skipwith that has been in the habit of transacting business with the french Government since the revolution began. He is on a good standing with them, and if the chance of the day should place you in the presidency you cannot do better than appoint him for any purpose you may have occasion for in France. He is an honest man and will do his country Justice, and that with civility and good manners to the government he is commissioned to act with; a faculty which that Northern Bear Timothy Pickering wanted, and which the Bear of that Bear, John Adams, never possessed.

"I know not much of Mr. Murray, otherwise than of his unfriendliness to every American who is not of his faction, but I am sure that Joel Barlow is a much fitter man to be in Holland than Mr. Murray. It is upon the fitness of the man to the place that I speak, for I have not communicated a thought upon the subject to Barlow, neither does he know, at the time of my writing this (for he is at Havre), that I have intention to do it.

"I will now, by way of relief, amuse you with some account of the progress of Iron Bridges. The french revolution and Mr. Burke's attack upon it, drew me off from any pontifical Works. Since my coming from England in '92, an Iron Bridge of a single arch 236 feet span versed sine 34 feet, has been cast at the Iron Works of the Walkers where my model was, and erected over the river Wear at Sunderland in the county of Durham in England. The two members in Parliament for the County, Mr. Bourdon and Mr. Milbank, were the principal subscribers; but the direction was committed to Mr. Bourdon. A very sincere friend of mine, Sir Robert Smyth, who lives in france, and whom Mr. Monroe well knows, supposing they had taken their plan from my model wrote to Mr.

Milbank upon the subject. Mr. Milbank answered the letter, which answer I have by me and I give you word for word the part concerning the Bridge : 'With respect to the Bridge over the river Wear at Sunderland it certainly is a Work well deserving admiration both for its structure, durability and utility, and I have good grounds for saying that the first Idea was taken from Mr. Paine's bridge exhibited at Paddington. But with respect to any compensation to Mr. Paine, however desirous of rewarding the labours of an ingenious man, I see not how it is in my power, having had nothing to do with his bridge after the payment of my subscription, Mr. Bourdon being accountable for the whole. But if you can point out any mode by which I can be instrumental in procuring for Mr. P. any compensation for the advantages which the public may have derived from his ingenious model, from which certainly the outlines of the Bridge at Sunderland was taken, be assured it will afford me very great satisfaction.'

"I have now made two other models, one is pasteboard, five feet span and five inches of height from the cords. It is in the opinion of every person who has seen it one of the most beautifull objects the eye can behold. I then cast a model in Metal following the construction of that in pasteboard and of the same dimensions. The whole was executed in my own Chamber. It is far superior in strength, elegance, and readiness in execution to the model I made in America, and which you saw in Paris. I shall bring those Models with me when I come home, which will be as soon as I can pass the seas in safety from the piratical John Bulls.

"I suppose you have seen, or have heard of the Bishop of Landaff's answer to my second part of the Age of reason. As soon as I got a copy of it I began a third part, which served also as an answer to the Bishop ; but as soon as the clerical Society for promoting *Christian Knowledge* knew of my intention to answer the Bishop, they prosecuted, as a Society, the printer of the first and second parts, to prevent that answer appearing. No other reason than this can be assigned for their prosecuting at the time they did, because the first part had been in circulation above three years and the second part more than one, and they prosecuted immediately on knowing that I was taking up their Champion. The Bishop's answer, like Mr. Burke's attack on the french revolution, served me as a back-ground to bring forward other subjects upon, with more advantage than if the background was not there. This is the motive that induced me to answer him, otherwise I should have gone on without taking any notice of him. I have made and am still making additions to the manuscript, and shall continue to do so till an opportunity arrive for publishing it.

"If any American frigate should come to france, and the direction of it fall to you, I will be glad you would give me the opportunity of returning. The abscess under which I suffered almost two years is entirely healed of itself, and I enjoy exceeding good health. This is the first of October, and Mr. Skipwith has just called to tell me the Commissioners set off for Havre tomorrow. This will go by the frigate but not with the knowledge of the Commissioners. Remember me with much affection to my friends and accept the same to yourself."

As the Commissioners did not leave when they expected, Paine added several other letters to Jefferson, on public affairs. In one (October 1st) he says he has information of increasing aversion in the English people to their government. "It was the hope of conquest, and is now the hope of peace that keeps it [Pitt's administration] up." Pitt is anxious about his paper money. "The credit of Paper is suspicion asleep. When suspicion wakes the credit vanishes as the dream would." "England has a large Navy, and the expense of it leads to her ruin." The English nation is tired of war, longs for peace, "and calculates upon defeat as it would upon victory." On October 4th, after the Commissioners had concluded a treaty, Paine alludes to an article said to be in it, requiring certain expenditures in France, and says that if he, Jefferson, be "in the chair, and not otherwise," he should offer himself for this business, should an agent be required. " It will serve to defray my expenses until I can return, but I wish it may be with the condition of returning. I am not tired of working for nothing, but I cannot afford it. This appointment will aid me in promoting the object I am now upon of a law of nations for the protection of neutral commerce." On October 6th he reports to Jefferson that at an entertainment given the American envoys, Consul Le Brun gave the toast : " À l'union de l'Amérique avec les puissances du Nord pour faire respecter la liberté des mers." On October 15th the last of his enclosures to Jefferson is written. He says that Napoleon, when asked if there would be more war, replied : " Nous n'aurions plus qu'une guerre d'écritoire." In all of Paine's writing about Napoleon, at this time, he seems as if watching a thundercloud, and trying to make out meteorologically its drift, and where it will strike.

CHAPTER XV.

THE LAST YEAR IN EUROPE.

On July 15, 1801, Napoleon concluded with Pius VII. the Concordat. Naturally, the first victim offered on the restored altar was Theophilanthropy. I have called Paine the founder of this Society, because it arose amid the controversy excited by the publication of "Le Siècle de la Raison," its manual and tracts reproducing his ideas aud language; and because he gave the inaugural discourse. Theism was little known in France save as iconoclasm, and an assault on the Church: Paine treated it as a Religion. But, as he did not speak French, the practical organization and management of the Society were the work of others, and mainly of a Russian named Hauëy. There had been a good deal of odium incurred at first by a society which satisfied neither the pious nor the freethinkers, but it found a strong friend on the Directory. This was Larévellière-Lépeaux, whose secretary, Antoine Vallée, and young daughter, had become interested in the movement. This statesman never joined the Society, but he had attended one of its meetings, and, when a distribution of religious edifices was made, Theophilanthropy was assigned ten parish churches. It is said that when Larevéllière-

Lépeaux mentioned to Talleyrand his desire for the spread of this Society, the diplomat said: "All you have to do is to get yourself hanged, and revive the third day." Paine, who had pretty nearly fulfilled that requirement, saw the Society spread rapidly, and he had great hopes of its future. But Pius VII. also had an interested eye on it, and though the Concordat did not go into legal operation until 1802, Theophilanthropy was offered as a preliminary sacrifice in October, 1801.

The description of Paine by Walter Savage Landor, and representations of his talk, in the "Imaginary Conversations," so mix up persons, times, and places, that I was at one time inclined to doubt whether the two had met. But Mr. J. M. Wheeler, a valued correspondent in London, writes me: "Landor told my friend Mr. Birch of Florence that he particularly admired Paine, and that he visited him, having first obtained an interview at the house of General Dumouriez. Landor declared that Paine was always called 'Tom,' not out of disrespect, but because he was a jolly good fellow." An interview with Paine at the house of Dumouriez could only have occurred when the General was in Paris, in 1793. This would account for what Landor says of Paine taking refuge from trouble in brandy. There had been, as, Rickman testifies, and as all the facts show, nothing of this kind since that period. It would appear therefore that Landor must have mixed up at least two interviews with Paine, one in the time of Dumouriez, the other in that of Napoleon. Not even such an artist as Landor could invent the language ascribed to Paine concerning the French and Napoleon.

"The whole nation may be made as enthusiastic about a salad as about a constitution; about the colour of a cockade as about a consul or a king. You will shortly see the real strength and figure of Bonaparte. He is wilful, headstrong, proud, morose, presumptuous; he will be guided no longer; he has pulled the pad from his forehead, and will break his nose or bruise his cranium against every table, chair, and brick in the room, until at last he must be sent to the hospital."

Paine prophesies that Napoleon will make himself emperor, and that "by his intemperate use of power and thirst of dominion" he will cause the people to "wish for their old kings, forgetting what beasts they were." Possibly under the name "Mr. Normandy" Landor disguises Thomas Poole, referred to on a preceding page. Normandy's sufferings on account of one of Paine's books are not exaggerated. In Mrs. Sanford's work is printed a letter from Paris, July 20, 1802, in which Poole says: "I called one morning on Thomas Paine. He is an original, amusing fellow. Striking, strong physiognomy. Said a great many quaint things, and read us part of a reply which he intends to publish to Watson's 'Apology.'"

Paine seems to have had no relation with the ruling powers at this time, though an Englishman who visited him is quoted by Rickman (p. 198) as remarking his manliness and fearlessness, and that he spoke as freely as ever after Bonaparte's supremacy. One communication only to any member of the government appears; this was to the

[1] "Thomas Poole and His Friends," ii., p. 85.

Minister of the Interior concerning a proposed iron bridge over the Seine.[1] Political France and Paine had parted.

Under date of March 18, 1801, President Jefferson informs Paine that he had sent his manuscripts (Maritime Compact) to the printer to be made into a pamphlet, and that the American people had returned from their frenzy against France. He adds :

"You expressed a wish to get a passage to this country in a public vessel. Mr. Dawson is charged with orders to the captain of the Maryland to receive and accommodate you back if you can be ready to depart at such short warning. Rob. R. Livingston is appointed minister plenipotentiary to the republic of France, but will not leave this till we receive the ratification of the convention by Mr. Dawson.[2] I am in hopes you will find us returned generally to sentiments worthy of former times. In these it will be your glory to have steadily labored, and with as much effect as any man living. That you may long live to continue your useful labors and to reap the reward in the thankfulness of nations, is my sincere prayer. Accept assurances of my high esteem and affectionate attachment."

---

[1] "THE MINISTER OF THE INTERIOR TO THOMAS PAINE : I have received, Citizen, the observations that you have been so good as to address to me upon the construction of iron bridges. They will be of the greatest utility to us when the new kind of construction goes to be executed for the first time. With pleasure I assure you, Citizen, that you have rights of more than one kind to the gratitude of nations, and I give you, cordially, the expression of my particular esteem.—CHAPTAL."

It is rather droll, considering the appropriation of his patent in England, and the confiscation of a thousand pounds belonging to him, to find Paine casually mentioning that at this time a person came from London with plans and drawings to consult with him about an iron arch of 600 feet, over the Thames, then under consideration by a committee of the House of Commons.

[2] "Beau Dawson," an eminent Virginia Congressman.

The subjoined notes are from letters of Paine to Jefferson :

Paris, June 9, 1801. " Your very friendly letter by Mr. Dawson gave me the real sensation of happy satisfaction, and what served to increase it was that he brought it to me himself before I knew of his arrival. I congratulate America on your election. There has been no circumstance with respect to America since the times of her revolution that excited so much attention and expectation in France, England, Ireland, and Scotland as the pending election for President of the United States, nor any of which the event has given more general joy :

" I thank you for the opportunity you give me of returning by the Maryland, but I shall wait the return of the vessel that brings Mr. Livingston."

Paris, June 25, 1801. " The Parliamentaire, from America to Havre, was taken in going out, and carried into England. The pretence, as the papers say, was that a Swedish Minister was on board for America. If I had happened to have been there, I suppose they would have made no ceremony in conducting me on shore."

Paris, March 17, 1802. " As it is now Peace, though the definitive Treaty is not yet signed, I shall set off by the first opportunity from Havre or Dieppe, after the equinoctial gales are over. I continue in excellent health, which I know your friendship will be glad to hear of.—Wishing you and America every happiness, I remain your former fellow-labourer and much obliged fellow-citizen.

Paine's determination not to return to America in a national vessel was owing to a paragraph he saw in a Baltimore paper, headed " Out at Last." It stated that Paine had written to the President, expressing a wish to return by a national ship, and that " permission was given." There was here an indication that Jefferson's invitation to Paine by the Hon. John Dawson had become known to the President's enemies, and that Jefferson, on being attacked, had apologized by making the matter appear an act of charity. Paine would not believe that the President was personally responsible for the apologetic paragraph, which seemed inconsistent with the cordiality of the letter brought by Dawson; but, as he afterwards wrote to Jefferson, "it determined me not to come by a national ship."[1] His request had been made at a time when any other than a national American ship was pretty certain to land him in an English prison. There was evidently no thought of any *éclat* in the matter, but no doubt a regard for economy as well as safety.

The following to the eminent deist lecturer in New York, Elihu Palmer, bears the date, "Paris, February 21, 1802, since the Fable of Christ":

"DEAR FRIEND, I received, by Mr. Livingston, the letter you wrote me, and the excellent work you have published ["The Principles of Nature"]. I see you have thought deeply on the subject, and expressed your thoughts in a strong and clear style. The hinting and intimating manner of writing that was formerly used on subjects of this kind, produced skepticism, but not conviction. It is necessary to be bold. Some people can be reasoned into sense, and others must be shocked into it. Say a bold thing that will stagger them, and they will begin to think.

---

[1] It was cleared up afterwards. Jefferson had been charged with sending a national ship to France for the sole purpose of bringing Paine home, and Paine himself would have been the first to condemn such an assumption of power. Although the President's adherents thought it right to deny this, Jefferson wrote to Paine that he had nothing to do with the paragraph. "With respect to the letter [offering the ship] I never hesitate to avow and justify it in conversation. In no other way do I trouble myself to contradict anything which is said. At that time, however, there were anomalies in the motions of some of our friends which events have at length reduced to regularity."

"There is an intimate friend of mine, Colonel Joseph Kirkbride of Bordentown, New Jersey, to whom I would wish you to send your work. He is an excellent man, and perfectly in our sentiments. You can send it by the stage that goes partly by land and partly by water, between New York and Philadelphia, and passes through Bordentown.

"I expect to arrive in America in May next. I have a third part of the Age of Reason to publish when I arrive, which, if I mistake not, will make a stronger impression than any thing I have yet published on the subject.

"I write this by an ancient colleague of mine in the French Convention, the citizen Lequinio, who is going [as] Consul to Rhode Island, and who waits while I write.[1] Yours in friendship."

The following, dated July 8, 1802, to Consul Rotch, is the last letter I find written by Paine from Paris:

"MY DEAR FRIEND,—The bearer of this is a young man that wishes to go to America. He is willing to do anything on board a ship to lesson the expense of his passage. If you know any captain to whom such a person may be usefull I will be obliged to you to speak to him about it.

"As Mr. Otte was to come to Paris in order to go to America, I wanted to take a passage with him, but as he stays in England to negociate some arrangements of Commerce, I have given up that idea. I wait now for the arrival of a person from England whom I want to see,[2] after which, I shall bid adieu to restless and wretched Europe. I am with affectionate esteem to you and Mrs. Rotch,

"Yours,
"THOMAS PAINE."

The President's cordial letter had raised a happy vision before the eyes of one sitting amid the ruins

---

[1] J. M. Lequinio, author of "Prejudices Destroyed," and other rationalistic works, especially dealt with in Priestley's "Letters to the Philosophers of France."

[2] No doubt Clio Rickman.

of his republican world. As he said of Job, he had "determined, in the midst of accumulating ills, to impose upon himself the hard duty of contentment." Of the comrades with whom he began the struggle for liberty in France but a small circle remained. As he wrote to Lady Smith,—from whom he must now part,—"I might almost say like Job's servant, 'and I only am escaped.'" Of the American and English friends who cared for him when he came out of prison few remain.

The President's letter came to a poor man in a small room, furnished only with manuscripts and models of inventions. Here he was found by an old friend from England, Henry Redhead Yorke, who, in 1795, had been tried in England for sedition. Yorke has left us a last glimpse of the author in "wretched and restless Europe." The "rights of man" had become so antiquated in Napoleon's France, that Yorke found Paine's name odious on account of his antislavery writings, the people "ascribing to his espousal of the rights of the negroes of St. Domingo the resistance which Leclercq had experienced from them." He found Paine in No. 4 Rue du Théâtre Français. A "jolly-looking woman" (in whom we recognize Madame Bonneville) scrutinized Yorke severely, but was smiling enough on learning that he was Paine's old friend. He was ushered into a little room heaped with boxes of documents, a chaos of pamphlets and journals. While Yorke was meditating on the contrast between this habitation of a founder of two great republics and the mansions of their rulers, his old friend entered, dressed in a long flannel gown.

"Time seemed to have made dreadful ravages over his whole frame, and a settled melancholy was visible on his countenance. He desired me to be seated, and although he did not recollect me for a considerable time, he conversed with his usual affability. I confess I felt extremely surprised that he should have forgotten me; but I resolved not to make myself known to him, as long as it could be avoided with propriety. In order to try his memory, I referred to a number of circumstances which had occurred while we were in company, but carefully abstained from hinting that we had ever lived together. He would frequently put his hand to his forehead, and exclaim, 'Ah! I know that voice, but my recollection fails!' At length I thought it time to remove his suspense, and stated an incident which instantly recalled me to his mind. It is impossible to describe the sudden change which this effected; his countenance brightened, he pressed me by the hand, and a silent tear stole down his cheek. Nor was I less affected than himself. For some time we sat without a word escaping from our lips. 'Thus are we met once more, Mr. Paine,' I resumed, 'after a long separation of ten years, and after having been both of us severely weather-beaten.' 'Aye,' he replied, 'and who would have thought that we should meet in Paris?' He then enquired what motive had brought me here, and on my explaining myself, he observed with a smile of contempt, 'They have shed blood enough for liberty, and now they have it in perfection. This is not a country for an honest man to live in; they do not understand any thing at all of the principles of free government, and the best way is to leave them to themselves. You see they have conquered all Europe, only to make it more miserable than it was before.' Upon this, I remarked that I was surprised to hear him speak in such desponding language of the fortune of mankind, and that I thought much might yet be done for the Republic. 'Republic!' he exclaimed, 'do you call this a Republic? Why they are worse off than the slaves of Constantinople; for there, they expect to be bashaws in heaven by submitting to be slaves below, but here they believe neither in heaven nor hell, and yet are slaves by choice. I know of no Republic in the world except America, which is the only country for such men as you and I. It is my intention to get away from this place as soon as possible, and I hope to be off in the autumn ; you are a young man and may see better times, but I have done with Europe, and its slavish politics.'

"I have often been in company with Mr. Paine, since my arrival here, and I was not a little surprised to find him wholly indifferent about the public spirit in England, or the remaining influence of his doctrines among its people. Indeed he seemed to dislike the mention of the subject; and when, one day, in order to provoke discussion, I told him I had altered my opinions upon many of his principles, he answered, 'You certainly have the right to do so ; but you cannot alter the nature of things ; the French have alarmed all honest men ; but still truth is truth. Though you may not think that my principles are practicable in England, without bringing on a great deal of misery and confusion, you are, I am sure, convinced of their justice.' Here he took occasion to speak in terms of the utmost severity of Mr ——, who had obtained a seat in parliament, and said that 'parsons were always mischievous fellows when they turned politicians.' This gave rise to an observation respecting his 'Age of Reason,' the publication of which I said had lost him the good opinion of numbers of his English advocates. He became uncommonly warm at this remark, and in a tone of singular energy declared that he would not have published it if he had not thought it calculated to 'inspire mankind with a more exalted idea of the Supreme Architect of the Universe, and to put an end to villainous imposture.' He then broke out with the most violent invectives against our received opinions, accompanying them at the same time with some of the most grand and sublime conceptions of an Omnipotent Being, that I ever heard or read of. In the support of his opinion, he avowed himself ready to lay down his life, and said 'the Bishop of Llandaff may roast me in Smithfield if he likes, but human torture cannot shake my conviction.' He reached down a copy of the Bishop's work, interleaved with remarks upon it, which he read me ; after which he admitted the liberality of the

Bishop, and regretted that in all controversies among men a similar temper was not maintained. But in proportion as he appeared listless in politics, he seemed quite a zealot in his religious creed; of which the following is an instance. An English lady of our acquaintance, not less remarkable for her talents than for elegance of manners, entreated me to contrive that she might have an interview with Mr. Paine. In consequence of this I invited him to dinner on a day when we were to be favoured with her company. But as she is a very rigid Roman Catholic I cautioned Mr. Paine, beforehand, against touching upon religious subjects, assuring him at the same time that she felt much interested to make his acquaintance. With much good nature he promised to be *discreet*. . . . For above four hours he kept every one in astonishment and admiration of his memory, his keen observation of men and manners, his numberless anecdotes of the American Indians, of the American war, of Franklin, Washington, and even of his Majesty, of whom he told several curious facts of humour and benevolence. His remarks on genius and taste can never be forgotten by those present. Thus far everything went on as I could wish; the sparkling champagne gave a zest to his conversation, and we were all delighted. But alas! alas! an expression relating to his 'Age of Reason' having been mentioned by one of the company, he broke out immediately. He began with Astronomy,—addressing himself to Mrs. Y.,—he declared that the least inspection of the motion of the stars was a convincing proof that Moses was a liar. Nothing could stop him. In vain I attempted to change the subject, by employing every artifice in my power, and even attacking with vehemence his political principles. He returned to the charge with unabated ardour. I called upon him for a song though I never heard him sing in my life. He struck up one of his own composition; but the instant he had finished it he resumed his favourite topic. I felt extremely mortified, and remarked that he had forgotten his promise, and that it was not fair to wound so deeply the opinions of the ladies. 'Oh! ' said he, 'they'll come again. What a pity it is that people should be so prejudiced!' To which I retorted that their prejudices might be virtues. 'If so,' he replied, 'the blossoms may be beautiful to the eye, but the root is weak.' One of the most extraordinary properties belonging to Mr. Paine is his power of retaining everything he has written in the course of his life. It is a fact that he can repeat word for word every sentence in his 'Common Sense,' 'Rights of Man,' etc., etc. The Bible is the only book which he has studied, and there is not a verse in it that is not familiar to him. In shewing me one day the beautiful models of two bridges he had devised he observed that Dr. Franklin once told him that 'books are written to please, houses built for great men, churches for priests, but no bridges for the people.' These models exhibit an extraordinary degree not only of skill but of taste; and are wrought with extreme delicacy entirely by his own hands. The largest is nearly four feet in length; the iron works, the chains, and every other article belonging to it, were forged and manufactured by himself. It is intended as the model of a bridge which is to be constructed across the Delaware, extending 480 feet with only one arch. The other is to be erected over a lesser river, whose name I forget, and is likewise a single arch, and of his own workmanship, excepting the chains, which, instead of iron, are cut out of pasteboard, by the fair hand of his correspondent the 'Little Corner of the World,' whose indefatigable perseverance is extraordinary. He was offered £3000 for these models and refused it. The iron bars, which I before mentioned that I noticed in a corner of his room, were also forged by himself, as the model of a crane, of a new description. He put them together, and exhibited the power of the lever to a most surprising degree."[1]

About this time Sir Robert Smith died, and another of the ties to Paris was snapped. His beloved Bonnevilles promised to follow him to the New World. His old friend Rickman has come over to see him off, and observed that "he did not drink spirits, and wine he took moderately; he even objected to any spirits being laid in as a part of his

[1] "Letters from France," etc., London, 1804, 2 vols., 8vo. Thirty-three pages of the last letter are devoted to Paine.

sea-stock." These two friends journeyed together to Havre, where, on September 1st, the way-worn man begins his homeward voyage. Poor Rickman, the perpetually prosecuted, strains his eyes till the sail is lost, then sits on the beach and writes his poetical tribute to Jefferson and America for recalling Paine, and a touching farewell to his friend:

> " Thus smooth be thy waves, and thus gentle the breeze,
>   As thou bearest my Paine far away;
>   O waft him to comfort and regions of ease,
>   Each blessing of freedom and friendship to seize,
>   And bright be his setting sun's ray."

Who can imagine the joy of those eyes when they once more beheld the distant coast of the New World! Fifteen years have passed,—years in which all nightmares became real, and liberty's sun had turned to blood,—since he saw the happy land fading behind him. Oh, America, thine old friend who first claimed thy republican independence, who laid aside his Quaker coat and fought for thy cause, believing it sacred, is returning to thy breast! This is the man of whom Washington wrote: "His writings certainly had a powerful effect on the public mind,—ought they not then to meet an adequate return? He is poor! He is chagrined!" It is not money he needs now, but tenderness, sympathy; for he comes back from an old world that has plundered, outlawed, imprisoned him for his love of mankind. He has seen his dear friends sent to the guillotine, and others are pining in British prisons for publishing his "Rights of Man,"—principles pronounced by President

Jefferson and Secretary Madison to be those of the United States. Heartsore, scarred, white-haired, there remains to this veteran of many struggles for humanity but one hope, a kindly welcome, a peaceful haven for his tempest-tossed life. Never for an instant has his faith in the heart of America been shaken. Already he sees his friend Jefferson's arms extended; he sees his old comrades welcoming him to their hearths; he sees his own house and sward at Bordentown, and the beautiful Kirkbride mansion beside the Delaware,—river of sacred memories, soon to be spanned by his graceful arch. How the ladies he left girls,—Fanny, Kitty, Sally,—will come with their husbands to greet him! How will they admire the latest bridge-model, with Lady Smith's delicate chain-work for which (such is his estimate of friendship) he refused three thousand pounds, though it would have made his mean room palatial! Ah, yes, poor heart, America will soothe your wounds, and pillow your sinking head on her breast! America, with Jefferson in power, is herself again. They do not hate men in America for not believing in a celestial Robespierre. Thou stricken friend of man, who hast appealed from the god of wrath to the God of Humanity, see in the distance that Maryland coast, which early voyagers called Avalon, and sing again your song when first stepping on that shore twenty-seven years ago:

> " I come to sing that summer is at hand,
> The summer time of wit, you 'll understand;
> Plants, fruits, and flowers, and all the smiling race
> That can the orchard or the garden grace;

The Rose and Lily shall address the fair,
And whisper sweetly out, ' My dears, take care : '
With sterling worth the Plant of Sense shall rise,
And teach the curious to philosophize !'
The frost returns ? We 'll garnish out the scenes
With stately rows of Evergreens,
Trees that will bear the frost, and deck their tops
With everlasting flowers, like diamond drops."[1]

[1] "The Snowdrop and Critic," *Pennsylvania Magazine*, 1775. Couplets are omitted between those given.

CHAPTER XVI.

THE AMERICAN INQUISITION.

On October 30th Paine landed at Baltimore. More than two and a half centuries had elapsed since the Catholic Lord Baltimore appointed a Protestant Governor of Maryland, William Stone, who proclaimed in that province (1648) religious freedom and equality. The Puritans, crowding thither, from regions of oppression, grew strong enough to exterminate the religion of Lord Baltimore who had given them shelter, and imprisoned his Protestant Governor. So, in the New World, passed the Inquisition from Catholic to Protestant hands.

In Paine's first American pamphlet, he had repeated and extolled the principle of that earliest proclamation of religious liberty. "Diversity of religious opinions affords a larger field for Christian kindness." The Christian kindness now consists in a cessation of sectarian strife that they may unite in stretching the author of the "Age of Reason" on their common rack, so far as was possible under a Constitution acknowledging no deity. This persecution began on the victim's arrival.

Soon after landing Paine wrote to President Jefferson : " I arrived here on Saturday from Havre, after a passage of sixty days. I have several cases of models, wheels, etc., and as soon as I can get them from the vessel and put them on board the packet for Georgetown I shall set off to pay my respects to you. Your much obliged fellow-citizen, —THOMAS PAINE."

On reaching Washington City Paine found his dear friend Monroe starting off to resume his ministry in Paris, and by him wrote to Mr. Este, banker in Paris (Sir Robert Smith's son-in-law), enclosing a letter to Rickman, in London. "You can have no idea," he tells Rickman, "of the agitation which my arrival occasioned." Every paper is "filled with applause or abuse."

"My property in this country has been taken care of by my friends, and is now worth six thousand pounds sterling; which put in the funds will bring me £400 sterling a year. Remember me in friendship and affection to your wife and family, and in the circle of our friends. I am but just arrived here, and the minister sails in a few hours, so that I have just time to write you this. If he should not sail this tide I will write to my good friend Col. Bosville, but in any case I request you to wait on him for me.[1] Yours in friendship."

[1] Paine still had faith in Bosville. He was slow in suspecting any man who seemed enthusiastic for liberty. In this connection it may be mentioned that it is painful to find in the "Diary and Letters of Gouverneur Morris," (ii., p. 426) a confidential letter to Robert R. Livingston, Minister in France, which seems to assume that Minister's readiness to receive slanders of Jefferson, who appointed him, and of Paine whose friendship he seemed to value. Speaking of the President, Morris says: "The employment of and confidence in adventurers from abroad will sooner or later rouse the pride and indignation of this country." Morris' editor adds: "This was probably an allusion to Thomas Paine, who had recently returned to America and was supposed to be an intimate friend of Mr. Jefferson, who, it was said, received him warmly, dined him at the White House, and could be seen walking arm in arm with him on the street any fine afternoon." The allusion to "adventurers" was no doubt meant for Paine, but not to his reception by Jefferson, for Morris' letter was written on August 27th, some two months before

The defeated Federalists had already prepared their batteries to assail the President for inviting Paine to return on a national ship, under escort of a Congressman. It required some skill for these adherents of John Adams, a Unitarian, to set the Inquisition in motion. It had to be done, however, as there was no chance of breaking down Jefferson but by getting preachers to sink political differences and hound the President's favorite author. Out of the North, stronghold of the "British Party," came this partisan crusade under a pious flag. In Virginia and the South the "Age of Reason" was fairly discussed, its influence being so great that Patrick Henry, as we have seen, wrote and burnt a reply. In Virginia, Deism, though largely prevailing, had not prevented its adherents from supporting the Church as an institution. It had become their habit to talk of such matters only in private. Jefferson had not ventured to express his views in public, and was troubled at finding himself mixed up with the heresies of Paine.[1] The author on

---

Paine's arrival. It was probably meant by Morris to damage Paine in Paris, where it was known that he was intimate with Livingston, who had been introduced by him to influential men, among others to Sir Robert Smith and Este, bankers. It is to be hoped that Livingston resented Morris' assumption of his treacherous character. Morris, who had shortly before dined at the White House, tells Livingston that Jefferson "is descending to a condition which I find no decent word to designate." Surely Livingston's descendants should discover his reply to that letter.

[1] To the Rev. Dr. Waterhouse (Unitarian) who had asked permission to publish a letter of his, Jefferson, with a keen remembrance of Paine's fate, wrote (July 19, 1822): "No, my dear Sir, not for the world. Into what a hornet's nest would it thrust my head!—The *genus irritabile vatum*, on whom argument is lost, and reason is by themselves disdained in matters of religion. Don Quixote undertook to redress the bodily wrongs of the world, but the redressment of mental vagaries would be an enterprise more than Quixotic. I should as soon undertake to bring the crazy skulls of Bedlam to

reaching Lovell's Hotel, Washington, had made known his arrival to the President, and was cordially received; but as the newspapers came in with their abuse, Jefferson may have been somewhat intimidated. At any rate Paine so thought. Eager to disembarrass the administration, Paine published a letter in the *National Intelligencer*, which had cordially welcomed him, in which he said that he should not ask or accept any office.[1] He meant to continue writing and bring forward his mechanical projects. None the less did the "federalist" press use Paine's infidelity to belabor the President, and the author had to write defensive letters from the moment of his arrival. On October 29th, before Paine had landed, the *National Intelligencer* had printed (from a Lancaster, Pa., journal) a vigorous letter, signed "A Republican," showing that the denunciations of Paine were not religious, but political, as John Adams was also unorthodox. The "federalists" must often have wished that they had taken this warning,

sound understanding as to inculcate reason into that of an Athanasian. I am old, and tranquillity is now my *summum bonum*. Keep me therefore from the fire and faggot of Calvin and his victim Servetus. Happy in the prospect of a restoration of a primitive Christianity, I must leave to younger athletes to lop off the false branches which have been engrafted into it by the mythologists of the middle and modern ages."—MS. belonging to Dr. Fogg of Boston.

[1] The *National Intelligencer* (Nov. 3d), announcing Paine's arrival at Baltimore, said, among other things: "Be his religious sentiments what they may, it must be their [the American people's] wish that he may live in the undisturbed possession of our common blessings, and enjoy them the more from his active participation in their attainment." The same paper said, Nov. 10th: "Thomas Paine has arrived in this city [Washington] and has received a cordial reception from the Whigs of Seventy-six, and the republicans of 1800, who have the independence to feel and avow a sentiment of gratitude for his eminent revolutionary services."

for Paine's pen was keener than ever, and the opposition had no writer to meet him. His eight "Letters to the Citizens of the United States" were scathing, eloquent, untrammelled by partisanship, and made a profound impression on the country,—for even the opposition press had to publish them as part of the news of the day.[1]

On Christmas Day Paine wrote the President a suggestion for the purchase of Louisiana. The French, to whom Louisiana had been ceded by Spain, closed New Orleans (November 26th) against foreign ships (including American), and prohibited deposits there by way of the Mississippi. This caused much excitement, and the "federalists" showed eagerness to push the administration into a belligerent attitude toward France. Paine's "common sense" again came to the front, and he sent Jefferson the following paper:

"OF LOUISIANA.

"Spain has ceded Louisiana to france, and france has excluded the Americans from N. Orleans and the navigation of the Mississippi; the people of the Western Territory have complained of it to their Government, and the governt. is of consequence involved and interested in the affair The question then is—What is the best step to be taken?

"The one is to begin by memorial and remonstrance against an infraction of a right. The other is by accommodation, still keeping the right in view, but not making it a groundwork.

"Suppose then the Government begin by making a proposal to france to repurchase the cession, made to her by Spain, of

---

[1] They were published in the *National Intelligencer* of November 15th, 22d, 29th, December 6th, January 25th, and February 2d, 1803. Of the others one appeared in the *Aurora* (Philadelphia), dated from Bordentown, N. J., March 12th, and the last in the Trenton *True American*, dated April 21st.

Louisiana, provided it be with the consent of the people of Louisiana or a majority thereof.

"By beginning on this ground any thing can be said without carrying the appearance of a threat,—the growing power of the western territory can be stated as matter of information, and also the impossibility of restraining them from seizing upon New Orleans, and the equal impossibility of france to prevent it.

"Suppose the proposal attended to, the sum to be given comes next on the carpet. This, on the part of America, will be estimated between the value of the Commerce, and the quantity of revenue that Louisiana will produce.

"The french treasury is not only empty, but the Government has consumed by anticipation a great part of the next year's revenue. A monied proposal will, I believe, be attended to; if it should, the claims upon france can be stipulated as part of the payment, and that sum can be paid here to the claimants.

"——I congratulate you on the *birthday of the New Sun*, now called christmas-day; and I make you a present of a thought on Louisiana.

"T. P"

Jefferson next day told Paine, what was as yet a profound secret, that he was already contemplating the purchase of Louisiana.[1]

---

[1] "The idea occurred to me," Paine afterwards wrote to the President, "without knowing it had occurred to any other person, and I mentioned it to Dr. Leib who lived in the same house (Lovell's); and, as he appeared pleased with it, I wrote the note and showed it to him before I sent it. The next morning you said to me that measures were already taken in that business. When Leib returned from Congress I told him of it. 'I knew that,' said he. 'Why then,' said I, 'did you not tell me so, because in that case I would not have sent the note.' 'That is the very reason,' said he; 'I would not tell you, because two opinions concurring on a case strengthen it.' I do not, however, like Dr. Leib's motion about Banks. Congress ought to be very cautious how it gives encouragement to this speculating project of banking, for it is now carried to an extreme. It is but another kind of striking paper money. Neither do I like the notion respecting the recession of the territory [District of Columbia.]." Dr. Michael Leib was a representative from Pennsylvania.

The "New Sun" was destined to bring his sun-strokes on Paine. The pathetic story of his wrongs in England, his martyrdom in France, was not generally known, and, in reply to attacks, he had to tell it himself. He had returned for repose and found himself a sort of battlefield. One of the most humiliating circumstances was the discovery that in this conflict of parties the merits of his religion were of least consideration. The outcry of the country against him, so far as it was not merely political, was the mere ignorant echo of pulpit vituperation. His well-considered theism, fruit of so much thought, nursed amid glooms of the dungeon, was called infidelity or atheism. Even some from whom he might have expected discriminating criticism accepted the vulgar version and wrote him in deprecation of a work they had not read. Samuel Adams, his old friend, caught in this *schwärmerei*, wrote him from Boston (November 30th) that he had "heard" that he had "turned his mind to a defence of infidelity." Paine copied for him his creed from the "Age of Reason," and asked, "My good friend, do you call believing in God infidelity?"

This letter to Samuel Adams (January 1, 1803) has indications that Paine had developed farther his theistic ideal.

"We cannot serve the Deity in the manner we serve those who cannot do without that service. He needs no service from us. We can add nothing to eternity. But it is in our power to render a service acceptable to him, and that is, not by praying, but by endeavoring to make his creatures happy. A man does not serve God by praying, for it is himself he is trying to serve;

and as to hiring or paying men to pray, as if the Deity needed instruction, it is in my opinion an abomination. I have been exposed to and preserved through many dangers, but instead of buffeting the Deity with prayers, as if I distrusted him, or must dictate to him, I reposed myself on his protection; and you, my friend, will find, even in your last moments, more consolation in the silence of resignation than in the murmuring wish of a prayer."

Paine must have been especially hurt by a sentence in the letter of Samuel Adams in which he said: "Our friend, the president of the United States, has been calumniated for his liberal sentiments, by men who have attributed that liberality to a latent design to promote the cause of infidelity." To this he did not reply, but it probably led him to feel a deeper disappointment at the postponement of the interviews he had hoped to enjoy with Jefferson after thirteen years of separation. A feeling of this kind no doubt prompted the following note (January 12th) sent to the President:

"I will be obliged to you to send back the Models, as I am packing up to set off for Philadelphia and New York. My intention in bringing them here in preference to sending them from Baltimore to Philadelphia, was to have some conversation with you on those matters and others I have not informed you of. But you have not only shown no disposition towards it, but have, in some measure, by a sort of shyness, as if you stood in fear of federal observation, precluded it. I am not the only one, who makes observations of this kind."

Jefferson at once took care that there should be no misunderstanding as to his regard for Paine. The author was for some days a guest in the President's family, where he again met Maria Jefferson (Mrs. Eppes) whom he had known in Paris. Randall says the devout ladies of the family had been shy of Paine, as was but natural, on account of the President's reputation for rationalism, but "Paine's discourse was weighty, his manners sober and inoffensive; and he left Mr. Jefferson's mansion the subject of lighter prejudices than he entered it."[1]

Paine's defamers have manifested an eagerness to ascribe his maltreatment to personal faults. This is not the case. For some years after his arrival in the country no one ventured to hint anything disparaging to his personal habits or sobriety. On January 1, 1803, he wrote to Samuel Adams: "I have a good state of health and a happy mind; I take care of both by nourishing the first with temperance, and the latter with abundance." Had not this been true the "federal" press would have noised it abroad. He was neat in his attire. In all portraits, French and American, his dress is in accordance with the fashion. There was not, so far as I can discover, a suggestion while he was at Washington, that he was not a suitable guest for any drawing-room in the capital. On February 23, 1803, probably, was written the following which I find among the Cobbett papers:

From Mr. Paine to Mr. Jefferson, on the occasion of a toast being given at a federal dinner at Washington, of "MAY THEY NEVER KNOW PLEASURE WHO LOVE PAINE."

"I send you, Sir, a tale about some Feds,
Who, in their wisdom, got to loggerheads.

---

[1] "Life of Jefferson," ii., 642 *seq.* Randall is mistaken in some statements. Paine, as we have seen, did not return on the ship placed at his service by the President; nor did the President's letter appear until long after his return, when he and Jefferson felt it necessary in order to disabuse the public mind of the most absurd rumors on the subject.

> The case was this, they felt so flat and sunk,
> They took a glass together and got drunk.
> Such things, you know, are neither new nor rare,
> For some will hary themselves when in despair.
> It was the natal day of Washington,
> And that they thought a famous day for fun;
> For with the learned world it is agreed,
> The better day the better deed.
> They talked away, and as the glass went round
> They grew, in point of wisdom, more profound;
> For at the bottom of the bottle lies
> That kind of sense we overlook when wise.
> Come, here's a toast, cried one, with roar immense,
> May none know pleasure who love Common Sense.
> Bravo! cried some,—no, no! some others cried,
> But left it to the waiter to decide.
> I think, said he, the case would be more plain,
> To leave out Common Sense, and put in Paine.
> On this a mighty noise arose among
> This drunken, bawling, senseless throng.
> Some said that Common Sense was all a curse,
> That making people wiser made them worse;
> It learned them to be careful of their purse,
> And not be laid about like babes at nurse,
> Nor yet believe in stories upon trust,
> Which all mankind, to be well governed must;
> And that the toast was better at the first,
> And he that did n't think so might be cursed.
> So on they went, till such a fray arose
> As all who know what Feds are may suppose."

On his way northward, to his old home in Bordentown, Paine passed many a remembered spot, but found little or no greeting on his journey. In Baltimore a "New Jerusalemite," as the Swedenborgian was then called, the Rev. Mr. Hargrove, accosted him with the information that the key to scripture was found, after being lost 4,000 years.

"Then it must be very rusty," answered Paine. In Philadelphia his old friend Dr. Benjamin Rush never came near him. "His principles," wrote Rush to Cheetham, "avowed in his 'Age of Reason,' were so offensive to me that I did not wish to renew my intercourse with him." Paine made arrangements for the reception of his bridge models at Peale's Museum, but if he met any old friend there no mention of it appears. Most of those who had made up the old circle—Franklin, Rittenhouse, Muhlenberg—were dead, some were away in Congress; but no doubt Paine saw George Clymer. However, he did not stay long in Philadelphia, for he was eager to reach the spot he always regarded as his home, Bordentown. And there, indeed, his hope, for a time, seemed to be fulfilled. It need hardly be said that his old friend Colonel Kirkbride gave him hearty welcome. John Hall, Paine's bridge mechanician, "never saw him jollier," and he was full of mechanical "whims and schemes" they were to pursue together. Jefferson was candidate for the presidency, and Paine entered heartily into the canvass; which was not prudent, but he knew nothing of prudence. The issue not only concerned an old friend, but was turning on the question of peace with France. On March 12th he writes against the "federalist" scheme for violently seizing New Orleans. At a meeting in April, over which Colonel Kirkbride presides, Paine drafts a reply to an attack on Jefferson's administration, circulated in New York. On April 21st he writes the refutation of an attack on Jefferson, *àpropos* of the national vessel offered for his return, which had been coupled with a charge that Paine had proposed to the Directory an invasion of America! In June he writes about his bridge models (then at Peale's Museum, Philadelphia), and his hope to span the Delaware and the Schuylkill with iron arches.

Here is a letter written to Jefferson from Bordentown (August 2d) containing suggestions concerning the beginning of government in Louisiana, from which it would appear that Paine's faith in the natural inspiration of *vox populi* was still imperfect:

"I take it for granted that the present inhabitants know little or nothing of election and representation as constituting government. They are therefore not in an immediate condition to exercise those powers, and besides this they are perhaps too much under the influence of their priests to be sufficiently free.

"I should suppose that a Government *provisoire* formed by Congress for three, five, or seven years would be the best mode of beginning. In the meantime they may be initiated into the practice by electing their Municipal government, and after some experience they will be in train to elect their State government. I think it would not only be good policy but right to say, that the people shall have the right of electing their Church Ministers, otherwise their Ministers will hold by authority from the Pope. I do not make it a compulsive article, but to put it in their power to use it when they please. It will serve to hold the priests in a stile of good behavior, and also to give the people an idea of elective rights. Anything, they say, will do to learn upon, and therefore they may as well begin upon priests.

"The present prevailing language is french and spanish, but it will be necessary to establish schools to teach english as the laws ought to be in the language of the Union.

"As soon as you have formed any plan for settling the Lands I shall be glad to know it. My motive for this is because there are thousands and tens of thousands in England and Ireland and also in Scotland who are friends of mine by principle, and who would gladly change their present country and condition. Many among them, for I have friends in all ranks of life in those countries, are capable of becoming monied purchasers to any amount.

"If you can give me any hints respecting Louisiana, the quantity in square miles, the population, and amount of the present Revenue I will find an opportunity of making some use of it. When the formalities of the cession are compleated, the next thing will be to take possession, and I think it would be very consistent for the President of the United States to do this in person.

"What is Dayton gone to New Orleans for? Is he there as an Agent for the British as Blount was said to be?"

Of the same date is a letter to Senator Breckenridge, of Kentucky, forwarded through Jefferson:

"My Dear Friend,—Not knowing your place of Residence in Kentucky I send this under cover to the President desiring him to fill up the direction.

"I see by the public papers and the Proclamation for calling Congress, that the cession of Louisiana has been obtained. The papers state the purchase to be 11,250,000 dollars in the six per cents and 3,750,000 dollars to be paid to American claimants who have furnished supplies to France and the french Colonies and are yet unpaid, making on the whole 15,000,000 dollars.

"I observe that the faction of the Feds who last Winter were for going to war to obtain possession of that country and who attached so much importance to it that no expense or risk ought be spared to obtain it, have now altered their tone and say it is not worth having, and that we are better without it than with it. Thus much for their consistency. What follows is for your private consideration.

"The second section of the 2d article of the constitution says, The 'President shall have Power by and with the consent of the senate to make Treaties provided two thirds of the senators present concur.'

"A question may be supposed to arise on the present case, which is, under what character is the cession to be considered and taken up in congress, whether as a treaty, or in some other shape ? I go to examine this point.

"Though the word, Treaty, as a Word, is unlimited in its meaning and application, it must be supposed to have a defined meaning in the constitution. It there means Treaties of alliance or of navigation and commerce—Things which require a more profound deliberation than common acts do, because they entail on the parties a future reciprocal responsibility and become afterwards a supreme law on each of the contracting countries which neither can annull. But the cession of Louisiana to the United States has none of these features in it. It is a sale and purchase. A sole act which when finished, the parties have no more to do with each other than other buyers and sellers have. It has no future reciprocal consequences (which is one of the marked characters of a Treaty) annexed to it ; and the idea of its becoming a supreme law to the parties reciprocally (which is another of the characters of a Treaty) is inapplicable in the present case. There remains nothing for such a law to act upon.

"I love the restriction in the constitution which takes from the Executive the power of making treaties of his own will : and also the clause which requires the consent of two thirds of the Senators, because we cannot be too cautious in involving and entangling ourselves with foreign powers ; but I have an equal objection against extending the same power to the senate in cases to which it is not strictly and constitutionally applicable, because it is giving a nullifying power to a minority. Treaties, as already observed, are to have future consequences and whilst they remain, remain always in execution externally as well as internally, and therefore it is better to run the risk of losing a good treaty for the want of two thirds of the senate than be exposed to the danger of ratifying a bad one by a small majority. But in the present case no operation is to follow but what acts itself within our own Territory and under our own laws. We are the sole power concerned after the cession is accepted and the money paid, and therefore the cession is not a Treaty in the constitutional meaning of the word subject to be rejected by a minority in the senate.

"The question whether the cession shall be accepted and the bargain closed by a grant of money for the purpose, (which I take to be the sole question) is a case equally open to both houses of congress, and if there is any distinction of *formal right*, it ought according to the constitution, as a money transaction, to begin in the house of Representatives.

"I suggest these matters that the senate may not be taken unawares, for I think it not improbable that some Fed, who intends to negative the cession, will move to take it up as if it were a Treaty of Alliance or of Navigation and Commerce.

"The object here is an increase of territory for a valuable consideration. It is altogether a home concern—a matter of domestic policy. The only real ratification is the payment of the money, and as all verbal ratification without this goes for nothing, it would be a waste of time and expense to debate on the verbal ratification distinct from the money ratification. The shortest way, as it appears to me, would be to appoint a committee to bring in a report on the President's Message, and for that committee to report a bill for the payment of the money. The french Government, as the seller of the property, will not consider anything ratification but the payment of the money contracted for.

"There is also another point, necessary to be aware of, which is, to accept it in toto. Any alteration or modification in it, or annexed as a condition is so far fatal, that it puts it in the power of the other party to reject the whole and propose new Terms. There can be no such thing as ratifying in part, or with a condition annexed to it and the ratification to be binding. It is still a continuance of the negociation.

"It ought to be presumed that the American ministers have done to the best of their power and procured the best possible terms, and that being immediately on the spot with the other party they were better Judges of the whole, and of what could, or could not be done, than any person at this distance, and unacquainted with many of the circumstances of the case, can possibly be.

"If a treaty, a contract, or a cession be good upon the whole, it is ill policy to hazard the whole, by an experiment to get some trifle in it altered. The right way of proceeding in such case is to make sure of the whole by ratifying it, and then instruct the minister to propose a clause to be added to the Instrument to obtain the amendment or alteration wished for. This was the method Congress took with respect to the Treaty of Commerce with France in 1778. Congress ratified the whole and proposed two new articles which were agreed to by France and added to the Treaty.

"There is according to newspaper account an article which admits french and spanish vessels on the same terms as American vessels. But this does not make it a commercial Treaty. It is only one of the Items in the payment: and it has this advantage, that it joins Spain with France in making the cession and is an encouragement to commerce and new settlers.

"With respect to the purchase, admitting it to be 15 millions dollars, it is an advantageous purchase. The revenue alone purchased as an annuity or rent roll is worth more—at present I suppose the revenue will pay five per cent for the purchase money.

"I know not if these observations will be of any use to you. I am in a retired village and out of the way of hearing the talk of the great world. But I see that the Feds, at least some of them, are changing their tone and now reprobating the acquisition of Louisiana; and the only way they can take to lose the affair will be to take it up as they would a Treaty of Commerce and annull it by a Minority; or entangle it with some condition that will render the ratification of no effect.

"I believe in this state (Jersey) we shall have a majority at the next election. We gain some ground and lose none anywhere. I have half a disposition to visit the Western World next spring and go on to New Orleans. They are a new people and unacquainted with the principles of representative government and I think I could do some good among them.

"As the stage-boat which was to take this letter to the Post-office does not depart till to-morrow, I amuse myself with continuing the subject after I had intended to close it.

"I know little and can learn but little of the extent and present population of Louisiana. After the cession be compleated and the territory annexed to the United States it will, I suppose, be formed into states, one, at least, to begin with.

The people, as I have said, are new to us and we to them and a great deal will depend on a right beginning. As they have been transferred backward and forward several times from one European Government to another it is natural to conclude they have no fixed prejudices with respect to foreign attachments, and this puts them in a fit disposition for their new condition. The established religion is roman ; but in what state it is as to exterior ceremonies (such as processions and celebrations), I know not. Had the cession to france continued with her, religion I suppose would have been put on the same footing as it is in that country, and there no ceremonial of religion can appear on the streets or highways ; and the same regulation is particularly necessary now or there will soon be quarrells and tumults between the old settlers and the new. The Yankees will not move out of the road for a little wooden Jesus stuck on a stick and carried in procession nor kneel in the dirt to a wooden Virgin Mary. As we do not govern the territory as provinces but incorporated as states, religion there must be on the same footing it is here, and Catholics have the same rights as Catholics have with us and no others. As to political condition the Idea proper to be held out is, that we have neither conquered them, nor bought them, but formed a Union with them and they become in consequence of that union a part of the national sovereignty.

" The present Inhabitants and their descendants will be a majority for some time, but new emigrations from the old states and from Europe, and intermarriages, will soon change the first face of things, and it is necessary to have this in mind when the first measures shall be taken. Everything done as an expedient grows worse every day, for in proportion as the mind grows up to the full standard of sight it disclaims the expedient. America had nearly been ruined by expedients in the first stages of the revolution, and perhaps would have been so, had not 'Common Sense' broken the charm and the Declaration of Independence sent it into banishment.

"Yours in friendship

" remember me in the circle of your friends."

" THOMAS PAINE.[1]

---

[1] The original is in possession of Mr. William F. Havermeyer, Jr.

Mr. E. M. Woodward, in his account of Bordentown, mentions among the "traditions" of the place, that Paine used to meet a large number of gentlemen at the "Washington House," kept by Debora Applegate, where he conversed freely "with any proper person who approached him."

"Mr. Paine was too much occupied in literary pursuits and writing to spend a great deal of his time here, but he generally paid several visits during the day. His drink was invariably brandy. In walking he was generally absorbed in deep thought, seldom noticed any one as he passed, unless spoken to, and in going from his home to the tavern was frequently observed to cross the street several times. It is stated that several members of the church were turned from their faith by him, and on this account, and the general feeling of the community against him for his opinions on religious subjects, he was by the mass of the people held in odium, which feeling to some extent was extended to Col. Kirkbride."

These "traditions" were recorded in 1876. Paine's "great power of conversation" was remembered. But among the traditions, even of the religious, there is none of any excess in drinking.

Possibly the turning of several church-members from their faith may not have been so much due to Paine as to the parsons, in showing their "religion" as a gorgon turning hearts to stone against a benefactor of mankind. One day Paine went with Colonel Kirkbride to visit Samuel Rogers, the Colonel's brother-in-law, at Bellevue, across the river. As he entered the door Rogers turned his back, refusing his old friend's hand, because it had written the "Age of Reason." Presently Bordentown was placarded with pictures of the Devil flying away with Paine. The pulpits set up a chorus of vituperation. Why should the victim spare the altar on which he is sacrificed, and justice also? Dogma had chosen to grapple with the old man in its own way. That it was able to break a driven leaf Paine could admit as truly as Job; but he could as bravely say: Withdraw thy hand from me, and I will answer thee, or thou shalt answer me! In Paine too it will be proved that such outrages on truth and friendship, on the rights of thought, proceed from no God, but from the destructive forces once personified as the adversary of man.

Early in March Paine visited New York, to see Monroe before his departure for France. He drove with Kirkbride to Trenton; but so furious was the pious mob, he was refused a seat in the Trenton stage. They dined at Government House, but when starting for Brunswick were hooted. These were the people for whose liberties Paine had marched that same road on foot, musket in hand. At Trenton insults were heaped on the man who by camp-fires had written the *Crisis*, which animated the conquerors of the Hessians at that place, in "the times that tried men's souls." These people he helped to make free,—free to cry *Crucify!*

CHAPTER XVII

DEATH AND RESURRECTION.

THE blow that Paine received by the refusal of his vote at New Rochelle was heavy. Elisha Ward, a Tory in the Revolution, had dexterously gained power enough to give his old patrons a good revenge on the first advocate of independence. The blow came at a time when his means were low, and Paine resolved to apply to Congress for payment of an old debt. The response would at once relieve him, and overwhelm those who were insulting him in New York. This led to a further humiliation, and one or two letters to Congress, of which Paine's enemies did not fail to make the most.[1]

[1] Paine had always felt that Congress was in his debt for his voyage to France for supplies with Col. Laurens (i., p. 171). In a letter (Feb. 20, 1782) to Robert Morris, Paine mentions that when Col. Laurens proposed that he should accompany him, as secretary, he was on the point of establishing a newspaper. He had purchased twenty reams of paper, and Mr. Izard had sent to St. Eustatia for seventy more. This scheme, which could hardly fail of success, was relinquished for the voyage. It was undertaken at the urgent solicitation of Laurens, and Paine certainly regarded it as official. He had ninety dollars when he started, in bills of exchange; when Col. Laurens left him, after their return, he had but two louis d'or. The Memorial sent by Paine to Congress (Jan. 21, 1808) recapitulated facts known to my reader. It was presented by the Hon. George Clinton, Jr., February 4, and referred to the Committee of Claims. On February 14th Paine wroth a statement concerning the $3,000 given him (1785) by Congress, which he maintained was an indemnity for injustice done him in the Deane case. Laurens had long been dead. The Committee consulted the

The letters are those of a broken-hearted man, and it seems marvellous that Jefferson, Madison, and the Clintons did not intervene and see that some recognition of Paine's former services, by those who should not have forgotten them, was made without the ill-judged memorial. While they were enjoying their grandeur the man who, as Jefferson wrote, "steadily laboured, and with as much effect as any man living," to secure America freedom, was living—or rather dying—in a miserable lodging-house, 63 Partition Street. He had gone there for economy; for he was exhibiting that morbid apprehension about his means which is a well-known symptom of decline in those who have suffered poverty in early life. Washington, with 40,000 acres, wrote in his last year as if facing ruin. Paine had only a little farm at New Rochelle. He had for some time suffered from want of income, and at last had to sell the farm he meant for the Bonnevilles for $10,000; but the purchaser died, and at his widow's appeal the contract was cancelled. It was at this time that he appealed to Congress. It appears, however,

President, whose reply I know not. Vice-President Clinton wrote (March 23, 1808) that "from the information I received at the time I have reason to believe that Mr. Paine accompanied Col. Laurens on his mission to France in the course of our revolutionary war, for the purpose of negotiating a loan, and that he acted as his secretary on that occasion; but although I have no doubt of the truth of this fact, I cannot assert it from my own actual knowledge." There was nothing found on the journals of Congress to show Paine's connection with the mission. The old author was completely upset by his longing to hear the fate of his memorial, and he wrote two complaints of the delay, showing that his nerves were shattered. "If," he says, March 7th, "my memorial was referred to the Committee of Claims for the purpose of losing it, it is unmanly policy. After so many years of service my heart grows cold towards America."

that Paine was not anxious for himself, but for the family of Madame Bonneville, whose statement on this point is important.

The last letter that I can find of Paine's was written to Jefferson, July 8, 1808:

"The british Ministry have out-schemed themselves. It is not difficult to see what the motive and object of that Ministry were in issuing the orders of Council. They expected those orders would force all the commerce of the United States to England, and then, by giving permission to such cargoes as they did not want for themselves to depart for the Continent of Europe, to raise a revenue out of those countries and America. But instead of this they have lost revenue; that is, they have lost the revenue they used to receive from American imports, and instead of gaining all the commerce they have lost it all.

"This being the case with the british Ministry it is natural to suppose they would be glad to tread back their steps, if they could do it without too much exposing their ignorance and obstinacy. The Embargo law empowers the President to suspend its operation whenever he shall be satisfied that our ships can pass in safety. It therefore includes the idea of empowering him to use means for arriving at that event. Suppose the President were to authorise Mr. Pinckney to propose to the british Ministry that the United States would negociate with France for rescinding the Milan Decree, on condition the English Ministry would rescind their orders of Council; and in that case the United States would recall their Embargo. France and England stand now at such a distance that neither can propose any thing to the other, neither are there any neutral powers to act as mediators. The U. S. is the only power that can act.

"Perhaps the british Ministry if they listen to the proposal will want to add to it the Berlin decree, which excludes english commerce from the continent of Europe; but this we have nothing to do with, neither has it any thing to do with the Embargo. The british Orders of Council and the Milan decree are parallel cases, and the cause of the Embargo. Yours in friendship."

Paine's last letters to the President are characteristic. One pleads for American intervention to stay the hand of French oppression among the negroes in St. Domingo; for the colonization of Louisiana with free negro laborers; and his very last letter is an appeal for mediation between France and England for the sake of peace.

Nothing came of these pleadings of Paine; but perhaps on his last stroll along the Hudson, with his friend Fulton, to watch the little steamer, he may have recognized the real mediator beginning its labors for the federation of the world.

Early in July, 1808, Paine removed to a comfortable abode, that of Mrs. Ryder, near which Madame Bonneville and her two sons resided. The house was on Herring Street (afterwards 293 Bleecker), and not far, he might be pleased to find, from "Reason Street." Here he made one more attempt to wield his pen,—the result being a brief letter "To the Federal Faction," which he warns that they are endangering American commerce by abusing France and Bonaparte, provoking them to establish a navigation act that will exclude American ships from Europe. "The United States have flourished, unrivalled in commerce, fifteen or sixteen years. But it is not a permanent state of things. It arose from the circumstances of the war, and most probably will change at the close of the present war. The Federalists give provocation enough to promote it."

Apparently this is the last letter Paine ever sent to the printer. The year passed peacefully away; indeed there is reason to believe that from the middle of July, 1808, to the end of January, 1809, he fairly enjoyed existence. During this time he made acquaintance with the worthy Willett Hicks, watchmaker, who was a Quaker preacher. His conversations with Willett Hicks — whose cousin, Elias Hicks, became such an important figure in the Quaker Society twenty years later—were fruitful.

Seven serene months then passed away. Towards the latter part of January, 1809, Paine was very feeble. On the 18th he wrote and signed his Will, in which he reaffirms his theistic faith. On February 1st the Committee of Claims reported unfavorably on his memorial, while recording, "That Mr. Paine rendered great and eminent services to the United States during their struggle for liberty and independence cannot be doubted by any person acquainted with his labours in the cause, and attached to the principles of the contest." On February 25th he had some fever, and a doctor was sent for. Mrs. Ryder attributed the attack to Paine's having stopped taking stimulants, and their resumption was prescribed. About a fortnight later symptoms of dropsy appeared. Towards the end of April Paine was removed to a house on the spot now occupied by No. 59 Grove Street, Madame Bonneville taking up her abode under the same roof. The owner was William A. Thompson, once a law partner of Aaron Burr, whose wife, *née* Maria Holdron, was a niece of Elihu Palmer. The whole of the back part of the house (which was in a lot, no street being then cut) was given up to Paine.[1] Reports of neglect of Paine by Madame Bonneville

---

[1] The topographical facts were investigated by John Randel, Jr., Civil Engineer, at the request of David C. Valentine, Clerk of the Common Council, New York, his report being rendered April 6, 1864.

have been credited by some, but are unfounded. She gave all the time she could to the sufferer, and did her best for him. Willett Hicks sometimes called, and his daughter (afterwards Mrs. Cheeseman) used to take Paine delicacies. The only procurable nurse was a woman named Hedden, who combined piety and artfulness. Paine's physician was the most distinguished in New York, Dr. Romaine, but nurse Hedden managed to get into the house one Dr. Manly, who turned out to be Cheetham's spy. Manly afterwards contributed to Cheetham's book a lying letter, in which he claimed to have been Paine's physician. It will be seen, however, by Madame Bonneville's narrative to Cobbett, that Paine was under the care of his friend, Dr. Romaine. As Manly, assuming that he called as many did, never saw Paine alone, he was unable to assert that Paine recanted, but he converted the exclamations of the sufferer into prayers to Christ.[1]

The god of wrath who ruled in New York a hundred years, through the ministerial prerogatives, was guarded by a Cerberean legend. The three alternatives of the heretic were, recantation, special judgment, terrible death. Before Paine's arrival

[1] Another claimant to have been Paine's physician has been cited. In 1876 (*N. Y. Observer*, Feb. 17th) Rev. Dr. Wickham reported from a late Dr. Matson Smith, of New Rochelle, that he had been Paine's physician, and witnessed his drunkenness. Unfortunately for Wickham he makes Smith say it was on his farm where Paine "spent his latter days." Paine was not on his farm for two years before his death. Smith could never have attended Paine unless in 1803, when he had a slight trouble with his hands,—the only illness he ever had at New Rochelle,—while the guest of a neighbor, who attests his sobriety. Finally, a friend of Dr. Smith is living, Mr. Albert Willcox, who writes me his recollection of what Smith told him of Paine. Neither drunkenness, nor any item of Wickham's report is mentioned. He said Paine was afraid of death, but could only have heard it.

in America, the excitement on his approach had tempted a canny Scot, Donald Fraser, to write an anticipated "Recantation" for him, the title-page being cunningly devised so as to imply that there had been an actual recantation. On his arrival in New York, Paine found it necessary to call Fraser to account. The Scotchman pleaded that he had vainly tried to earn a living as fencing-master, preacher, and school-teacher, but had got eighty dollars for writing the "Recantation." Paine said: "I am glad you found the expedient a successful shift for your needy family; but write no more concerning Thomas Paine. I am satisfied with your acknowledgment—try something more worthy of a man."[1] The second mouth of Cerberus was noisy throughout the land; revivalists were describing in New Jersey how some "infidel" had been struck blind in Virginia, and in Virginia how one was struck dumb in New Jersey. But here was the very head and front of what they called "infidelity," Thomas Paine, who ought to have gathered in his side a sheaf of thunderbolts, preserved by more marvellous "providences" than any sectarian saint. Out of one hundred and sixty carried to the guillotine from his prison, he alone was saved, by the accident of a chalk mark affixed to the wrong side of his cell door. On two ships he prepared to return to America, but was prevented; one sank at sea, the other was searched by the British for him particularly. And at the very moment when New Rochelle disciples were calling down fire on his head, Christopher

[1] Dr. Francis' "Old New York," p. 139.

Dederick tried vainly to answer the imprecation; within a few feet of Paine, his gun only shattered the window at which the author sat. "Providence must be as bad as Thomas Paine," wrote the old deist. This amounted to a sort of contest like that of old between the prophets of Baal and those of Jehovah. The deists were crying to their antagonists: "Perchance he sleepeth." It seemed a test case. If Paine was spared, what heretic need tremble? But he reached his threescore years and ten in comfort; and the placard of Satan flying off with him represented a last hope.

Skepticism and rationalism were not understood by pious people a hundred years ago. In some regions they are not understood yet. Renan thinks he will have his legend in France modelled after Judas. But no educated Christian conceives of a recantation or extraordinary death-bed for a Darwin, a Parker, an Emerson. The late Mr. Bradlaugh had some fear that he might be a posthumous victim of the "infidel's legend." In 1875, when he was ill in St. Luke's Hospital, New York, he desired me to question the physicians and nurses, that I might, if necessary, testify to his fearlessness and fidelity to his views in the presence of death. But he has died without the "legend," whose decline dates from Paine's case; that was its crucial challenge.

The whole nation had recently been thrown into a wild excitement by the fall of Alexander Hamilton in a duel with Aaron Burr. Hamilton's worldliness had been notorious, but the clergymen (Bishop Moore and the Presbyterian John Mason) reported his dying words of unctuous piety and orthodoxy. In a public letter to the Rev. John Mason, Paine said:

"Between you and your rival in communion ceremonies, Dr. Moore of the Episcopal church, you have, in order to make yourselves appear of some importance, reduced General Hamilton's character to that of a feeble-minded man, who in going out of the world wanted a passport from a priest. Which of you was first applied to for this purpose is a matter of no consequence. The man, sir, who puts his trust and confidence in God, that leads a just and moral life, and endeavors to do good, does not trouble himself about priests when his hour of departure comes, nor permit priests to trouble themselves about him."

The words were widely commented on, and both sides looked forward, almost as if to a prize-fight, to the hour when the man who had unmade thrones, whether in earth or heaven, must face the King of Terrors. Since Michael and Satan had their legendary combat for the body of Moses, there was nothing like it. In view of the pious raids on Paine's death-bed, freethinkers have not been quite fair. To my own mind, some respect is due to those humble fanatics, who really believed that Paine was approaching eternal fires, and had a frantic desire to save him.[1]

Paine had no fear of death; Madame Bonneville's narrative shows that his fear was rather of

[1] Nor should it be forgotten that several liberal Christians, like Hicks, were friendly towards Paine at the close of his life, whereas his most malignant enemies were of his own "Painite" household, Carver and Cheetham. Mr. William Erving tells me that he remembers an English clergyman in New York, named Cunningham, who used to visit his (Erving's) father. He heard him say that Paine and he were friends; and that "the whole fault was that people hectored Paine, and made him say things he would never say to those who treated him as a gentleman."

living too long. But he had some such fear as that of Voltaire when entering his house at Fernay after it began to lighten. He was not afraid of the lightning, he said, but of what the neighboring priest would make of it should he be struck. Paine had some reason to fear that the zealots who had placarded the devil flying away with him might fulfil their prediction by body-snatching. His unwillingness to be left alone, ascribed to superstitious terror, was due to efforts to get a recantation from him, so determined that he dare not be without witnesses. He had foreseen this. While living with Jarvis, two years before, he desired him to bear witness that he maintained his theistic convictions to the last. Jarvis merrily proposed that he should make a sensation by a mock recantation, but the author said, "Tom Paine never told a lie." When he knew that his illness was mortal he solemnly reaffirmed these opinions in the presence of Madame Bonneville, Dr. Romaine, Mr. Haskin, Captain Pelton, and Thomas Nixon.[1] The nurse Hedden, if the Catholic Bishop of Boston (Fenwick) remembered accurately thirty-seven years later, must have conspired to get him into the patient's room, from which, of course, he was stormily expelled. But the Bishop's story is so like a pious novelette that, in the absence of any mention of his visit by Madame Bonneville, herself a Catholic, one cannot be sure that the interview he waited so long to report did not take place in some slumberous episcopal chamber in Boston.[2]

[1] See the certificate of Nixon and Pelton to Cobbett (Vale, p. 177).

[2] Bishop Fenwick's narrative (*U. S. Catholic Magazine*, 1846) is quoted in the *N. Y. Observer*, September 27, 1877. (Extremes become friends when a freethinker is to be crucified.)

It was rumored that Paine's adherents were keeping him under the influence of liquor in order that he might not recant,—so convinced, at heart, or enamoured of Calvinism was this martyr of Theism, who had published his "Age of Reason" from the prison where he awaited the guillotine.[1]

Of what his principles had cost him Paine had near his end a reminder that cut him to the heart. Albert Gallatin had remained his friend, but his connections, the Fews and Nicholsons, had ignored the author they once idolized. The woman for whom he had the deepest affection, in America, had been Kitty Nicholson, now Mrs. Few. Henry Adams, in his biography of Gallatin, says: "When confined to his bed with his last illness he [Paine] sent for Mrs. Few, who came to see him, and when they parted she spoke some words of comfort and religious hope. Poor Paine only turned his face to the wall, and kept silence." What is Mr. Adams' authority for this? According to Rickman, Sherwin, and Vale, Mr. and Mrs. Few came of their own accord, and "Mrs. Few expressed a wish to renew their former friendship." Paine said to her, "very impressively, 'You have neglected me, and I beg that you will leave the room.' Mrs. Few went into the garden and wept bitterly." I doubt this tradition also, but it was cruelly tantali-

[1] Engineer Randel (orthodox), in his topographical report to the Clerk of the City Council (1864), mentions that the "very worthy mechanic," Amasa Wordsworth, who saw Paine daily, told him "there was no truth in such report, and that Thomas Paine had declined saying anything on that subject [religion]." "Paine," testifies Dr. Francis, "clung to his infidelity to the last moment of his natural life." Dr. Francis (orthodox) heard that Paine yielded to King Alcohol, but says Cheetham wrote with "settled malignity," and suspects "sinister motives" in his "strictures on the fruits of unbelief in the degradation of the wretched Paine."

zing for his early friend, after ignoring him six years, to return with Death.

If, amid tortures of this kind, the annoyance of fanatics and the "Painites" who came to watch them, and the paroxysms of pain, the sufferer found relief in stimulants, the present writer can only reflect with satisfaction that such resource existed. For some time no food would stay on his stomach. In such weakness and helplessness he was for a week or so almost as miserable as the Christian spies could desire, and his truest friends were not sorrowful when the peace of death approached. After the years in which the stories of Paine's wretched end have been accumulating, now appears the testimony of the Catholic lady,— persons who remember Madame Bonneville assure me that she was a perfect lady,—that Paine's mind was active to the last, that shortly before death he made a humorous retort to Dr. Romaine, that he died after a tranquil night.

Paine died at eight o'clock on the morning of June 8, 1809. Shortly before, two clergymen had invaded his room, and so soon as they spoke about his opinions Paine said: "Let me alone; good morning!" Madame Bonneville asked if he was satisfied with the treatment he had received in her house, and he said "Oh yes." These were the last words of Thomas Paine.

On June 10th Paine's friends assembled to look on his face for the last time. Madame Bonneville took a rose from her breast and laid it on that of her dead benefactor. His adherents were busy men, and mostly poor; they could not undertake the then difficult journey (nearly twenty-five miles) to the grave beyond New Rochelle. Of the *cortége* that followed Paine a contemptuous account was printed (Aug. 7th) in the London *Packet:*

"Extract of a letter dated June 20th, Philadelphia, written by a gentleman lately returned from a tour : 'On my return from my journey, when I arrived near Harlem, on York island, I met the funeral of Tom Paine on the road. It was going on to East Chester. The followers were two negroes, the next a carriage with six drunken Irishmen, then a riding chair with two men in it, one of whom was asleep, and then an Irish Quaker on horseback. I stopped my sulkey to ask the Quaker what funeral it was; he said it was Paine, and that his friends as well as his enemies were all glad that he was gone, for he had tired his friends out by his intemperance and frailties. I told him that Paine had done a great deal of mischief in the world, and that, if there was any purgatory, he certainly would have a good share of it before the devil would let him go. The Quaker replied, he would sooner take his chance with Paine than any man in New York, on that score. He then put his horse on a trot, and left me.'"

The funeral was going to West Chester; one of the vehicles contained Madame Bonneville and her children; and the Quaker was not an Irishman. I have ascertained that a Quaker did follow Paine, and that it was Willett Hicks. Hicks, who has left us his testimony that Paine was "a good man, and an honest man," may have said that Paine's friends were glad that he was gone, for it was only humane to so feel, but all said about "intemperance and frailties" is doubtless a gloss of the correspondent, like the "drunken Irishmen" substituted for Madame Bonneville and her family.

Could the gentleman of the sulky have appreciated the historic dignity of that little *cortége* he would have turned his horse's head and followed it. Those two negroes, travelling twenty-five miles on foot, represented the homage of a race for whose deliverance Paine had pleaded from his first essay written in America to his recent entreaty for the President's intervention in behalf of the slaughtered negroes of Domingo.[1] One of those vehicles bore the wife of an oppressed French author, and her sons, one of whom was to do gallant service to this country in the War of 1812, the other to explore the unknown West. Behind the Quaker preacher, who would rather take his chance in the next world with Paine than with any man in New York, was following invisibly another of his family and name, who presently built up Hicksite Quakerism, the real monument of Paine, to whom unfriendly Friends refused a grave.

The grand people of America were not there, the clergy were not there; but beside the negroes stood the Quaker preacher and the French Catholic woman. Madame Bonneville placed her son Benjamin—afterwards General in the United States army—at one end of the grave, and standing herself at the other end, cried, as the earth fell on the coffin: "Oh, Mr. Paine, my son stands here as testimony of the gratitude of America, and I for France!"[2]

[1] " On the last day men shall wear
On their heads the dust,
As ensign and as ornament
Of their lowly trust."—*Hafiz*.

[2] No sooner was Paine dead than the ghoul sat gloating upon him. I found in the Rush papers a letter from Cheetham (July 31st) to Benjamin Rush: "Since Mr. Paine's arrival in this city from Washington, when on his way you very properly avoided him, his life, keeping the lowest com-

The day of Paine's death was a day of judgment. He had not been struck blind or dumb; Satan had not carried him off; he had lived beyond his threescore years and ten and died peacefully in his bed. The self-appointed messengers of Zeus had managed to vex this Prometheus who brought fire to men, but could not persuade him to whine for mercy, nor did the predicted thunderbolts come. This immunity of Thomas Paine brought the deity of dogma into a dilemma. It could be explained only on the the theory of an apology made and accepted by the said deity. Plainly there had to be a recantation somewhere. Either Paine had to recant or Dogma had to recant.

The excitement was particularly strong among

pany, has been an uninterrupted scene of filth, vulgarity, and drunkenness. As to the reports, that on his deathbed he had something like compunctious visitings of conscience with regard to his deistical writings and opinions, they are altogether groundless. He resisted very angrily, and with a sort of triumphant and obstinate pride, all attempts to draw him from those doctrines. Much as you must have seen in the course of your professional practice of everything that is offensive in the poorest and most depraved of the species, perhaps you have met with nothing excelling the miserable condition of Mr. Paine. He had scarcely any visitants. It may indeed be said that he was totally neglected and forgotten. Even Mrs. Bournville [*sic*], a woman, I cannot say a Lady, whom he brought with him from Paris, the wife of a Parisian of that name, seemed desirous of hastening his death. He died at Greenwich, in a small room he had hired in a very obscure house. He was hurried to his grave with hardly an attending person. An ill-natured epitaph, written on him in 1796, when it was supposed he was dead, very correctly describes the latter end of his life. He

" Blasphemes the Almighty, lives in filth like a hog,
Is abandoned in death and interr'd like a dog."

The object of this letter was to obtain from Rush, for publication, some abuse of Paine; but the answer honored Paine, save for his heresy, and is quoted by freethinkers as a tribute.

Within a year the grave opened for Cheetham also, and he sank into it branded by the law as the slanderer of a woman's honor, and scourged by the community as a traitor in public life.

the Quakers, who regarded Paine as an apostate Quaker, and perhaps felt compromised by his desire to be buried among them. Willett Hicks told Gilbert Vale that he had been beset by pleading questions. "Did thee never hear him call on Christ?" "As for money," said Hicks, "I could have had any sum." There was found, later on, a Quakeress, formerly a servant in the family of Willett Hicks, not proof against such temptations. She pretended that she was sent to carry some delicacy to Paine, and heard him cry "Lord Jesus have mercy upon me"; she also heard him declare "if the Devil has ever had any agency in any work he has had it in my writing that book [the 'Age of Reason']."[1] Few souls are now so belated as to credit such stories; but my readers may form some conception of the mental condition of the community in which Paine died from the fact that such absurdities were printed, believed, spread through the world. The Quaker servant became a heroine, as the one divinely appointed witness of Tom Paine's recantation.

[1] "Life and Gospel Labors of Stephen Grellet." This "valuable young Friend," as Stephen Grellet calls her, had married a Quaker named Hinsdale. Grellet, a native of France, convert from Voltaire, led the anti-Hicksites, and was led by his partisanship to declare that Elias promised him to suppress his opinions! The cant of the time was that "deism might do to live by but not to die by." But it had been announced in Paine's obituaries that "some days previous to his demise he had an interview with some Quaker gentlemen on the subject [of burial in their graveyard] but as he declined a renunciation of his deistical opinions his anxious wishes were not complied with." But ten years later, when Hick's deism was spreading, death-bed terrors seemed desirable, and Mary (Roscoe) Hinsdale, formerly Grellet's servant also, came forward to testify that the recantation refused by Paine to the "Quaker gentlemen," even for a much desired end, had been previously confided to her for no object at all! The story was published by one Charles Collins, a Quaker, who afterwards admitted to Gilbert Vale his doubts of its truth, adding "some of our *friends* believe she indulges in opiates" (Vale, p. 186).

DEATH AND RESURRECTION. 343

But in the end it was that same Mary that hastened the resurrection of Thomas Paine. The controversy as to whether Mary was or was not a calumniator; whether orthodoxy was so irresistible that Paine must needs surrender at last to a servant-girl who told him she had thrown his book into the fire; whether she was to be believed against her employer, who declared she never saw Paine at all; all this kept Paine alive. Such boiling up from the abysses, of vulgar credulity, grotesque superstition, such commanding illustrations of the Age of Unreason, disgusted thoughtful Christians.[1]

Such was the religion which was supposed by some to have won Paine's heart at last, but which, when mirrored in the controversy over his death, led to a tremendous reaction. The division in the

---

[1] The excitement of the time was well illustrated in a notable caricature by the brilliant artist John Wesley Jarvis. Paine is seen dead, his pillow "Common Sense," his hand holding a manuscript, "A rap on the knuckles for John Mason." On his arm is the label, "Answer to Bishop Watson." Under him is written: "A man who devoted his whole life to the attainment of two objects—rights of man and freedom of conscience—had his vote denied when living, and was denied a grave when dead!" The Catholic Father O'Brian (a notorious drunkard), with very red nose, kneels over Paine, exclaiming, "Oh you ugly drunken beast!" The Rev. John Mason (Presbyterian) stamps on Paine, exclaiming, "Ah, Tom! Tom! thou'lt get thy frying in hell; they'll roast thee like a herring.

> "They'll put thee in the furnace hot,
> And on thee bar the door:
> How the devils all will laugh
> To hear thee burst and roar!"

The Rev. Dr. Livingston kicks at Paine's head, exclaiming, "How are the mighty fallen, Right fol-de-riddle-lol!" Bishop Hobart kicks the feet, singing:

> "Right fol-de-rol, let's dance and sing,
> Tom is dead, God save the king—
> The infidel now low doth lie—
> Sing Hallelujah—hallelujah!"

A Quaker turns away with a shovel, saying, "I'll not bury thee."

Quaker Society swiftly developed. In December, 1826, there was an afternoon meeting of Quakers of a critical kind, some results of which led directly to the separation. The chief speaker was Elias Hicks, but it is also recorded that "Willet Hicks was there, and had a short testimony, which seemed to be impressive on the meeting." He had stood in silence beside the grave of the man whose chances in the next world he had rather take than those of any man in New York; but now the silence is broken.[1]

I told Walt Whitman, himself partly a product of Hicksite Quakerism, of the conclusion to which I had been steadily drawn, that Thomas Paine rose again in Elias Hicks, and was in some sort the origin of our one American religion. I said my visit was mainly to get his "testimony" on the subject for my book, as he was born in Hicks' region, and mentions in "Specimen Days" his acquaintance with Paine's friend, Colonel Fellows. Walt said, for I took down his words at the time:

"In my childhood a great deal was said of Paine in our neighborhood, in Long Island. My father, Walter Whitman, was

[1] Curiously enough, Mary (Roscoe) Hinsdale turned up again. She had broken down under the cross-examination of William Cobbett, but he had long been out of the country when the Quaker separation took place. Mary now reported that a distinguished member of the Hicksite Society, Mary Lockwood, had recanted in the same way as Paine. This being proved false, the hysterical Mary sank and remained in oblivion, from which she is recalled only by the Rev. Rip Van Winkle. It was the unique sentence on Paine to recant and yet be damned. This honor belies the indifference expressed in the rune taught children sixty years ago:

"Poor Tom Paine! there he lies:
Nobody laughs and nobody cries:
Where he has gone or how he fares,
Nobody knows and nobody cares!"

rather favorable to Paine. I remember hearing Elias Hicks preach; and his look, slender figure, earnestness, made an impression on me, though I was only about eleven. He died in 1830. He is well represented in the bust there, one of my treasures. I was a young man when I enjoyed the friendship of Col. Fellows,—then a constable of the courts; tall, with ruddy face, blue eyes, snowy hair, and a fine voice; neat in dress, an old-school gentleman, with a military air, who used to awe the crowd by his looks; they used to call him 'Aristides.' I used to chat with him in Tammany Hall. It was a time when, in religion, there was as yet no philosophical middle-ground; people were very strong on one side or the other; there was a good deal of lying, and the liars were often well paid for their work. Paine and his principles made the great issue. Paine was double-damnably lied about. Col. Fellows was a man of perfect truth and exactness; he assured me that the stories disparaging to Paine personally were quite false. Paine was neither drunken nor filthy; he drank as other people did, and was a high-minded gentleman. I incline to think you right in supposing a connection between the Paine excitement and the Hicksite movement. Paine left a deep, clear-cut impression on the public mind. Col. Fellows told me that while Paine was in New York he had a much larger following than was generally supposed. After his death a reaction in his favor appeared among many who had opposed him, and this reaction became exceedingly strong between 1820 and 1830, when the division among the Quakers developed. Probably William Cobbett's conversion to Paine had something to do with it. Cobbett lived in the neighborhood of Elias Hicks, in Long Island, and probably knew him. Hicks was a fair-minded man, and no doubt read Paine's books carefully and honestly. I am very glad you are writing the Life of Paine. Such a book has long been needed. Paine was among the best and truest of men."

Paine's risen soul went marching on in England also. The pretended recantation proclaimed there was exploded by William Cobbett, and the whole controversy over Paine's works renewed. One after another deist was sent to prison for publishing

Paine's works, the last being Richard Carlile and his wife. In 1819, the year in which William Cobbett carried Paine's bones to England, Richard Carlile and his wife, solely for this offence, were sent to prison,—he for three years, with fine of £1,500, she for two years, with fine of £500.[1] This was a suicidal victory for bigotry. When these two came out of prison they found that wealthy gentlemen had provided for them an establishment in Fleet Street, where these books were thenceforth sold unmolested. Mrs. Carlile's petition to the House of Commons awakened that body and the whole country. When Richard Carlile entered prison it was as a captive deist; when he came out the freethinkers of England were generally atheists.

But what was this atheism? Merely another Declaration of Independence. Common sense and common justice were entering into religion as they were entering into government. Such epithets as "atheism," "infidelity," were but labels of outlawry which the priesthood of all denominations

[1] I have before me an old fly-leaf picture, issued by Carlile in the same year. It shows Paine in his chariot advancing against Superstition. Superstition is a snaky-haired demoness, with poison-cup in one hand and dagger in the other, surrounded by instruments of torture, and treading on a youth. Behind her are priests, with mask, crucifix, and dagger. Burning faggots surround them with a cloud, behind which are worshippers around an idol, with a priest near by, upholding a crucifix before a man burning at the stake. Attended by fair genii, who uphold a banner inscribed, "Moral Rectitude." Paine advances, uplifting in one hand the mirror of Truth, in the other his "Age of Reason." There are ten stanzas describing the conflict, Superstition being described as holding

"in vassalage a doating World,
Till Paine and Reason burst upon the mind,
And Truth and Deism their flag unfurled."

pronounced upon men who threatened their throne, precisely as "sedition" was the label of outlawry fixed by Pitt on all hostility to George III. In England, atheism was an insurrection of justice against any deity diabolical enough to establish the reign of terror in that country or any deity worshipped by a church which imprisoned men for their opinions. Paine was a theist, but he arose legitimately in his admirer Shelley, who was punished for atheism. Knightly service was done by Shelley in the struggle for the Englishman's right to read Paine. If any enlightened religious man of to-day had to choose between the godlessness of Shelley and the godliness that imprisoned good men for their opinions, he would hardly select the latter. The genius of Paine was in every word of Shelley's letter to Lord Ellenborough on the punishment of Eaton for publishing the "Age of Reason."[1]

In America "atheism" was never anything but the besom which again and again has cleared the

[1] "Whence is any right derived, but that which power confers, for persecution? Do you think to convert Mr. Eaton to your religion by embittering his existence? You might force him by torture to profess your tenets, but he could not believe them except you should make them credible, which perhaps exceeds your power. Do you think to please the God you worship by this exhibition of your zeal? If so the demon to whom some nations offer human hecatombs is less barbarous than the Deity of civilized society. . . . Does the Christian God, whom his followers eulogize as the deity of humility and peace—he, the regenerator of the world, the meek reformer—authorise one man to rise against another, and, because lictors are at his beck, to chain and torture him as an infidel? When the Apostles went abroad to convert the nations, were they enjoined to stab and poison all who disbelieved the divinity of Christ's mission? . . . The time is rapidly approaching—I hope that you, my Lord, may live to behold its arrival—when the Mahometan, the Jew, the Christian, the Deist, and the Atheist will live together in one community, equally sharing the benefits which arrive from its association, and united in the bonds of charity and brotherly love."

human mind of phantasms represented in outrages on honest thinkers. In Paine's time the phantasm which was called Jehovah represented a grossly ignorant interpretation of the Bible; the revelation of its monstrous character, represented in the hatred, slander, falsehood, meanness, and superstition, which Jarvis represented as crows and vultures hovering near the preachers kicking Paine's dead body, necessarily destroyed the phantasm, whose pretended power was proved nothing more than that of certain men to injure a man who out-reasoned them. Paine's fidelity to his unanswered argument was fatal to the consecrated phantasm. It was confessed to be ruling without reason, right, or humanity, like the King from whom "Common Sense," mainly, had freed America, and not by any "Grace of God" at all, but through certain reverend Lord Norths and Lord Howes. Paine's peaceful death, the benevolent distribution of his property by a will affirming his Theism, represented a posthumous and potent conclusion to the "Age of Reason."

Paine had aimed to form in New York a Society for Religious Inquiry, also a Society of Theophilanthropy. The latter was formed, and his posthumous works first began to appear, shortly after his death, in an organ called *The Theophilanthropist*. But his movement was too cosmopolitan to be contained in any local organization. "Thomas Paine," said President Andrew Jackson to Judge Hertell, "Thomas Paine needs no monument made by hands; he has erected a monument in the hearts of all lovers of liberty." The like may be said of his religion : Theophilanthropy, under a hundred translations and forms, is now the fruitful branch of every religion and every sect. The real cultivators of skepticism,—those who ascribe to deity biblical barbarism, and the savagery of nature,—have had their day.

The removal and mystery of Paine's bones appear like some page of Mosaic mythology.[1] An English caricature pictured Cobbett seated on Paine's coffin, in a boat named RIGHTS OF MAN, rowed by NEGRO SLAVES.

"A singular coincidence [says Dr. Francis] led me to pay a visit to Cobbett at his country seat, within a couple of miles of the city, on the island, on the very day that he had exhumed the bones of Paine, and shipped them for England. I will here repeat the words which Cobbett gave utterance to at the friendly interview our party had with him. 'I have just performed a duty, gentlemen, which has been too long delayed : you have neglected too long the remains of Thomas Paine. I have done myself the honor to disinter his bones. I have removed them from New Rochelle. I have dug them up ; they are now on their way to England. When I myself return, I shall cause them to speak the common sense of the

[1] The bones of Thomas Paine were landed in Liverpool November 21, 1819. The monument contemplated by Cobbett was never raised. There was much parliamentary and municipal excitement. A Bolton town-crier was imprisoned nine weeks for proclaiming the arrival. In 1836 the bones passed with Cobbett's effects into the hands of a Receiver (West). The Lord Chancellor refusing to regard them as an asset, they were kept by an old day-laborer until 1844, when they passed to B. Tilley, 13 Bedford Square, London, a furniture dealer. In 1849 the empty coffin was in possession of J. Chennell, Guildford. The silver plate bore the inscription "Thomas Paine, died June 8, 1809, aged 72." In 1854, Rev. R. Ainslie (Unitarian) told E. Truelove that he owned "the skull and the right hand of Thomas Paine," but evaded subsequent inquiries. The removal caused excitement in America. Of Paine's gravestone the last fragment was preserved by his friends of the Bayeaux family, and framed on their wall. In November, 1839, the present marble monument at New Rochelle was erected.

great man; I shall gather together the people of Liverpool and Manchester in one assembly with those of London, and those bones will effect the reformation of England in Church and State.'"

Mr. Badeau, of New Rochelle, remembers standing near Cobbett's workmen while they were digging up the bones, about dawn. There is a legend that Paine's little finger was left in America, a fable, perhaps, of his once small movement, now stronger than the loins of the bigotry that refused him a vote or a grave in the land he so greatly served. As to his bones, no man knows the place of their rest to this day. His principles rest not. His thoughts, untraceable like his dust, are blown about the world which he held in his heart. For a hundred years no human being has been born in the civilized world without some spiritual tincture from that heart whose every pulse was for humanity, whose last beat broke a fetter of fear, and fell on the throne of thrones.